ON THE GENEALOGY OF
MORALITY

ON THE GENEALOGY OF MORALITY: A POLEMICAL TRACT

Friedrich Nietzsche

edited by Gregory Maertz
translated by Ian Johnston

broadview editions

BROADVIEW PRESS – www.broadviewpress.com
Peterborough, Ontario, Canada

Founded in 1985, Broadview Press remains a wholly independent publishing house. Broadview's focus is on academic publishing; our titles are accessible to university and college students as well as scholars and general readers. With over 800 titles in print, Broadview has become a leading international publisher in the humanities, with world-wide distribution. Broadview is committed to environmentally responsible publishing and fair business practices.

Library and Archives Canada Cataloguing in Publication

Title: On the genealogy of morality : a polemical tract / Friedrich Nietzsche ; edited by Gregory
    Maertz ; translated by Ian Johnston.
Other titles: Zur Genealogie der Moral. English
Names: Nietzsche, Friedrich Wilhelm, 1844-1900, author. | Maertz, Gregory, 1958- editor. |
    Johnston, Ian (Ian Courtenay), 1938- translator.
Series: Broadview editions.
Description: Series statement: Broadview editions | Includes bibliographical references.
Identifiers: Canadiana (print) 20230439535 | Canadiana (ebook) 20230439594 | ISBN
    9781551119892 (softcover) | ISBN 9781460408308 (EPUB) | ISBN 9781770488984
    (PDF)
Subjects: LCSH: Ethics.
Classification: LCC B3313.Z73 E52023 | DDC 170—dc23

Advisory editor for this volume: Michel Pharand

Broadview Press handles its own distribution in North America:
PO Box 1243, Peterborough, Ontario K9J 7H5, Canada
555 Riverwalk Parkway, Tonawanda, NY 14150, USA
Tel: (705) 743-8990; Fax: (705) 743-8353
email: customerservice@broadviewpress.com

For all territories outside of North America, distribution is handled by Eurospan Group.

Broadview Press acknowledges the financial support of the Government of Canada for our publishing activities.

Canadä

Cover design and typesetting: George Kirkpatrick

PRINTED IN CANADA

Contents

Acknowledgements

My work on this edition of Friedrich Nietzsche's *The Genealogy of Morality* began at the idyllic Rockefeller Foundation Bellagio Center on Lake Como and continued in various locations, including Gravir on the Isle of Lewis and the village of Obereggen in the Dolomites, and was completed at my home in Princeton, New Jersey. This edition reflects my career-long engagement with German literature and culture which began in my undergraduate years. I am indebted to Don LePan for encouraging me to undertake this project and to Stephen Latta at Broadview Press for his steadfast support. I wish to thank Endrit Agolli for his research assistance and Michel Pharand for his expert copy editing. As ever, I am grateful for the support of my colleagues and students in the English Department at St. John's University in New York City.

Introduction

> Name almost any poet, man of letters, philosopher, who
> wrote in German during the twentieth century and attained
> to stature and influence—Rilke, George, Kafka, Thomas
> Mann, Ernst Jünger, Musil, Benn, Heidegger, or Jaspers—
> and you name at the same time Friedrich Nietzsche. He is
> to them all—whether or not they know and acknowledge
> it (and most of them do)—what St. Thomas Aquinas was
> to Dante: the categorical interpreter of a world which they
> contemplate poetically or philosophically without ever rad-
> ically upsetting its Nietzschean Structure.
>
> —Erich Heller[1]

As the influential critic Erich Heller (1911–90) taught generations of scholars and students, Friedrich Nietzsche (1844–1900)
consciously or unconsciously provided the intellectual backdrop
for leading writers and intellectuals in the German language tradition. But Nietzsche's impact is felt across linguistic boundaries.
Turning to French literature, we can see how Nietzsche inspired
the absurdism of Albert Camus and the existentialism of Jean-
Paul Sartre and André Gide. In English we can see Nietzsche's
fingerprints on the novels of Jack London, James Joyce, and D.H.
Lawrence, the poetry of Wallace Stevens and Robinson Jeffers,
and the plays of Eugene O'Neill. Nietzsche's influence on modern philosophy has been similarly far reaching, both in the work
of German thinkers and beyond. Besides Martin Heidegger, Karl
Jaspers, and Georg Simmel, there are figures in diverse fields,
such as the philosophers Ferdinand Tönnies and Max Scheler,
the psychologists Sigmund Freud and Carl Jung, the theologian
Martin Buber, and members of the Frankfurt School such as
Max Horkheimer and Theodor Adorno. Georg Simmel considered Nietzsche's contributions to ethics to be as consequential as
Copernicus was for cosmology, and the intellectual landscape ev-
erywhere reveals the impact craters of Nietzsche's explosive ideas.
Other French thinkers who emulated Nietzsche include Paul
Ricoeur, Gilles Deleuze, Félix Guattari, Jacques Derrida, and
Michel Foucault. In Russia, Andrei Bely, Dmitry Merezhkovsky,
and Vyacheslav Ivanov were prominent among the writers

---

1 "The Importance of Nietzsche" 2.

responding to Nietzsche. Among the composers who took inspiration from Nietzsche we must mention Gustav Mahler, Richard Strauss, Frederick Delius, and Alexander Scriabin.

As influential as the emulation of Nietzsche was in post-World War II intellectual history, the misappropriation of Nietzsche has been just as consequential. Despite Nietzsche's repeated forceful denunciations of German nationalism, antisemitism, and Teutonic pretensions of superiority, his works were enthusiastically embraced, and the meaning thereof routinely distorted, by nationalist, fascist, and proto-fascist admirers—from Benito Mussolini, the future dictator of Italy, and Adolf Hitler, who sanctioned the wholesale exploitation of Nietzsche in National Socialist Germany, to the Nobel Prize-winning Norwegian novelist and Nazi collaborator Knut Hamsun, and the extreme Japanese nationalist novelist Yukio Mishima. As we will see below in a discussion of the reception of Nietzsche, such appropriations reveal the perils associated with his writings.

Why Nietzsche Now? Why *On the Genealogy of Morality*?

Why is Nietzsche's work relevant to us at this time? What does *On the Genealogy of Morality* offer readers in the twenty-first century? Why do we need a new translation? We live in an era of radical transition (technological, societal, political, climatological), which has been likened to that of the industrial revolution of the late eighteenth and early nineteenth centuries, with similarly disruptive implications for social structures, work patterns, and moral choices, as well as crises—the COVID-19 pandemic, planetary warming, and the Russian invasion of Ukraine—that have exacerbated the crises fed by technological innovation but have also forced a concomitant ethical reckoning and repositioning. We also live in a time of mass disinformation that also happens to coincide with the rise of proto-fascist extreme nationalist authoritarian leaders, both at home and abroad, and a resurgence of white supremacist groups across North America and Europe. At such a time it is ever more urgent that we emulate Nietzsche's method of critical reading and subject our views and thought process to scrupulous analysis. This is where *On the Genealogy of Morality*, in a fresh, remarkably accessible translation with contextualizing appendices, can do its part.

The Genealogy is a history of ethics, a text about interpreting that history, and a primer on interpretation in general. There are also elements of archaeology, sociology, anthropology, psychology, and etymology, too. Nietzsche's history-based approach to the development of morality as well as his keen understanding of how power relations, especially the role played in this process by social, class, and racial divisions, continue to shape our definitions of ethical norms and standards of behavior. In our age of "alternative truths" and the rise of conspiracy theories and their capture of a large percentage of the population of the wealthiest and most powerful country in world history, Nietzsche's insight into the nature of interpretation is more valuable today than ever before. His reading of history and the human capacity for rationalization anticipated, influenced, and continues to underpin the interpretative techniques and strategies that emerged as dominant in the humanities and social sciences over the past several decades.

The Path to Authorship

Who was Friedrich Nietzsche? Why is he still so fascinating to us? Why do his thoughts seem so contemporary?

Nietzsche grew from a precocious schoolboy into an historically youthful professor of classical languages at the University of Basel, a Swiss institution that had become an important regional cultural center. His rise to a maverick intellectual who planted the seeds for an epistemological revolution—thanks to his pioneering methodology of interrogating facts and the foundations of cultural institutions and practices through the lens of language and how terms, labels, metaphors, similes, and names evolve and are employed in surprising and unexpected ways—was unforeseeable, but his polymathic range of skills and interests (accomplished pianist, composer, poet, crypto-novelist, philologist, philosopher, proto-anthropologist) promised that he would not be content in the limited range of inquiry of his academic discipline as well as in the heavy burdens of teaching.

Nietzsche's intellectual audacity was backed up by great personal courage when he volunteered to serve at the front in the Franco-Prussian War (1870–71). There he witnessed the conflict in all its brutality, carnage, and wastefulness. He manifested other qualities in his personal life and literary works—unquenchable wanderlust, a contrarian pugnacity, and an expansive appetite for natural beauty. His exultation in the mountains and his experience of the sublime serve as the launching pad for his concept of the *Übermensch* and the prophecy of Zarathustra, those pioneers of a new morality, born of the will to power. The ecstatic tone and style that characterize Nietzsche's works are the expression of the euphoria experienced at high altitude, the unobstructed views of the sun, blue skies, snow, glaciers, and perhaps even of the impact of untreated syphilis. The *Übermensch* is an aspirational projection—a bundling of characteristics and attitudes—an imaginative assertion of Nietzsche's own courageous longing—a mask, a persona, an embodiment of his spirit of adventure, his lust for discovery, his contrarian disposition, his instinctive tendency to challenge conventional beliefs and so-called truths, especially British Utilitarianism (i.e., what is most useful to the largest number, an attitude that Nietzsche felt had infected intellectual inquiry at the expense of the truth) and German bourgeois complacency.

The Genealogy represents Nietzsche's most emphatic attempt at disrupting traditional academic disciplinary boundaries and traditional conventions of scholarly discourse. Indeed, from *The Birth of Tragedy* (1872) onwards, Nietzsche's writings embody a rejection of the staid, conservative social stratum occupied by German academics. It was this professional caste, in just a few decades, that would provide crucial support for the radical right's overthrow of German democracy (the Weimar Republic) and then mobilize itself to serve Hitler's regime. It is supremely ironic, of course, that under National Socialism Nietzsche would be co-opted into the nazified academy—normalized, as a precursor, a crypto-Nazi, crypto-racist, ultra-nationalist, which, as we know, he was not. For Nietzsche was consistently a vocal and vehement critic of Germany's pursuit of empire—and he objected, above all, to German antisemitism.

Nietzsche's war service and his subsequent denunciation of German nationalism suggest the impact of a conversion experience, an awakening from the conventional mindset of German academics into a subversive one, and a journey toward the transcendence and transgression of disciplinary boundaries and formal stylistic conventions. Nietzsche is perceived by his colleagues as a class traitor of sorts, one who has rejected the privileges and prerogatives of his profession and ridiculed its claims to truth. Ulrich von Wilamowitz-Moellendorff's infamous review of *The Birth of Tragedy* harnesses the outrage and the incomprehension of his peers at Nietzsche's insurrection against his privileged status as a member of a genuine Brahmin caste in the modern world.[1] How dare he seek to subvert the authority

---

1 Ulrich von Wilamowitz-Moellendorff (1848–1931), leading German philologist, who transferred, along with Nietzsche, from

of academic discourse, of *Wissenschaft*—of scholarship itself—the chief idol which Nietzsche insists is facing the twilight of its unquestioned authority? Nietzsche was concerned that the state and its institutions, which included state-funded universities, inevitably appropriate the work of scholars to support, pursue, and propagandize on behalf of its agenda—however correct or socially improving that agenda may seem, it is unavoidably instrumentalized and serves as an expression of irresistible state power.

Nietzsche resisted this instrumentalization of his work and thus resigned his position at the University of Basel. He needed complete freedom and autonomy to explore the ambiguous, demonic, and unpalatable origins of morality, of the foundations of culture, which can be best encapsulated by Walter Benjamin's insight: "There is no document of civilization which is not at the same time a document of barbarism" (Theses VII "On the Concept of History"). Nietzsche sought to be free from all disciplinary and caste allegiances to follow his thoughts wheresoever they might lead him, without the constraints of civilization (a need to align himself with progressive ideas) or the social pressure on science to endorse progress (along with evolution).

The Making of a Revolutionary Thinker

The son and grandson of Lutheran pastors, Nietzsche was portentously named after King Friedrich Wilhelm IV of Prussia (r. 1840–61), with all the great expectations that this implied. A child prodigy and product of the renowned Schulpforta prep school (graduating in 1864 with a thesis written in Latin on the ancient Greek poet Theognis), Nietzsche matriculated at the University of Bonn with the intention of studying theology as preparation for entering the family business of the Lutheran ministry. But shortly after arriving in Bonn, Nietzsche broke free of family expectations and transferred to the University of Leipzig in order to study classical philology under the renowned scholar Friedrich Ritschl (1806–76). Then, just five years after leaving high school, Nietzsche was, on the strength of Ritschl's

---

the University of Bonn to the University of Leipzig to continue studying with their mentor, Friedrich Ritschl (1806–76). Wilamowitz-Moellendorff's extended review, entitled *Zukunftsphilologie* (*Philology of the Future*), was published as a book in Berlin in 1872.

recommendation alone, appointed a full professor of classical philology at Basel, in the German-speaking northwestern corner of Switzerland. This appointment confirmed his status as a wunderkind—hired without having completed his PhD dissertation or a *Habilitationsschrift* (a second scholarly monograph usually required for the professorial rank). To remedy the credential deficit, Ritschl arranged for Leipzig to award Nietzsche, then just twenty-four years old, an honorary doctorate.

However, once again, Nietzsche shapeshifts away from fulfilling the role expected of him by his prodigious talents and his mentor's recommendation and diverges from the pathway to the security and comforts of a conventional academic career. In this second metamorphosis, Nietzsche emerges from his chrysalis as a hybrid butterfly—a "philosopher" who rejects all systems because he rejects idealism and thus the existence of transcendental realms, denies metaphysical and transcendental systems and truths, and simultaneously critiques the scientific empiricism which seeks to replace the totalizing authority of religion with a new omniscient god in whose name conventions were established and norms were asserted.

Philosophical Context:
From Rebel to Canonical Philosopher

The Genealogy belongs to a tradition of radical approaches to the origins of human society and values reaching from Plato to Rousseau and beyond. Like all of Nietzsche's work, *The Genealogy* belongs to a hybrid genre, combining features of proto-anthropology, crypto-sociology, cultural history, religion, linguistics, and psychology. Generically, it more closely resembles the kind of speculative history produced a century earlier by Jean-Jacques Rousseau in his *Discourse on the Origins and Basis of Inequality Among Men* (1754). To this genre also belongs a work like Thomas Malthus's *An Essay on the Principle of Population* (1798), which, like Rousseau's little book, had a stimulating effect on subsequent thinkers, despite its predictive limitations. Rousseau (1712–78) begins with primitive humanity, which accounts for his book's following among proto-anthropologists (examples of such work are excerpted in the appendices), the era he deemed to be the Edenic period of happiness and innocence for homo sapiens. This period ended, however, with the agricultural revolt and the rise of cities. With these developments came the growth of culture (written literature, science, philosophy) and all that Rousseau considered inherently evil and foreign to our original human purpose: patriarchy, militaries, class, caste, gendered social structures, as well as the marginalization of "forest peoples" and nomads who had not yet adapted to agriculture and urban settlement. Recent twenty-first-century archaeology suggests the existence of thriving egalitarian societies (such as the culture that produced Stonehenge as a site for communal feasting and celebrations) without palaces and temples and other evidence of hierarchy and social stratification—societies which had as their organizing principles comity rather than competition, social conflict, arrogance, cruelty, and oppression, with no evidence of the presence of social elites. However, Nietzsche's vision of human nature and society is predicated upon the exercise of the will to power by aristocratic elites.

Nietzsche's system of moral evolution, which is thus dependent on inequality and the rise and domination of elites, is, of course, entirely Western/Indo-European in orientation, and while it serves as a brilliant example of his analytical acumen, its larger utility as a global historical template is questionable. Following Rousseau, who suggested that the rise of urban culture and a class of wealthy and powerful elites destroyed the primitivist utopia of hunter gatherers that led to the rise of elites who then ascribed moral values to the exercise of their hegemonic power, Nietzsche does, however, reveal the impact of assertions of strength and power on the construction of Western values. Such power expressed as values endures and continues to influence cultural and moral behavior long after the original elites have passed into historical obscurity. Therefore, our inheritance from these hegemonic elites as social and moral practice is freighted with history, with unspeakable violence, exploitation, the spilling of blood, and enforced toil. Our morals are therefore ghosts of such power relations. Nietzsche seeks a way out of this compromised history with its surviving vestiges of power, oppression, and brutality.

Nietzsche thus emphatically departs from Rousseau in rejecting any idealization of the primitive past, which exercised such a profound influence over the Romantic generation in Germany, Britain, and France. Instead, Nietzsche's approach to the distant past de-romanticized and de-idealized it as a paradise from which we have drifted. Rather, the distant past is the stage on which transpired the great struggle in the assertion of the will to power. Also, rather than embracing Rousseau's concept of the "noble savage"—in which is crystallized the West's worship of the "primitive" and the implicit condemnation of the decadence of modern humans whose hierarchical societies destroyed the aboriginal paradise—Nietzsche acknowledges and accepts as a productive ethical force the actual savage potential of human beings. In his view, human beings are hardwired to form hierarchies and to rationalize domination and difference as a function of intrinsic worth, strength, and beauty.

In Rousseau's wake comes the most prominent of his successors, the philosophical writing team of Karl Marx (1818–83) and Friedrich Engels (1820–95), whose Edenic world in *The Communist Manifesto* (1848) differs from Rousseau's only in that it is posited in the future rather than the past. In both cases, the pertinent overlap is that each of them offers a secular vision of human perfectibility. Nietzsche differentiates his speculative cultural history in *The Genealogy* from that of Rousseau and Marx and Engels by his recognition that the past was not a paradise disconnected from real time and its imperfections, and that future perfection was similarly unattainable. Rather than a broad-based social revolution, Nietzsche's transvaluation of values would occur on an individual level—a breaking away from the herd—the consequence of an individual epiphany instead of the group dynamics of the Rousseauvian and Marxist paradigms in which broad social revolutions necessarily submerged, muted, and de-emphasized the role of individual agency. Eschewing utopias, Nietzsche sought to remain resolutely realistic about the basis of human relations—POWER—and believed that human history and, above all, human values must always be read as the product of power relations. The will to power as Nietzsche conceives of it is an amoral force in human relations that empties morality of ethical content—only self-interest remains.

Major Influences

The most important precursor figures Nietzsche grappled with were the idealist philosophers Immanuel Kant (1724–1804) and Arthur Schopenhauer (1788–1860), according to whom ultimate truths were not immediately perceivable by human senses. Echoing Marcus Aurelius (121–180 CE), who wrote, "Everything we see is a perspective, not the truth," Nietzsche embraces the view of Schopenhauer, who insisted that human perception can only grasp at "representations"—emanations, phantasms, and reflections of ultimate reality (the will)—but not the core of reality itself. To complicate matters further, according to Nietzsche's notion of "perspectivism," everyone's perception of the will's representations is differentiated and distinct from every other—a hall of mirrors in which every person's perspective is merely a variation of Kant's "thing-in-itself"— "thing-in-itselfness" as it were—rather than a glimpse into unmediated reality or truth. The result is not an encounter with ultimate reality but a distorted sense of privileged insight. Hence Nietzsche's famous declaration in *On Truth and Falsity in Their Ultramoral Sense* (1873): "What is truth but a mobile army of metaphors?" Accordingly, in *The Genealogy* Nietzsche questions our definitions of "good" and "evil," the cornerstones of Western morality, as similarly subject to merely arbitrary, temporary, placeholding signifiers which are in turn subject to metamorphosis and transformation, depending on who is in charge and thus empowered to shroud their self-interest and prerogatives with a moral smokescreen. In addition, what we would denote as social, racial, ethnic, and caste distinctions originally crystalized around distinctions of power. Subjective value judgments become solidified and objectified as laws and universal truths. The possession of power thus translated the "signified"—patterns of behavior, social and class markers, physical appearance—into moral qualities which were deemed universal, transcendent codes of conduct. As another example, think of our culture's ideas of beauty, which were originally organized and derived from Eurocentric ideals of attractiveness—in other words, temporally and culturally determined rather than absolute, universal qualities. However, these temporally produced values become detached from their historical contexts and are posited via moral diktats as universals. Nietzsche's idea of the "transvaluation of values" is precisely this: that moral codes are never moored in unchanging, universally valid, transcendent values. This makes them capable of change, as does the tension between the content of morality and the pursuit of political power. The pathways to this process of objectification have been obscured by the institutionalization of morality (by the establishment of priesthood), in whose self-interest the maintenance of these values was identified. Thus, self-interest supersedes any simple good versus evil value assessment and dictates the conversion of values into their opposites in an ever-changing historical process. The lineage or genealogy of moral values is configured and traceable to these metamorphoses. Morality is thus to be seen as a dynamic, endlessly evolving, mutating set of values arbitrarily tied to the self-interest of power-holding elites.

Slave Morality

A significant portion of *The Genealogy* is devoted to analyzing the process by which what Nietzsche designates as "slave morality" achieves a position of dominance over its former masters. When a former underclass of subalterns and subservient groups, such as Jews and Christians, takes the reins of power, their values of submissiveness, quietude, meekness, self-abnegation, and servility—as exemplified by the Jesus of the Gospels—are established as positive virtues to be aspired to and embraced—a prizing of the transcendent world to come over the present life, earthly existence, and identifying the traits of mastery, strength, enjoyment of life's pleasures as behaviors condemned as "evil," pagan, barbarous, and transgressive: the actions and values, in short, of the "blond beast." The vehicle for the institutionalization of "slave morality" is the priestly class. This transition from pagan-aristocratic values to the "slave morality" as dominant moral code (distilled from the Judeo-Christian tradition) is the initial focus of *The Genealogy*. From here Nietzsche examines the transfer of the authority of the priestly class to the new secular "priesthood" of scientists who picked up the mantle of priestly authority and claimed it for themselves—along with the claims of objective truth that were once made by priests—perhaps with greater justification than priests but with no less overweening pride. Nietzsche's analysis of priestly authority extends from Judaic and Christian history to Hinduism and Buddhism—other religions associated with *ressentiment*—grievance and the thirst for revenge—as the main thrust of the will to power: to conquer, overcome, and supplant, by violence if necessary, the previous power-holding regime—for example, Oliver Cromwell's revolt against the English throne and Church of England—and characterized, following victory, by the emergence of new cultic leadership. The master morality, the dominant method of evaluation prior to the slave revolt in morality, reflected the ascendant class's perceived goodness, superiority, and self-esteem. It was not prescribed behavior for others—and this is the difference between the ethics of the blond beast and that of slave morality. Christianity represents the capacity of *ressentiment* when harnessed to the will to power to become creative and assert its own values. It is the vehicle of the oppressed for the acquisition of power by subverting the existing authority and power structure and its concomitant values. Thus, asceticism and *ressentiment* come to embody the expression of the will to power, and the triumph of Christianity represents the ultimate victory of Judaic quietism in the face of the previous dominant, oppressive, enslaving pagan Roman Empire.

The vehemence of the revenge of the oppressed and the enslaved is a product of repression and pent-up aggression. Not permitted to act of their own volition, slaves must thus content themselves with "imagined revenge," which fatally infects their "positive" actions and moral prescriptions with *ressentiment*. The result is a reversal of the concept of the master morality: the good, the beautiful, the strong are now evil; the evil, the ugly, the weak are now God. According to Matthew 19:24, success, wealth, fame, and pride are now the subject of contempt and condemnation: "And again I say unto you, it is easier for a camel to go through the eye of a needle than for a rich man to enter into the Kingdom of Heaven." It is this weaponizing of grievance, which is an essential ingredient of modern fascism, white supremacy, and, in Nietzsche's time and for another half-century, of German nationalism, that was so effectively exploited by Hitler and led to the marginalized and the aggrieved in German society to identify their self-interest and values with the Nazi movement.

Asceticism, aspects of which are associated with the major religions Nietzsche examines, represents the will to power turned upon life itself, as well as the physical body, and is thus translated into abstemiousness, self-mortification, and the life-denying vows of poverty, obedience, and chastity which, somewhat perversely as Nietzsche maintains, transform priests into leaders and paradigms for the new cultures founded upon and governed by the newly ascendant slave morality. One could easily apply Nietzsche's paradigm to the cults and religious extremists of our times—Evangelical Christians, the Taliban in Afghanistan, Islamic extremists, white nationalists, neo-Nazis, and the anti-vaccination death cults who embrace the freedom to risk death as a celebration of life.

As understood by Nietzsche, morality falsifies the complexity of reality, of human nature, and covers up the interdependency of good and evil throughout history. Traced back to its origins, morality is invariably derived from criminality that has been whitewashed and converted into the highest expression of moral action. In other words, every system of morality achieved dominance through immoral methods. The Nietzschean moral revolution is epitomized by Zarathustra, an idealized individual, to whom all social and moral restraints would be meaningless or ultimately overcome. Similarly, the *Übermensch* is one who would have the courage and strength to leap over all limitations and temptations—moral and psychological, emotional and somatic, especially those imposed by Christianity—and thereby give full expression to and indulgence in the human appetite for freedom from restraint, to live without the support of divine beings and moral systems justified in the aforesaid divinity's name, and to ignore and repudiate the strictures imposed by the priestly caste. The *Übermensch* represents not perfectibility but freedom from social constraints and especially freedom from the pains of conscience, the worst symptom of the internalization of priestly restraints associated, first, with the ancient Indian religion, followed by Judaism, and then, more universally, with Christianity—in which each iteration demonstrates the domination of a priestly class which seeks to domesticate, tame, and emasculate human drives. The *Übermensch* channels the audacity of pre-modern, pagan elites in the assertion of his strength of will, of his appetite for joy, of his determination to free himself from the self-imposed restraints of Christian morality. With the promulgation of the *Übermensch*, Nietzsche issues a challenge to prevailing orthodoxies by indicating how easily hegemonic value systems can be overthrown—by a mere leap of faith or by a joyous dance step.

For his prizing of this impulse Nietzsche was celebrated by conservative critics, including those intellectuals associated with fascism and National Socialism, as a counter-revolutionary force to the tradition of 1789, and for his apparent anti-utopian resistance to liberalism. Thus he was recruited for inclusion in the Nazi pantheon. Nietzsche was also popular with anti-progressive modernists who had embraced—in part because of the horrors of World War I and the collapse of religious faith—cultural pessimism and therefore abandoned, *pace* Max Nordau in *Degeneration* (1892), belief in the progressive march of civilization.

Human Context

An interesting contrast is formed between Nietzsche's historical personage, who was affable, sociable, and maintained an extensive network of friends from childhood, Schulpforta, and Basel, and the persona suggested by his books—the lonely, tortured, endlessly wandering philosopher isolated from humanity. While Nietzsche suffered from numerous persistent physical complaints—headaches, vision problems, digestion issues, as well as undiagnosed aches and pains—he was nonetheless an intensely social creature who attended openings at the Bayreuth festival, was a ritual presence at various literary salons, and lived communally in Basel and afterwards with his friend Paul Rée (1849–1901) and his love interest Lou Andreas-Salomé (1861–1937). He also conducted a vast correspondence right up to the onset of his psychological breakdown.

In Basel, Nietzsche joined a cluster of intellectual figures comparable to other such collections of cultural luminaries in German history, such as Goethe's Weimar, Jena and Heidelberg during the Romantic period, and Berlin during the Weimar Republic. These thinkers included Franz Overbeck (1837–1905), who, like Lou Salomé, was born to German parents in St. Petersburg, enjoyed a cosmopolitan childhood, and studied theology at German universities. Overbeck arrived in Basel in 1870—the same year as Nietzsche—as a professor of New Testament theology. He and Nietzsche lived in the same boarding house from 1870 to 1875, and the two remained friends after Nietzsche's departure from Basel in 1879. The publication of Overbeck's book *How Christian Is Our Present-Day Theology* (1873) coincided with the appearance of the first of Nietzsche's *Untimely Meditations*—"David Strauss: The Confessor and the Writer" (1873). Both works respond to Strauss's *The Old and the New Faith: A Confession* (1871). Over the years, Overbeck visited Nietzsche and remained one of his most loyal friends. Indeed, in early January 1889, after Overbeck received one of Nietzsche's infamous "Wahnzettel" (notes of madness), he immediately traveled to Turin to attend to his friend and retrieve his manuscripts. Subsequently, Overbeck rejected Elisabeth Förster-Nietzsche's (1846–1935) distorted edition of *The Will to Power* (see Appendix A8) and renounced the cult that grew up around Nietzsche under Förster-Nietzsche's leadership.

The classical philologist Erwin Rohde (1845–98) was another friend with whom Nietzsche maintained an extensive correspondence. They met at the University of Bonn and left for Leipzig together to study with Professor Friedrich Ritschl. In 1872 Rohde entered the fray caused by the publication of Nietzsche's *The Birth of Tragedy* (1872) by defending Nietzsche against the withering critique of Wilamowitz-Moellendorff. Unlike Overbeck, however, Rohde assisted Förster-Nietzsche with the Nietzsche Archive and its publications.

Johann Heinrich Köselitz (1854–1918), who went by Peter Gast, a pseudonym given to him by Nietzsche, was a composer and writer who, along with Overbeck, was Nietzsche's most dedicated friend as well as his trusted amanuensis. In 1875 he transferred to the University of Basel, where he attended the lectures of Jacob Burckhardt, Overbeck, and Nietzsche. From 1899 to 1909, Gast worked at the Nietzsche Archive in Weimar, co-edited with Förster-Nietzsche the much-criticized *The Will to Power*, and assisted in the publication of other posthumous writings. Gast was deemed essential to this process as it was determined that he was the only person who could decipher Nietzsche's notoriously illegible handwriting. Until breaking with Förster-Nietzsche in 1909, Gast had fully allied himself with her, perhaps out of financial necessity or a misplaced sense of loyalty to her brother, even against Overbeck.

One of Nietzsche's closest friends, Paul Rée was a physician and also a philosopher in his own right. Like Nietzsche, he studied at Leipzig and was an admirer of Schopenhauer. Rée's book *The Origin of the Moral Sensations* (1877), with its plain, accessible style and emphasis on "moral Darwinism," influenced Nietzsche, as did Rée's attempt to explain the emergence of altruistic impulses and how altruism came to be described as moral behavior. In response, reflecting the dialogic nature of Nietzsche's work, *The Genealogy* adopts Ree's emphasis on Darwinian natural selection and presents the emergence of altruism as an expression of slave morality in opposition to the ethics of strength associated with the "blond beast." However, while Rée followed Darwin (1809–82) in tracing morality to biocentric causes, Nietzsche in the Prologue to *The Genealogy* rejects this position, insisting instead that morality boils down to choices that involve the will to power—and these choices overwhelm any inborn or congenital biological impulses or causes. Nonetheless, even though he vehemently disagreed with his friend,[1] Nietzsche's later characteristic style and patterns of argument emerge in response to Rée's treatment of the birth of conscience, selfless behavior, and moral lines of inquiry. Indeed, central to Nietzsche's thought, from *Human, All-Too Human* onwards, is the concept of the history or prehistory of morality, which he gleaned from Rée's book (see Appendix A2).

---

1 From the Prologue: "I have perhaps never read anything which I would have denied, statement by statement, conclusion by conclusion, as I did with this book, but entirely without any annoyance or impatience."

Jacob Burckhardt (1818–97) was the *primus inter pares* of the luminaries on the Basel faculty. Best known for his masterpiece *The Culture of the Renaissance in Italy* (1860), Burckhardt single-handedly invented the discipline of cultural history as a fusion of literature, art, architecture, and politics, and he is justly considered one of the intellectual giants of the period. Like Nietzsche, Burckhardt was the son of a Lutheran minister, and the two of them bonded over their mutual admiration for the philosophy of Schopenhauer and Richard Wagner's music dramas. Nietzsche found Burckhardt's writings and lectures sympathetic because in them Burckhardt opposed the teleological approach to history associated with Hegel as well as other reductionist interpretive methods, such as those that focused solely on economic forces and more rigidly positivistic techniques adopted from the natural sciences.

Richard Wagner (1813–83) was both a friend and patron to the young Nietzsche, who became a regular member of the household at Tribschen, the Wagner estate on Lake Lucerne. Nietzsche frequently attended performances at Bayreuth and became so convinced of the cultural value of Wagner's compositions that he placed Wagner's music at the center of his first book, *The Birth of Tragedy*. Ostensibly a study of classical tragedy, its emergence and decline, Nietzsche's undeniably lyrical if historically dubious book is presented as an analysis of the causes of the decadence of modernity and offers a tonic for cultural rebirth—a return to the mythical roots of German culture. Nietzsche claims that Wagner's music dramas are a sign that this rebirth has begun. Wagner was flattered by the young devotee's attention as they bonded over their shared admiration for Schopenhauer and their mutual hatred of illiberal autocracy. However, Nietzsche and Wagner drifted apart over the composer's increasingly overt expressions of antisemitism and his undisguised celebration of Roman Catholic mysticism in the late opera *Parsifal* (1882). It is, of course, *The Birth of Tragedy*, with Nietzsche's implicit sympathy for a "Blut und Boden" German cultural revival, along with Förster-Nietzsche's corrupt edition of *The Will to Power*, that attracted the admiration of German nationalists and, later, fascists.

Nietzsche and Women

Despite the infamous epigraph found in *Zarathustra* ("You are going to women? Do not forget the whip"), Nietzsche's misogyny would best be described as one of his poses or masks rather than as an expression of genuine hostility to women. Indeed, he was connected to several remarkable women who were instrumental in introducing him to eminent cultural figures as well as fostering his intellectual growth. Malwida von Meysenburg (1816–1903), the first woman nominated for a Nobel Prize in literature, met Nietzsche at the cornerstone laying of the Bayreuth Festspielhaus (festival concert hall) in 1872. In the autumn of 1876, she invited Rée and Nietzsche to live and work in her house in Sorrento. It was there that Rée wrote *The Origin of the Moral Sensations* (see Appendix A2) and Nietzsche started working on *Human, All-Too Human* (see Appendix A4).

Cosima Wagner (1837–1930), the daughter of composer and virtuoso pianist Franz Liszt (1811–86), founded with her second husband Richard Wagner the Bayreuth Festival, which opened in 1876, and she ran the festival after Wagner's death in 1883 until 1906. Cosima befriended Nietzsche, hosted his many visits over the years, and exercised a positive maternal presence in his life, which stood in stark contrast to his strained relations with his mother and sister.

Lou Salomé was a St. Petersburg-born psychoanalyst and writer whose presence in Nietzsche's life would loom large. In April 1882 Salomé, Rée, and Nietzsche met in Rome and over the next several months traveled together through Italy, Switzerland, and Germany. Nietzsche, having fallen in love with Salomé at first sight, proposed marriage to her on multiple occasions but was rejected each time. Then, in October 1882, after the trio had cohabited for three weeks, Rée and Salomé departed together, leaving Nietzsche in a state of emotional despair. Five years after Nietzsche's mental collapse, Salomé published her own study of Nietzsche (1894).

Close to her brother in childhood, Elisabeth Förster-Nietzsche, whom he affectionately called "Llama" after the notoriously obstreperous animal, suffered a break with Nietzsche over her engagement and marriage to Bernhard Förster (1843–89), a prominent German nationalist and antisemite. In 1887 Elisabeth and Förster launched "Nueva Germania" (New Germany), a colony of German settlers in the remote Paraguayan wilderness. Advertised with great fanfare as an opportunity to demonstrate the superiority of German blood and culture, the venture turned out to be a catastrophic failure. In 1889, after the full extent of the colony's disastrous finances became clear, Bernhard Förster hanged himself. Elisabeth returned to Germany in 1893 to find her brother incapacitated. Despite her limited understanding of her brother's work, Förster-Nietzsche assumed control of his literary legacy and established the Nietzsche Archive in 1894. It was because of his sister's intentional distortions of his posthumous papers that Nietzsche became associated with German militarism and National Socialism. Indeed, after Förster-Nietzsche joined the Nazi Party in 1930, Adolf Hitler visited the Weimar archive, provided financial support, and in 1935 attended Förster-Nietzsche's funeral, which was observed with full state honors.

Scientific Context

In *The Genealogy* Nietzsche expresses anxiety about the possibility that a truth-creating system, like science or philosophy, could devolve into a system for enabling the power for a new priesthood. As Alexander Nehemas explains, "[Nietzsche] does not object to science itself ... but rather to an interpretation which refuses to acknowledge that science itself is an interpretation in the sense that it provides a revisable description of a part of the world which is no more [ultimately] real than any other ... Nietzsche attacks only this privileging of the methods and objects of science and not its methods and objects themselves" (65).

In other words, Nietzsche insists that scientists acknowledge that what they are engaging in is not an absolute lawgiving or the identification of everlasting truths, but rather offering interpretations of phenomena that are subject to human limitations, biases, psychology, and even the individual perception of the scientists. Here Nietzsche echoes Kant as well as Plato, both of whom insisted that an encounter with absolute truth cannot take place through human sense perception. Thus, if science depends on faith in the metaphysical, then it too is vulnerable to Nietzsche's critique that it is one of the forms of nihilism and therefore not fully empirical: like previous forms of idealism, modern science sets itself up as a new religion with claims of absolute authority which one is required to accept on faith. Nietzsche's position is a radical step—unique in the nineteenth century—for science was seen by secular intellectuals as a cure for the excesses of metaphysics and a replacement for belief in a supernatural realm. *The*

Genealogy makes explicit the connection between this critique of metaphysics and modern science as both being essentially nihilistic. Put another way, Nietzsche is concerned that science, as a replacement for religion, is not free of confirmation bias—subjectivity or perspectivism—for the ultimate reality behind every façade of authority or claim to moral superiority is the will to power. Nietzsche views science from a revolutionary perspective: despite the claims of empiricism and objectivity, all scientific interpretations of experience and phenomena are necessarily carried out under human perception, according to which no one can achieve total objectivity; the phenomenon and the knowing subject are combined in the act of seeing and experiencing. One's vision or perception is indistinguishable from projections of the imagination (the knower's contribution to perception) and of one's individual and unique perspective. Nietzsche's critique of science anticipates Thomas Kuhn's *The Structure of Scientific Revolutions* (1962), in which scientific perspectives are described as paradigms rather than knowledge, as well as even the more radical critiques of knowledge and authority-affirming discourses associated with the writings of Michel Foucault (1925–84) and Jacques Derrida (1930–2004). Nietzsche doesn't dispute scientific facts per se, but he does critique the function of science in a society decoupled from religion and the authority it once wielded over human morals and institutions. He foresees the risks involved with science overtaking religion and establishing its own authority, value-system, and quasi-priestly caste. In short, Nietzsche seeks to decouple science from the pseudo-science of ethics because moral or immoral behavior is more properly derived from cultural and linguistic praxis.

Nietzsche observed that rejection of the physical world—"hostility to life"—was common to religious asceticism and science. The scientist as priest is a replacement and continuation of the ascetic project (rejection of life) while appearing to be in favor of life—because of the innate anti-metaphysical bias of science. For example, the various social lockdowns recommended by the scientific community during the COVID-19 pandemic were taken by some as attempts to suppress the "life force"—the desire to give expression to life-enhancing activities even if they turn out to be self-destructive and potentially deadly. Similarly, *ressentiment*, as a counter-expression and response on the part of the enslaved and the oppressed to the aristocratic-pagan, blond beast, predatory *carpe diem* morality, was nonetheless an expression of the will to power directed at itself self-destructively, suicidally, as the otherwise healthy expression of self-assertion. By undermining and subverting "healthy" instincts as a manifestation of strength and power and by pathologizing such behavior as "immoral" or inferior which was once deemed "moral" or superior—is the ultimate expression of slave morality and its innate denial of self and abstemiousness.

Nietzsche strenuously objected to Darwin's theory of evolution (see Appendices D4–D5) because it was driven by a biocentric force, namely, "natural selection." This assignment of a physical basis for human evolution was then, in the work of Darwin's contemporaries and successors—such as Henry Thomas Buckle (1821–62), Sir John Lubbock (1834–1913; see Appendix D6), and Herbert Spencer (1820–1903; see Appendix D7)—readily applied to all aspects of human culture, including the emergence and development of morality and ethics. While this observational approach represented a signal advance over unempirical pre-modern methods, such as corpse medicine (eating pieces of dead bodies to treat a wide range of ailments) and Galen's ancient Greek humor-based system (good health required maintaining a balance of four basic fluids: blood, yellow bile, black bile, and phlegm), in opposition to Darwin and his followers, Nietzsche postulated an alternative model of human ethical development based on the role of the will to power in shaping human destiny. Nietzsche was also opposed to Darwinism on account of the political uses to which this interpretation of the world and its phenomena could potentially be exploited by nationalist, proto-fascist political parties in Germany, for example, parties founded and nourished on myths of German racial and hygienic superiority over other nations. In this way, Nietzsche anticipated the emergence of Social Darwinism, a thought and social movement based on a profound misreading of the concept of "natural selection," which was vulgarly interpreted to mean "the survival of the fittest," which, under the Nazis, would also be linked to oversimplified and distorted biopolitical interpretations of the meaning of the will to power.

Literary Context

Writing after the era of the polymaths Kant, Goethe (1749–1832), and Hegel (1770–1831), predecessors who were products of a classical education and an intellectual tradition in which science (natural philosophy) was not strictly distinguished from philosophy, and prior to the fragmentation of academic disciplines into discrete departments, Nietzsche audaciously presents his work as that of a polymath encroaching on multiple areas of learning, at the same time writing with verve and stylistic flamboyance in a truly original voice. In *The Genealogy* we see Nietzsche move away from the aphoristic style of *Human, All-Too Human* and *Beyond Good and Evil* (see Appendix A6) and return to the essayistic style of *The Birth of Tragedy.*

Nietzsche's writing, like *The Genealogy* itself, defies easy categorization, but it is undeniably literary in its use of irony, ventriloquism, polyvocalism, role-playing, and incessant wordplay. In the persona that emerges from his authorial voice we see that Nietzsche has adopted the guise of a late-born Stoic—such as Marcus Aurelius—who is not a systematic philosopher. *The Genealogy* is, as Nietzsche calls it, a *Streitschrift* (polemical tract), a text that directly engages in conflict, in a war of ideas. The advantage of this Broadview translation, in its freshness and clarity, is in the unfettered access it affords to Nietzsche's argument, examples, and style.

Along with Goethe, Nietzsche has the distinction of being considered one of the most original and influential literary stylists in the German language. Also like Goethe, Nietzsche is almost untranslatable in his subtle, at times recondite, wordplay. It is this stylistic genius that makes Nietzsche's thoughts seem fresh and contemporary as well as far more trenchant, ironic, self-deprecating, fearless, and more approachably human than his successors and epigones such as Martin Heidegger (1889–1976), Foucault, and Derrida. While their works are easily pigeonholed as the writings of a particular time and place, reflecting a fashion, a trend, a taste for a particular style of subversiveness, Nietzsche's voice still resonates with us, bypassing the horrific creeds (such as Nazism) or merely annoying or intentionally baffling intellectual fads (poststructuralism) that once claimed Nietzsche as their progenitor.

The impact of Nietzsche's discovery of Arthur Schopenhauer was decisive, not just for the emphasis in Schopenhauer's thought on the will but also for Nietzsche's development as a writer: unlike Schopenhauer's nemesis and rival, Hegel, who is notoriously difficult to understand, let alone translate into English, Schopenhauer is a writer of astonishing lucidity and power—a tremendous role model for any aspiring writer. Schopenhauer, who was partially educated in England, combined with the ever-present Goethe and the invocation of French and English authors in *The Genealogy*, ensured that Nietzsche would follow these exemplars of clarity and precision rather than the opaque Hegel and his copycat minions. In addition to Goethe, Schopenhauer (see Appendix A1), and authors of classical antiquity, it is important to consider the influence of his friend Paul Rée (whose *The Origins of the Moral Sensations* is excerpted in Appendix A2), whose plain style Nietzsche admired and emulated in *The Genealogy*. In addition, Stendhal's (1783–1842) major novels, *The Red and the Black* (1830) and *The Charterhouse of Parma* (1839), were among Nietzsche's favorites. The pairing of acute, penetrating psychological insights with intense feeling and emotion is another feature that entered Nietzsche's own writing, directly or indirectly, from French literature and thought.

Nearly as important as Schopenhauer was for Nietzsche was his discovery of the novels of the Russian realistic novelist Fyodor Dostoevsky (1821–81), best known for *Notes from Underground* (1864), *Crime and Punishment* (1866), and *The Brothers Karamazov* (1879–80). According to Nietzsche, Dostoevsky was "the only psychologist ... from whom I had something to learn; he ranks among the most beautiful strokes of fortune in my life" (*Twilight of the Idols*). Nietzsche recognized with Dostoevsky that art reflects the dark world of the subconscious out of which culture emerges, and Nietzsche identified with the figure of the artist who stands between the world of civilization and culture and is as yet home in neither. Nietzsche might justly be welcome in the company of contemporary writers who dare approach the demonic, the illiberal, and the dangerous, such as W.G. Sebald (1944–2001), Roberto Bolaño (1953–2003), Michel Houellebecq (b. 1956), Elena Ferrante (b. 1943), and Karl Ove Knausgård (b. 1968).

Reception

Nietzsche's true progenitor was Niccolò Machiavelli (1469–1527), who said, "I'm not interested in preserving the status quo; I want to overthrow it." And it is in this spirit of revolution that so many of Nietzsche's admirers—on the right and left—read him and claimed him as one of their own. Thus, the history of the reception of *The Genealogy* is revealing as to its audiences and the seeming inexhaustible capacity of the book to generate controversy and to stimulate reflection and debate. The twentieth-century reception of Nietzsche, especially of *The Genealogy*, constitutes a series of (mis)readings and (mis)representations that successively marked the development of his posthumous reputation. These interpretations can be loosely described as cultic, fascist/Nazi, and post-World War II right- and left-wing efforts to reintegrate Nietzsche into the Western canon, which made works like *The Genealogy* either the means to achieve liberation from bourgeois morality or an intellectual safe haven for middle-class North American university students. Thus, a normalized, domesticated Nietzsche was co-opted to serve a liberal capitalist academic culture in the decades after the defeat of Nazi Germany.

From the late nineteenth century into the 1930s, there was a distinct lack of unanimity among German critics of Nietzsche. Indeed, Nietzsche's violation of academic norms and his stylistic eccentricities were deemed either problematic or liberating, depending upon the writer's perspective. Max Nordau (1849–1923; see Appendix E1), arch-defender of Enlightenment rationalism, identified Nietzsche's works as symptomatic of decadence and cultural decline, while Stefan George (1868–1933; see Appendix E2) and Ernst Bertram (1884–1957; see Appendix E3) idolized Nietzsche as an authentic messiah and instigator of German cultural rebirth. Similarly, Oswald Spengler (1880–1936; see Appendix E4), seen mostly as an apostle of the decline of Western civilization, saw in Nietzsche the catalyst for its revival.

The transfer of the Nietzsche Archive from Naumburg to Weimar in 1896 was decisive in the twentieth-century reception of Nietzsche. The relocated archive served as both a National Socialist pilgrimage site and a counterpoint to the city's long association with Goethe, the central figure of German Classicism, whose humanism and celebration of *Weltliteratur* clashed all too clearly with Adolf Hitler's ultra-nationalist ideology. The reception of Nietzsche in Nazi Germany was also tone deaf to Nietzsche's critique of value-creating hegemonic structures whose sole claim to this privilege is superior power and dominance. *The Genealogy* does not celebrate such power but offers an investigation and a laying bare of the origins and the linguistic infrastructure of morality formation as an expression of brute, tyrannical strength. Similarly, Nietzsche's subversive sense of humor and irony were lost on Förster-Nietzsche's Nazi patrons, who sought a thinker of his stature to lend credibility to the genocide of the Jews and others deemed sub-human enemies of the German volk.

That Nietzsche, the ultimate outsider and subverter of disciplinary boundaries and arbitrary authority, should have been venerated and placed at the center of the Nazi philosophical canon (along with fellow academic outsider Schopenhauer) is indeed highly ironic. Only a heavily redacted, expurgated, and censored text, such as Förster-Nietzsche's edition of *The Will to Power*, could make Nietzsche unobjectionable for a pro-Nazi reader. However, the version of Nietzsche that emerges in Förster-Nietzsche's bowdlerization of her brother's texts made him the perfect precursor figure to Hitler himself—a kind of Old Testament prophet to Hitler's messiah. That the anti-nationalist, anti-antisemite Nietzsche could be made to serve the opposite positions suggests how vulnerable all discourse is to abuse and misuse.

Surprisingly, Nietzsche's canonization under National Socialism was not revoked with the post-war denazification of German intellectual life. His survival as a totemic figure in West Germany is another instance of the continuity between the culture of Nazi Germany and the post-war era. Not only was Nietzsche's niche in the canon sustained, but it was also burnished and solidified chiefly by German-speaking Jewish refugees from Hitler's conquest of Europe—Walter Kaufmann (1921–80), Theodor Adorno (1903–69), Max Horkheimer (1895–1973), Karl Löwith (1897–1973), and Erich Heller—along with unrepentant NSDAP member Martin Heidegger. Strange bedfellows, indeed.

Chiefly, two different "Nietzsches" emerged in the post-war era who represented the political and interpretative investments of so-called "right" and "left" Nietzsche scholars, intellectuals, and writers. According to Ernst Nolte (1923–2016), the nationalist historian and philosopher, Nietzsche was the anti-modernist leader of a "counter-Enlightenment" and the icon of "anti-emancipation politics." Such divisive figures as Julius Evola (1898–1974), the Italian theorist of fascism, and the Russian-American novelist Ayn Rand (1905–82) joined Nolte's camp. The right Nietzscheans were opposed on the left principally by the French poststructuralist philosophers Michel Foucault and Jacques Derrida, who saw in Nietzsche the chief precursor of their assault on Western logocentrism and related methods of interpretation and social control. Nietzsche's works epitomized self-deconstructing artifacts that first state and then refute their stated assumptions. Because of the leading role played by *The Genealogy* in the 1960s and 1970s philosophical debate centered in France, it remains an integral part of the history of interpretation.

In the middle ground are independent figures like Heller, whose strength as an interpreter lay in his unrivaled familiarity with Nietzsche's texts, his eschewing of ideological commitments, and his essential grasp of Nietzsche's flirtation with intellectual danger. Heller, too, was a habitual wanderer of high-altitude landscapes, especially the Latemar and Rosengarten groups in the Dolomites. It was there that Heller composed many of the interpretive essays that form the best initiation into Nietzsche's thought. A text-based approach to Nietzsche, as exemplified by Heller, is especially suited to *The Genealogy*, for it is here that Nietzsche seeks to expose the biases latent in all values-endowed hermeneutics—biases that are contingent, subjective, and thus lacking in transcendent authority. Nietzsche especially distrusted the perspective of the outsider, the pariah, who, once in power, imposes their grievance-based interpretation of the world and its phenomena, insisting upon its universal validity.

It seems inevitable that Nietzsche will continue to be subject to enthusiastic attempts at cooptation by various politically motivated interpreters, both now and in the future. This is all the more reason to read *The Genealogy* with the same spirit of fearless adventure that characterized Nietzsche's way of living and thinking. When we read *The Genealogy* today, we partake in a dialogue much like the one we encounter in Plato, Marcus Aurelius, or Schopenhauer. We become Nietzsche's partner in dialogue as we interrogate the emergence and evolution of moral ideas and practices.

Hotel Bewallerhof
Obereggen, South Tyrol

Friedrich Nietzsche: A Brief Chronology

1844   Friedrich Wilhelm Nietzsche is born on 15 October at Röcken (a small village located mid-way between Leipzig and Naumburg) in present-day Saxony-Anhalt, the first child born to Franziska and Carl Ludwig Nietzsche, a Lutheran minister. Nietzsche is named after the Prussian King Friedrich Wilhelm IV, whose birthday he shares.

1846   Nietzsche's sister Elisabeth is born.

1849   30 July: Carl Ludwig Nietzsche dies.

1858   After being homeschooled on account of his poor health and delicacy, he starts secondary education at Schulpforta. Famous alumni include poet Friedrich Gottlieb Klopstock, philosopher Johann Gottlieb Fichte, historian Leopold von Ranke, and American Transcendentalist writer Frederic Henry Hedge.

1864   Matriculates at the University of Bonn, where he continues his study of classical languages. Around this time, he experiences a loss of faith, which is significant for the son, grandson, and nephew of Lutheran pastors.

1865   Follows the famous professor of philology Friedrich Wilhelm Ritschl to the University of Leipzig, where he befriends fellow student and philologist Erwin Rohde. Buys a used copy of *Die Welt als Wille und Vorstellung* (*The World as Will and Representation*) by Arthur Schopenhauer, which ignites an intense, life-long engagement with the philosopher's ideas.

1866   Reads Friedrich Albert Lange's *Geschichte des Materialismus* (*History of Materialism*), which provides an introduction to Darwin's theory of evolution and reinforces the core teaching of Immanuel Kant and Schopenhauer: knowledge of the essence of things is beyond the grasp of human senses.

1867   October: enlists as a volunteer in a Prussian artillery regiment stationed in Naumburg.

1868	April: promoted to lance corporal. Later in the year he is injured in a horseback riding accident. He is discharged and returns to his studies.
1869	January: at only age 24 and without completing his doctorate, Nietzsche is appointed an assistant professor of classical philology at the University of Basel. May: has his first meeting with the composer Richard Wagner at the latter's estate at Tribschen, initiating a complicated friendship.
1870	11 August: receives permission from the University of Basel to enlist in the Prussian Army. Swiss neutrality in the Franco-Prussian War dictates that he can serve only as a non-combatant, so he joins the medical corps. While he spends only a week at the front, he contracts diphtheria. Returning to Basel, he is promoted to professor ordinarius—the highest rank—in classical philology. Fellow professor Franz Overbeck moves into the same boarding house as Nietzsche and remains a lifelong friend. Other Basel colleagues who were instrumental in Nietzsche's intellectual development include Neo-Kantian philosopher Afrikan Spir and art historian Jacob Burckhardt. The latter serves as an informal mentor and father figure to the young professor Nietzsche.
1871	16 November: meets with E.W. Fritzsch, his new publisher, in Leipzig.
1872	Early January: the publication of Nietzsche's first book, *Die Geburt der Tragödie aus dem Geiste der Musik* (*The Birth of Tragedy from the Spirit of Music*), is received with skepticism by Nietzsche's colleagues in classical philology. Even his dissertation mentor Ritschl is unimpressed and dismisses it as "geistreiche Schiemelei" (clever inebriation). May: a devastating review by Ulrich von Wilamowitz-Moellendorf is published as a book, *Zukunftsphilologie* (*Philology of the Future*)—a play on Nietzsche's description of Wagner's compositions as "music of the future."
1873	May: meets writer Paul Rée, with whom he will develop a close friendship. Rée is best known for his work *Der Ursprung der moralischen Empfindungen*

(*The Origin of the Moral Sensations*), in which he introduces Darwin's concept of "natural selection" to
German philosophical discourse. Nietzsche begins
to have eye trouble and starts lecturing without
notes.

July: dictates *Über Wahrheit und Lüge im ausser-
moralischen Sinn* (*On Truth and Falsity in Their
Ultramoral Sense*) to Rée.

August: the essay "David Strauss: der Bekenner
und der Schriftsteller" ("David Strauss: The
Confessor and the Writer"), the first of the
Unzeitgemässe Betrachtungen (*Untimely Meditations*),
is published. The eventual publication of all four
essays constitutes a critique of the Schopenhauer-
Wagner German nationalist cultural orientation
gaining currency at the time.

Begins working on his last musical composition,
Hymnus an die Freundschaft (*Hymn on Friendship.
Piano for Four Hands*).

1874   October: "Schopenhauer als Erzieher"
("Schopenhauer as Educator"), the third of the
Untimely Meditations, is published. Begins read-
ing Spir's *Denken und Wirklichkeit: Versuch einer
Erneuerung der kritischen Philosophie* (*Thought and
Reality: An Attempt at a Renewal of the Critical
Philosophy*).

1875   April: a review of the first three *Untimely
Meditations* appears in the *Westminster Review and
Foreign Quarterly Review*, the first notice Nietzsche
receives in Britain.

Christmas Day: suffers a collapse.

1876   January: is released from the onerous duty of teaching university preparatory courses to high school
students.

February: takes leave from teaching at the
University.

April: travels to Geneva, where he impulsively pro-
poses to Mathilde Trampedach, who rejects him.
Finishes work on the fourth *Untimely Meditation*,
"Richard Wagner in Bayreuth."

12 August: attends the first performance of
the Ring Cycle. Begins to write *Menschliches,
Allzumenschliches: Ein Buch für freie Geister* (*Human,

All-Too Human: A Book for Free Spirits).
October: Nietzsche and Rée stay in Sorrento as
guests of Malwida von Meysenbug, the first woman
nominated for the Nobel Prize in literature.
November: meets Wagner in Sorrento. This is their
last meeting.

1877 Summer: continues to work on *Human, All-Too
Human*. Reads the New Testament and Rée's *The
Origin of the Moral Sensations.*

1878 January: sends the manuscript of *Human, All-
Too Human* to his publisher. Befriends Heinrich
Köselitz, author and composer, later known
as Peter Gast, a pseudonym given to him by
Nietzsche.
Late summer: falls ill and Wagner attacks him in
the *Bayreuther Blätter*, a local newspaper.
December: the second part of *Human, All-Too
Human* ("Mixed Opinions and Maxims") is
published.

1879 January: Nietzsche's physical condition worsens.
14 June: his resignation from the University is accepted. Afterwards Nietzsche settles in St. Moritz.
December: the third part of *Human, All-Too Human*
("The Wanderer and His Shadow") is published.

1880 January-November: works on *Morgenröte: Gedanken
über die moralischen Vorurteile (The Dawn: Thoughts
on Moral Prejudices)*, dictating it to Gast. Reads
Herbert Spencer and John Stuart Mill as well as the
work of the polymathic Sir John Lubbock, whose
*The Origin of Civilization and the Primitive Condition
of Man* was highly influential in its time.

1881 February: *The Dawn* is completed and sent to Gast.
July: travels to Sils Maria. Bernhard Förster, his
future brother-in-law, lectures in Berlin on "Das
Verhältnis der modernen Judentums zur deutschen
Kunst" ("The Relationship between Modern
Judaism and German Art"). While in Sils Maria,
Nietzsche conceives of *Zarathustra* and the idea of
"die ewige Wiederkehr" ("the eternal recurrence").
Over the winter, some text originally written
for *The Dawn* is developed into *Die fröhliche
Wissenschaft (The Joyful Wisdom).*

1882 February-March: *The Joyful Wisdom* is completed.

March: Rée arrives in Genoa and proposes a
Zusammensein (a "being together" or celibate
cohabitation) with Nietzsche and the writer Lou
Salomé.
June: *The Joyful Wisdom* is published.
August: Salomé arrives in Tautenburg for a period
of mutual study and conversation.
October: Salomé, Rée, and Nietzsche stay in
Leipzig, but only a month later, Nietzsche is aban-
doned by his friends.

1883   January: *Also Sprach Zarathustra* (*Thus Spoke
Zarathustra, Part I*) is published.
February: learns of Wagner's death. He seeks but
is denied an appointment in philosophy at the
University of Leipzig.

1884   Returns to Sils Maria to work over the summer,
which is followed by the publication of *Zarathustra,
Part II* and *Part III*. Breaks with his sister and
Förster over their antisemitic activism.

1885   Self-publishes *Zarathustra, Part IV*.
May: Elisabeth Nietzsche marries Förster.
June: begins working on *Jenseits von Gut und Böse:
Vorspiel einer Philosopher der Zukunft* (*Beyond Good
and Evil: Prologue to a Philosophy of the Future*)
and reads Rée's *Die Entstehung des Gewissens* (*The
Emergence of the Conscience*).

1886   January: *Beyond Good and Evil* is finished.
August: following an argument with new publisher
Ernst Schmeitzner over his antisemitism, self-pub-
lishes *Beyond Good and Evil*.
October: writes the fifth book of *The Joyful Wisdom*.
He winters in Nice, where he discovers the novels
of Fyodor Dostoevsky.

1887   Summer: returns to Sils Maria, where he writes
Zur Genealogie der Moral: Eine Streitschrift (*On the
Genealogy of Morality: A Polemical Tract*).
September-late October: works with Peter Gast
on the page proofs of *On the Genealogy of Morality*,
which is published in November.

1888   April: settles in Turin and reads Dostoevsky.
May: begins writing *Der Fall Wagner: Ein
Musikanten-Problem* (*The Wagner Case: A Musician's
Problem*).

June: returns to Sils Maria and finishes working on *Götzen-Dämmerung oder wie man mit dem Hammer philosophirt* (*Twilight of the Idols, or How One Philosophizes with a Hammer*).

September: having completed writing *The Wagner Case*, starts work on *Der Antichrist: Fluch auf das Christentum* (*The Antichrist: A Curse on Christianity*).

September: the Danish critic Georg Brandes gives the first public lectures on Nietzsche's philosophy in Copenhagen.

15 October: celebrates his 44th birthday by writing the first pages of the autobiographical book *Ecce Homo: Wie man wird, was man ist* (*Ecce Homo: How One Becomes What One Is*), which will not be published until 1908.

1889   3 January: after witnessing the flogging of a horse in Turin, collapses on the street. He is said to have run to the horse and thrown his arms around its neck to protect it, and then fallen to the ground senseless. This incident mirrors a scene in Dostoevsky's *Crime and Punishment* in which Raskolnikov dreams of an episode from his childhood in which drunken peasants beat a horse to death. Nietzsche had read that scene not long before in a French translation of the novel.

3–6 January: sends several of his so-called *Wahnzettel* (madness letters) to friends, including Cosima Wagner (widow of the composer), Burckhardt, and Overbeck. Is escorted back to Basel by Overbeck and undergoes medical treatment.

Mid-January: taken to Jena for further treatment.

3 June: Bernhard Förster commits suicide in Paraguay. Publication of *Twilight of the Idols*.

November: the art historian Julius Langbehn arrives in Jena and takes Nietzsche into his care for the next six months.

1891   On a visit back to Germany, Elisabeth Förster-Nietzsche blocks publication of *Zarathustra, Part IV.*

1892   The Köselitz/Gast edition of Nietzsche's collected works begins to appear.

1893	September: Förster-Nietzsche returns from Paraguay for good. Nietzsche's condition continues to deteriorate.
	18 November: Förster-Nietzsche establishes the Nietzsche Archive in a room in the family house in Naumburg and blocks the further publication of the Köselitz/Gast edition. Fritz Kögel, a businessman and hobby poet, is Förster-Nietzsche's choice to replace Gast as editor of Nietzsche's works.
1894	4 February: the official announcement of the founding of the Nietzsche Archive in Naumburg is made.
	December: the Kögel edition of Nietzsche's works, in eight volumes, appears.
1895	Förster-Nietzsche publishes the first volume of her biography of Nietzsche, in which she embellishes her relationship with her brother and alienates his friends in Basel.
	December: Nietzsche's mother signs over all rights to his work, opening the way for Förster-Nietzsche to gain complete control over her brother's work and legacy.
1896	Rudolf Steiner, best known today as the founder of anthroposophy and the Waldorf holistic educational system, is hired at the Archive to organize Nietzsche's personal library.
	1 August: the Nietzsche Archive is moved to Weimar.
	27 November: the tone poem *Also Sprach Zarathustra*, composed by Richard Strauss, is premiered in Frankfurt am Main.
1897	The second volume of Förster-Nietzsche's biography is published.
	June: the publication of the Kögel edition is interrupted and the editor is dismissed.
	17 July: Nietzsche is moved to Weimar.
1898	Wagner expert and dramaturge Arthur Seidl replaces Kögel as editor of Nietzsche's works.
1899	Strauss visits the Archive. Seidl resigns his post and is succeeded by the brothers Horneffer, Ernst and August, philologists whose collected edition joins the preexisting Gast and Kögel editions. The first

English translation of *On the Genealogy of Morality* appears in Britain.
Peter Gast moves to Weimar to edit Nietzsche's correspondence.

1900   25 August: Nietzsche dies of complications from pneumonia and a stroke.

1901   28 October: Paul Rée dies by accident or suicide in a fall while hiking in the Swiss Alps.

Translator's Note

This translation (2023), a revised version of an earlier text (2013) is based on the first German edition of Friedrich Nietzsche's *Zur Genealogie der Moral* (Leipzig, 1887). Nietzsche frequently uses italics to emphasize a word or phrase in his text. These have all been preserved. I have also italicized all foreign words in the text (e.g., *a priori*, *ressentiment*) and all book titles, for both of which Nietzsche in most cases uses a normal font. I have also used italics for all explanatory words and phrases inserted in the text and for the occasional insertion of Nietzsche's original German phrasing into the English text (all such insertions are in square brackets). In the text I have translated Nietzsche's longer quotations from foreign languages into English and placed the original quotation in an endnote (at the end of each essay). When he quotes a Greek word, I have left the original Greek in the text and added, in square brackets, a version of the word in the Roman alphabet and a translation. In those places where Nietzsche refers to his own earlier works with page numbers, I have added section numbers, too (again, in square brackets), so that readers may consult any edition of the relevant text. Nietzsche's punctuation is often quite idiosyncratic (especially his use of dashes, ellipsis dots, and question marks), but it is an important feature of his style. I have retained most of it, as best I can, in order to convey this aspect of his style. But in some places I have not followed it faithfully.

Ian Johnston
Vancouver Island University

ON THE GENEALOGY OF MORALITY:

A POLEMICAL TRACT

PROLOGUE

1

We don't know ourselves, we knowledgeable people—we are personally ignorant about ourselves.[1] And there's good reason for that. We've never looked for ourselves[2]—how could it happen that one day we'd *discover* ourselves? With justice it's been said, "Where your treasure is, there shall your heart be also."[3] *Our* treasure lies where the beehives of our knowledge stand. We are always busy with our knowledge, as born winged creatures and collectors of intellectual honey. In our hearts we are concerned with really only one thing—to "bring something home." As far as the rest of life is concerned, what people call "experiences,"— who of us is serious enough for that? Or has enough time? In these matters, I fear, we've been "missing the point." Our hearts have simply not been engaged with that—nor, for that matter, have our ears! Instead, we've been more like someone divinely distracted and self-absorbed into whose ear the clock has just pealed the twelve strokes of noon with all its force and who all at once wakes up and asks himself "What exactly did that clock strike?"—so now and then we even rub our ears *afterwards* and ask, totally surprised and completely embarrassed—"What have we really just experienced?" And more: "Who *are* we really?" Then, as I've mentioned, we count—after the fact—all the twelve trembling strokes of the clock of our experience, of our lives, of our *being*—alas! in the process we keep losing count . . . We remain simply and necessarily strangers to ourselves, we do not understand ourselves, we *must* be confused about ourselves. For us this proposition holds for all eternity: "Each man is furthest from himself"[4]—where we ourselves are concerned, we are not "knowledgeable people" . . .

---

1 The Greek travel writer Pausanias (110–180 CE) in his *Description of Greece* (10.24.1) reports that "Know thyself" was one of the maxims inscribed outside the Temple of Apollo at Delphi.

2 Matthew 7:7: "Ask, and it shall be given you; seek and ye shall find; knock, and it shall be opened unto you."

3 Matthew 6:21: "Where your treasure is, there will your heart be also."

4 Nietzsche alters the passage from the Roman poet Terence (c. 195/185–c. 159 BCE), *Andria* (635): "Proximo sum egomet mihi" (I am closest to myself).

My thoughts about the *origin* of our moral prejudices—for this polemical tract is concerned about that origin—had their first brief, provisional expression in that collection of aphorisms which carried the title *Human, All-Too Human: A Book for Free Spirits*, which I started to write in Sorrento, during a winter when I had the chance to pause, just as a traveler stops, and to look over the wide and dangerous land through which my spirit had wandered up to that point. This happened in the winter of 1876–77, but the ideas themselves are older. In the main points, they were already the same ideas which I am taking up again in the present essays:—let's hope that the long interval of time has done them some good, that they have become riper, brighter, stronger, and more complete! But *the fact that* today I still stand by these ideas, that in the intervening time they themselves have constantly become more strongly associated with one another, in fact, have grown into each other and intertwined, that reinforces in me the joyful confidence that they may not have originally developed in me as single, random, or sporadic ideas, but up out of a common root, out of a *fundamental will* for knowledge ruling from deep within, always speaking with greater clarity, always demanding greater clarity. For that's the only thing appropriate to a philosopher. We have no right to be *isolated* in any way: we are not permitted either to make isolated mistakes or to run into truths in isolation. By contrast, our ideas, our values, our affirmations and denials, our *if*s and *whether*s grow out of us from the same necessity which makes a tree bear its fruit—totally related and interlinked among each other, witnesses of one will, one health, one soil, one sun.—As for the question whether these fruits of ours taste good to *you*—what does that matter to the trees! What concern is that to *us*, we philosophers!

3

Because of a doubt peculiar to my own nature, which I am reluctant to confess—for it concerns itself with *morality*, with everything which up to the present has been celebrated on earth as morality—a doubt which came into my life so early, so uninvited, so irresistibly, in such contradiction to my surroundings, my age, precedent, and my origin, that I would almost have the right to call it my "*a priori*" [Latin: from comes before][1]—because of this, my curiosity as well as my suspicion had to pause early on at the question of where our good and evil really *originated*. In fact, already as a thirteen-year-old lad, my mind was occupying itself with the problem of the origin of evil. At an age when one has "half children's play, half God in one's heart,"[2] I devoted my first childish literary trifle, my first written philosophical exercise, to this problem—and so far as my "solution" to it at that time is concerned, well, I gave the honor to God, as is reasonable, and made him the *father* of evil.[3] Is *that* precisely what my "*a priori*" demanded of me, that new immoral, at the very least unmoral "*a priori*" and the "categorical imperative"[4] which spoke out from it, alas, so anti-Kantian and so cryptic, which I have increasingly listened to ever since—and not just listened to? Luckily at an early stage I learned to separate theological prejudices from moral ones, and I no longer sought the origin of evil *behind* the world. Some education in history and philology, along with an inherently refined sense concerning psychological questions in general, quickly changed my problem into something else: Under what conditions did people invent for themselves those value judgments good and evil? *And what value do they inherently possess?* Have they hindered or fostered human wellbeing up to now? Are they a sign of some emergency, of impoverishment, of an atrophying life? Or is it the other way around? Do they indicate fullness, power, a will for life, its courage, its confidence, its future? To these questions I came across and proposed all sorts of answers for myself. I distinguished between ages, peoples, and different ranks of individuals. I kept refining my problem. Out of the answers arose new questions, investigations, assumptions, and probabilities, until, at last, I had my own country, my own

---

1 Commonly associated with the theories of the German philosopher Immanuel Kant (1724–1804), this Latin phrase refers to some concept or capacity that one possesses innately and not provided by experience. But for Nietzsche the meaning of the phrase has to do with the basis of an argument.

2 Goethe, *Faust*, Part I, 3781.

3 Nietzsche is likely referring to his schoolboy essay on the German Romantic poet Friedrich Hölderlin (1770–1843).

4 "Categorical imperative" is a key concept in Kant's *Critique of Practical Reason* (1788): "Act so that the maxim [which determines your will] may be capable of becoming a universal law for all rational beings."

soil, a totally secluded, flowering, blooming world, a secret garden, as it were, of which no one could have the slightest inkling. O how *lucky* we are, we knowledgeable people, provided only that we know how to stay silent long enough!

4

The initial stimulus to publish something of my hypotheses concerning the origin of morality was given to me by a lucid, tidy, clever, even precocious little book, in which for the first time I clearly ran into a topsy-turvy, perverse type of genealogical hypotheses—a genuinely *English* style. It drew me with that power of attraction that everything opposite, everything antipodal, contains. The title of this booklet was *The Origin of the Moral Feelings*, its author was Dr. Paul Rée, and it appeared in the year 1877.[1] I have perhaps never read anything which I would have denied, statement by statement, conclusion by conclusion, as I did with this book, but entirely without any annoyance or impatience. In the work I mentioned above, with which I was engaged at the time, I made opportune and inopportune references to statements in Dr. Rée's book, not in order to prove them wrong—what have I to do with preparing refutations!—but, as is appropriate to a positive spirit, to put in the place of something unlikely something more likely and, in some circumstances, in the place of some error another error. In that period, as I said, for the first time I brought into the light of day those hypotheses about genealogy to which these essays have been dedicated— but clumsily, as I myself would be the last to deny, still fettered, still without my own language for these concerns of mine, and with all sorts of retreating and vacillating. For particular details, you should compare what I say in *Human, All-Too Human*, p. 51 [Section 45], about the double nature of the prehistory of good and evil (that is, in the spheres of the nobility and the slaves); similarly, pages 119 ff. [Section 136], concerning the worth and origin of ascetic morality, as well as pages 78, 82, and II, 35 [Sections 96, 99, and Volume II, Section 89] concerning the "Morality of Custom," that much older and more primitive style of morality, which lies *toto coelo* [Latin: by all the heavens, i.e.,

---

1 Paul Rée (1849–1901), German philosopher and author of *The Origin of the Moral Sensations* (1877; see Appendix A2), which bears the influence of Charles Darwin, Herbert Spencer, and Sir John Lubbock.

absolutely] from the altruistic way of valuing (which Dr. Rée, like all English genealogists of morality, sees as the *very essence* of moral evaluation); similarly, page 74 [Section 1.92]; *Wanderer*, page 29 [Section 26]; and *The Dawn*, page 99 [Section 112], concerning the origin of justice as a compromise between approximately equal powers (equality as precondition of all contracts and therefore of all law); likewise concerning the origin of punishment in *Wanderer*, pages 25 and 34 [Sections 22 and 33], for which an intent to terrify is neither essential nor original (as Dr. Rée claims:—it is far more likely first brought in under a specific set of conditions and always as something incidental, something additional).[1]

5

Basically, at that point the real concern for me at heart was something much more important than coming up with the nature of hypotheses about the origin of morality, either my own or from other people (or, more precisely stated—this latter issue was important to me only for the sake of a goal to which it is one way out of many). For me the issue was the *value* of morality—and in that matter I had to take issue almost alone with my great teacher Schopenhauer, the one to whom, as if to a contemporary, that book, with its passion and hidden contradiction, addresses itself (—for it, too, was a "polemical tract").[2] The most specific issue was the worth of the "unegoistic," of the instincts for pity, for self-denial, and for self-sacrifice, of things which Schopenhauer himself had painted with gold, deified, and projected into another world [*verjenseitigt*] for so long that they finally remained for him "value as such" and the reason why he *said No* to life and even to himself, as well. But a constantly more fundamental suspicion of *these* very instincts voiced itself in me, a scepticism which always dug deeper! It was precisely here that I saw the *great* danger to humanity, its most sublime temptation and seduction.—But in what direction? To nothingness?—It was precisely here I saw the beginning of the end, the standing still,

---

1 *Human, All-Too Human* was published in 1878, *Wanderer* in 1880, and *The Dawn* in 1881.

2 Arthur Schopenhauer (1788–1860), German philosopher and author of *The World as Will and Representation* (1818/44), which exercised a profound influence on Nietzsche, especially the emphasis on the will and the importance attributed to art in Schopenhauer's thought.

the backward-glancing exhaustion, the will turning itself *against* life, the final illness tenderly and sadly announcing itself. I understood the morality of pity, which was always seizing more and more around it and which gripped even the philosophers and made them sick, as the most sinister symptom of our European culture, which itself had become sinister,[1] as its detour to a new Buddhism? to a European Buddhism?[2] to—*nihilism*?[3] ... This modern philosophical preference for and overvaluing of pity is really something new. Concerning the *worthlessness* of pity, philosophers up to now have been in agreement. I cite only Plato, Spinoza, La Rochefoucauld, and Kant—four spirits as different from one another as possible, but united in one thing, in the low value they set on pity.—[4]

6

This problem of the *value* of pity and of the morality of pity (—I'm an opponent of the disgraceful modern effeminacy of feeling—) appears at first to be only something isolated, a detached question mark. But anyone who remains here for a while and *learns* to ask questions will experience what happened to me:—a huge new vista opens up before him, a possibility grips him like an attack of dizziness, every kind of mistrust, suspicion, and fear springs up, his belief in morality, in all morality, totters—and finally he recognizes a new demand. Let's proclaim this *new*

---

1 Sinister or "uncanny." Nietzsche's use of *unheimlich* differs from Sigmund Freud's better-known definition: the many disguises assumed by the "will to power" of *ressentiment* toward existing institutions that thwart its self-expression.

2 Buddhism is a religion based on the teachings of Siddhartha Gautama Buddha (sixth to fourth century BCE), whose teachings lead to enlightenment by means of a liberating asceticism.

3 The belief in nothing (from the Latin *nihil*). Nietzsche ascribes nihilistic impulses to Christianity and socialism, which were previously considered to have been born of charitable, benevolent intentions.

4 Plato (428–348 BCE), the most important of the classical Greek philosophers and whose mouthpiece is Socrates. Baruch de Spinoza (1632–77), rationalist Jewish-Dutch philosopher whose work provided the foundation for the eighteenth-century Enlightenment. François de La Rochefoucauld (1613–80), French author famous for his maxims.

demand: we need a *critique* of moral values, *we must first question the very value of these values*—and for that we need a knowledge of the conditions and circumstances out of which these values grew, under which they have developed and changed (morality as consequence, as symptom, as mask, as *Tartufferie* [French: hypocrisy],[1] as illness, as misunderstanding, but also morality as cause, as means of healing, as stimulant, as scruple, as poison), a knowledge of a sort that has not been there up to this point, that has not even been wished for. We have taken the *worth* of these "values" as given, as self-evident, as beyond all dispute. Up until now people have not even had the slightest doubts about or wavered in setting up "the good man" as more valuable than "the evil man," of higher worth in the sense of improvement, usefulness, and prosperity with respect to humankind in general (along with the future of humanity). What about this? What if the truth were the other way around? Well? What if in the "good man" there even lay a symptom of regression, like a danger, a seduction, a poison, a narcotic, something which, for example, made the present live *at the cost of the future*? Perhaps in greater comfort and less danger, but also on a smaller scale and in a more demeaning way? ... So that morality itself would be guilty if the inherently possible *highest power and magnificence* of the human type were never attained? So that morality itself might be the danger of dangers? ...

7

Suffice it to say that once this insight revealed itself to me, I had reasons to look around me for learned, bold, and hard-working comrades (today I'm still searching). It's a matter of traveling through the immense, distant, and so secretive land of morality—morality which has really existed, which has really been lived—with nothing but new questions and, as it were, with new eyes. Isn't that almost like *discovering* this land for the first time? ... In this matter, it so happened that, among others I thought of, the above-mentioned Dr. Rée, because I had no doubts at all that by the very nature of his questions he would be driven on his own to a more correct methodology in order to arrive at any answers. Did I deceive myself in this? At any rate, my desire was to provide a better direction for such a keen and objective

---

1 Derived from *Tartuffe* (1664), a play about a religious hypocrite by the French comedic dramatist Molière (1622–73).

eye as his, a direction leading to a true *history of morality*, and to advise him in time against such an English way of making hypotheses *into the blue*. For, indeed, it's obvious which color must be a hundred times more important for a genealogist of morality than this blue: namely, *gray*, in other words, what has been documented, what can be established as the truth, what really took place, in short, the long and difficult-to-decipher hieroglyphic writing of the past in human morality.—*This* was unknown to Dr. Rée. But he had read Darwin:—and so to some extent in his hypotheses the Darwinian beast and the most modern modest and tender moral sensibility, which "no longer bites," politely extend their hands to each other in a way that is at least entertaining—with the latter bearing a facial expression revealing a certain good-natured and refined indolence, in which is even mixed a grain of pessimism and exhaustion, as if it is really not worth taking all these things—the problems of morality—so seriously.[1] But for me things appear reversed: there are no issues at all which provide *more incentives* to take them seriously; among the rewards, for example, is the fact that one day perhaps people will be permitted to take them *cheerfully*. For cheerfulness, or, to say it in my own language, *the joyful wisdom*,[2] is a reward, a reward for a lengthy, brave, hard-working, and underground seriousness, which, of course, is not something for everyone. But on that day when, from full hearts, we say "Forward! Our old morality also belongs *in a comedy*!" we'll have discovered a new complication and possibility for the Dionysian drama[3] of "the

---

1   Charles Darwin (1809–82), British natural scientist and author of *On the Origin of Species* (1859; see Appendix D4) and *The Descent of Man* (1871; see Appendix D5). Darwin's theories of evolution and "natural selection"—which seems to be what Nietzsche is referencing by "the Darwinian beast" above—revolutionized science, religion, and morality in the nineteenth century and beyond.

2   Nietzsche's *The Joyful Wisdom* was published in 1882. See Appendix A7.

3   The Greek god of wine and dramatic works, Dionysus plays a central role in Nietzsche's worldview. Complemented by Apollo, the god of poetry and individuated identity, Dionysus represents the intoxicated chaos and fluid, amorphous identity which predates the emergence of "you" and "I." The binary between Dionysus and Apollo first appears in Nietzsche's *The Birth of Tragedy* (1872). In his later works, Apollo is replaced by Christ, who serves as a symbol for ascetic denial of life versus Dionysus's affirmation of life inclusive of its pain and suffering.

fate of the soul":—and we can bet that he will put it to good use, the grand old immortal comic poet of our existence! ...

8

If this writing is incomprehensible to someone or other and hurts his ears, the blame for that, it strikes me, is not necessarily mine. The writing is sufficiently clear given the conditions I assume— that people have first read my earlier writings and have taken some trouble to do so, for, in fact, these works are not easily accessible. For example, so far as my *Zarathustra* is concerned, I don't consider anyone knowledgeable about it who has not at sometime or another been deeply wounded by and profoundly delighted with every word in it.[1]

For only then can he enjoy the privilege of sharing with reverence the halcyon element out of which that work was born, its sunny clarity, distance, breadth, and certainty. In other cases the aphoristic form creates difficulties. These stem from the fact that nowadays people do *not* take this form *seriously enough*. An aphorism, properly stamped and poured, has not yet been "deciphered" simply by being read. It's much more the case that only now can one begin *to explicate* it, and that requires an art of interpretation. In the third essay of this book I have set out a model of what I call an "interpretation" for such a case.—In this essay an aphorism is presented, and the essay itself is a commentary on it. Of course, in order to practice this style of reading as *art*, one thing is above all essential, something that today especially has been preferably forgotten—and so it will require still more time before my writings are "readable"—something for which one almost needs to be a cow, at any rate *not* a "modern man"—*rumination*.[2]

Sils-Maria, Oberengadin
July 1887

---

1 Nietzsche's *Thus Spoke Zarathustra* was written between 1883 and 1885. Adapted from Zoroaster, the Iranian prophet, priest, and founder of Zoroastrianism, the leading religion of the region until the arrival of Islam, Zarathustra serves as a mouthpiece for Nietzsche.

2 Nietzsche advises his readers to read his words deliberately, in the manner of a bovine animal chewing its cud.

FIRST ESSAY

GOOD AND EVIL, GOOD AND BAD

1

—These English psychologists, whom we have to thank for the only attempts up to this point to produce a history of the origins of morality—in themselves they serve up to us no small riddle.[1] By way of a living riddle, they even offer, I confess, something substantially more than their books—*they are interesting in themselves!* These English psychologists—what do they really want? We find them, willingly or unwillingly, always at the same work, that is, shoving the *partie honteuse* [French: shameful part] of our inner world into the foreground and looking for the truly effective and operative factor which has determined our development in the very place where man's intellectual pride would least *wish* to find it (for example, in the *vis inertiae* [Latin: force of inertia] of habit or in forgetfulness or in a blind, contingent, mechanical joining of ideas or in something purely passive, automatic, reflex, molecular, and fundamentally stupid)—what is it that really drives these psychologists always in *this* particular direction? Is it a secret, malicious, and common instinct, perhaps one which cannot be acknowledged even to itself, for belittling humanity? Or something like a pessimistic suspicion, the mistrust of idealists who've become disappointed, gloomy, venomous, and green? Or a small underground hostility and *rancune* [French: rancor] towards Christianity (and Plato),[2] which perhaps has never once managed to cross the threshold of consciousness? Or even a lecherous taste for what is odd or painfully paradoxical, for what in

---

1 Nietzsche refers to the empirical psychology of John Locke (1632–1704) as well as the utilitarian ethics of Jeremy Bentham (1748–1832) and John Stuart Mill (1806–73). Herbert Spencer (1820–1903) and Henry Buckle (1821–62) are also mentioned below as representatives of what Nietzsche considers to be the empiricism typical of British science and historiography in the nineteenth century.

2 From Nietzsche's perspective, Christianity has absorbed Plato's devaluing of the real work in preference to an ideal, transcendent realm (heaven). Nietzsche considers the combined impact of Christianity, Judaism, socialism, feminism, etc., as destructive of one's enjoyment and appreciation of life.

existence is questionable and ridiculous? Or finally—a bit of all of these: a little vulgarity, a little gloominess, a little hostility to Christianity, a little thrill, and a need for pepper? ... But I'm told that these men are simply old, cold, boring frogs, who creep and hop around and into people, as if they were in their own proper element, that is, in a *swamp*. I resist that idea when I hear it. What's more, I don't believe it. And if one is permitted to hope where one cannot know, then I hope from my heart that the situation with these men might be reversed, that these investigators and the ones peering at the soul through their microscopes may be thoroughly brave, generous, and proud animals, who know how to control their hearts and their pain and who at the same time have educated themselves to sacrifice all desirability for the sake of the truth, for the sake of *every* truth, even the simple, bitter, hateful, repellent, unchristian, immoral truth.... For there are such truths. —

2

So, all respect to the good spirits that may govern in these historians of morality! But it's certainly a pity that they lack the *historical spirit*, that they've been left in the lurch especially by all the good spirits of history itself! As a group they all think *essentially* unhistorically, in what is now the traditional manner of philosophers.[1] Of that there is no doubt. The incompetence of their genealogies of morals reveals itself at the very beginning, where the issue is to determine the origin of the idea and of the judgment "good." "People," so they proclaim, "originally praised unegoistic actions and called them good from the perspective of those for whom they were done, that is, those for whom such actions were *useful*. Later people *forgot* how this praise began, and simply because unegoistic actions had, *according to custom*, always been praised as good, people also felt them as good—as if they were something inherently good." We perceive right away that this initial derivation already contains all the typical characteristic idiosyncrasies of English psychologists—we have "usefulness," "forgetting," "habit," and finally "error," all as the foundation

---

1 Nietzsche requires the philosopher not only to deal with morality empirically, from the perspective of utility or even biologically, but also to take into consideration its development through the ages. Morality and moral ideas, too, have a history, a genealogy of ideological evolution.

for an evaluation in which the higher man up to this time has taken pride, as if it were a sort of privilege of men generally. This pride *is to be* humbled, this evaluation of worth emptied of value. Has that been achieved? ... Now, first of all, it's obvious to me that from this theory the essential source for the origin of the idea "good" has been sought for and established in the wrong place: the judgment "good" does *not* originate from those to whom "goodness" was shown! On the contrary, it was the "good people" themselves, that is, the noble, powerful, higher-ranking, and higher-thinking people who felt and set themselves and their actions up as good, that is to say, of the first rank, in opposition to everything low, low-minded, common, and vulgar. From this *pathos of distance*[1] they first arrogated to themselves the right to create values, to stamp out the names for values. What did they care about usefulness! Particularly in relation to such a hot pouring out of the highest rank-ordering, rank-setting judgments of value, the point of view which considers utility is as foreign and inappropriate as possible. Here the feeling has reached the very opposite of the low level of warmth which is a condition for that calculating shrewdness, that reckoning by utility—and not just for a moment, not for one exceptional hour, but permanently. The pathos of nobility and distance, as I mentioned, the lasting and dominating feeling, something total and fundamental, of a higher ruling nature in relation to a lower type, to a "beneath"— *that* is the origin of the opposition between "good" and "bad." (The right of the master to give names extends so far that we could permit ourselves to grasp the origin of language itself as an expression of the power of the rulers: they say "That *is* such and such"; they seal every object and event with a sound, and in the process, as it were, take possession of it.) Given this origin, the word "good" is from the start *in no way* necessarily tied up with "unegoistic" actions, as it is in the superstition of those genealogists of morality. Instead that occurs for the first time with the *decline* of aristocratic value judgments, when this entire contrast between "egoistic" and "unegoistic" presses itself ever more strongly into the human conscience—it is, to use my own words, the *instinct of the herd* which, through this contrast, finally gets its word (and its *words*). And even then, it takes a long time until this instinct in the masses becomes master, so that moral evaluation

---

1 Pathos of distance: Nietzsche's term for denoting the difference between the noble and the servile elements in society—in terms of rank, values, and taste.

remains thoroughly hung up on and bogged down in that opposition (as is the case, for example, in modern Europe: today the prejudice that takes "moralistic," "unegoistic," and "*désintéressé* [French: distinterested]"[1] as equally valuable ideas already governs with the force of a "fixed idea" and a disease of the brain).

3

Secondly, however, and quite apart from the fact that this hypothesis about the origin of the value judgment "good" is historically untenable, it suffers from an inherent psychological contradiction. The utility of the unegoistic action is supposed to be the origin of the praise it receives, and this origin has allegedly been *forgotten*:—but how is this forgetting even *possible*? Could the usefulness of such actions at some time or other perhaps just have stopped? The opposite is the case: this utility has rather been an everyday experience throughout the ages, and thus something that has always been constantly re-emphasized. Hence, instead of disappearing from consciousness, instead of becoming something forgettable, it must have pressed itself into the consciousness with ever-increasing clarity. How much more sensible is that contrasting theory (which is not therefore closer to the truth—) advocated, for example, by Herbert Spencer: he proposes that the idea "good" is essentially the same as the idea "useful" or "functional," so that in judgments "good" and "bad" human beings sum up and endorse the experiences they have *not forgotten* and *are unable to forget* concerning the useful-functional and the harmful-useless.[2] According to this theory, good is something which has always proved useful, so that it may assert its validity as "valuable in the highest degree," as "valuable in itself." This path to an explanation is, as I said, also false, but at least the account itself is inherently sensible and psychologically tenable.

---

1 Nietzsche alludes to Kant's idea that ethical and aesthetic values are disinterested and universally applicable.

2 Herbert Spencer, British philosopher and liberal political theorist who extended the application of Darwin's evolutionary theories into sociology and utilitarian ethics. From a Spencerian perspective, whatever supports or preserves life is considered good.

I was given a hint of the *right* direction by the following question: What, from an etymological perspective,[1] do the meanings of "good," as manifested in different languages, really signify? There I found that all of them lead back to the *same transformation of ideas*—that everywhere "noble" and "aristocratic" in a social sense is the fundamental idea out of which "good" in the sense of "spiritually noble," "aristocratic," "spiritually high-minded," "spiritually privileged" necessarily develops, a process which always runs in parallel with that other one that finally transforms "common," "vulgar," and "low" into the concept "bad." The most eloquent example of the latter is the German word "*schlecht* [bad]" itself, which is identical with the word "*schlicht* [plain]"—compare "*schlechtweg* [simply]" and "*schlechterdings* [simply]"[2]—and which originally designated the plain, common man, still without any suspicious side glance, simply in contrast to the noble man. Around the time of the Thirty Years' War[3] approximately, hence late enough, this sense changed into the one used now. As far as the genealogy of morals is concerned, this point strikes me as a *fundamental* insight; that it was first discovered so late we can ascribe to the repressive influence which democratic prejudice in the modern world exercises concerning all questions of origin. And this occurs in what appears to be the most objective realm of natural science and physiology, a point I can only hint at here. But the sort of mischief this prejudice can cause, once it has become unleashed and turned into hatred, particularly where morality and history are concerned, is revealed in the well-known case of Buckle: the *plebeian*[4] *nature* of the modern spirit, which originated in England, broke out once again on its home turf, as violently as a muddy volcano and with that salty, over-loud, and common

---

1 The application of the tools of etymological investigation into the origins and usage of ethical terms is the central purpose of *The Genealogy*. Nietzsche uses etymology to provide "legitimacy" for his privileging of aristocratic (noble) over slave morality.
2 Nietzsche's etymology in this instance is accurate.
3 A prolonged, devastating, and inconclusive pan-European war between Protestant and Catholic powers (1618–48).
4 Plebian: originally of the common people of ancient Rome. By analogy, Nietzsche refers to the leveling tendency of English ideas.

eloquence with which all previous volcanoes have spoken up to now.[1]

5

With respect to *our* problem—which for good reasons we can call a *quiet* problem and which addresses in a refined manner only a few ears—there is no little interest in establishing the point that often in those words and roots which designate "good" there still shines through the main nuance of what made the nobility feel they were men of higher rank. It's true that in most cases they perhaps name themselves simply after their superiority in strength (as "the powerful," "the masters," "those in command") or after the most visible sign of this superiority, for example, as "the rich" or "the owners" (that is the meaning of *arya* [Sanskrit: Aryan], and the corresponding words in Iranian and Slavic). But they also name themselves after a *typical characteristic*, and this is the case which is our concern here. For instance, they call themselves "the truthful," above all the Greek nobility, whose mouthpiece is the Megarian poet Theognis.[2] The word developed for this characteristic, ἐσθλός [esthlos: fine, noble, good, brave], indicates, according to its root meaning, a man who *is*, who possesses reality, who really exists, who is true. Then, with a subjective transformation, it indicates the true man as the truthful man. In this phase of conceptual transformation, it becomes the slogan and catch phrase for the nobility, and its sense shifts entirely over to mean "aristocratic," to mark a distinction from the *lying* common man, as Theognis takes and presents him—until finally, after the decline of the nobility, the word remains as a designation of spiritual *noblesse* [French: nobility] and becomes, as it were, ripe and sweet. In the word κακός [kakos: weak, worthless, evil, penniless], as in the word δειλός [deilos: cowardly, miserable, low-born] (the plebeian in contrast to the ἀγαθός [agathos: good man]), the cowardice is emphasized. This perhaps provides a hint about the direction in which

---

1 Henry Thomas Buckle, English historian and author of *The History of Civilization in England* (1862). Buckle's attempt to explain historical events and the development of nations as the result of certain mathematically precise laws made his name synonymous with mechanistic thinking.

2 Sixth-century BCE Aristocratic Greek poet from Megara whose work was the subject of Nietzsche's first published article.

we have to seek the etymological origin for the multiple meanings of αγαθός [agathos: good, high-born, brave, good, ethical].

In the Latin word *malus* [bad, evil, ugly] (which I place alongside μέλας [melas: black, dark, evil, ugly]) the common man could be designated as the dark-colored, above all as the dark-haired (*"hic niger est"* ["this soul is dark"]),[1] as the pre-Aryan inhabitant of Italian soil, who through this color stood out most clearly from those who became dominant, the blonds, that is, the conquering races of Aryans.[2] At any rate, Gaelic offers me an exactly corresponding example—the word *fin* (for example, in the name *Fin-Gal*[3]), the term designating nobility and finally the good, noble, and pure, originally referred to the blond-headed man in contrast to the dusky, dark-haired original inhabitants. Incidentally, the Celts were a thoroughly blond race. People are wrong when they link those traces of a basically dark-haired population, which are noticeable on the carefully prepared ethnographic maps of Germany, with any Celtic origin and mixing of blood, as Virchow still does.[4] It is much rather the case that in these places the *pre-Aryan* population of Germany predominates. (The same is true for almost all of Europe: essentially the conquered races have finally attained the upper hand for themselves once again,

---

1 Horace or Quintus Horatius Flaccus (65–8 BCE), Roman lyric poet. Nietzsche quotes Horace's *Satires*, I. iv. 85.

2 It is conjectured that the Aryan races included all those peoples who spoke Indo-European languages, from the Middle East to Northern Europe. Nietzsche contends that Nordic blond and pale warriors constituted an early aristocratic class of conquerors over the dark-haired and dark-skinned races whose predominance in Europe, particularly Southern Europe, had established them as the majority. The tendentious shift in the meaning of words that correspond to human qualities in the ancient world is here recalled and briefly examined by Nietzsche as the philologist he was. Also, Nietzsche makes the case that modern democracy has leveled and mixed the races to such an extent that the dark-haired people again have gained the upper hand in modern societies, which he blames on the impact of Christian "slave morality."

3 Fin-Gal, father of Ossian, the supposed author of the infamous literary forgery *Fingal, an Ancient Epic Poem* (1761), confected by the Scottish writer James Macpherson (1736–96).

4 Rudolf Virchow (1821–1902), pioneer of medical pathology, liberal advocate for public health, and leading German anti-evolutionist and opponent of Darwin.

in color, shortness of skull, perhaps even in the intellectual and social instincts. Who can confirm for us that modern democracy, the even more modern anarchism,[1] and indeed that preference for the "Commune," for the most primitive form of society, which all European socialists now share, does not indicate for the most part a monstrous *throwback* [*Nachschlag*]—and that the conquering *master race*, the race of Aryans, is not being physiologically defeated, too?). The Latin word *bonus* [good] I believe I can explicate as "the warrior," provided that I am correct in tracing *bonus* back to an older word *duonus* (compare *bellum* [war] = duellum [war] = *duen-lum*, which seems to me to contain that word *duonus*). Hence, *bonus* as a man of war, of division (duo [two]), as a warrior. We see what constituted a man's "goodness" in ancient Rome. What about our German word *"Gut"* [good] itself? Doesn't it indicate *"den Göttlichen"* [the god-like man], the man of *"göttlichen Geschlechts"* ["the family of gods]"? And isn't that identical to the people's (originally the nobles') name for the Goths? The reasons for this hypothesis do not belong here.—[2]

6

To this rule that the concept of political superiority always resolves itself into the concept of spiritual superiority, it is at first not an exception (although it may provide room for exceptions), when the highest caste is also the *priestly* caste and consequently for its overall description prefers an attribute which recalls its priestly function. Here, for example, the words "pure" and "impure" first appear as contrasting marks of one's social position, and here, too, a "good" and a "bad" also develop later with a meaning which no longer refers to social position. Incidentally, people should be warned not to begin by taking these ideas of

---

1 In this passage Nietzsche mounts a broad attack on left-wing movements in the nineteenth century. Anarchism, derived from the teachings of the French socialist Pierre-Joseph Proudhon (1809–65) and the Russian revolutionary Mikhail Bakunin (1814–76), seeks to replace centralized states with communal systems of power and property sharing. Nietzsche conflates anarchism and socialism and derides the 1871 Paris Commune as a failed anarchist experiment. Nietzsche shares Rée's contempt for the unrealistic social vision of communism.

2 Nietzsche scholars consider the etymology in this passage to be, at best, conjectural.

"pure" and "impure" too seriously, too broadly, or even sym-bolically. Instead, they should understand that all the ideas of ancient humanity, to a degree we can hardly imagine, are orig-inally much coarser, crude, superficial, narrow, blunt, and, in particular, *unsymbolic*. The "pure man" is initially simply a man who washes himself, who forbids himself certain foods that produce diseases of the skin, who doesn't sleep with the unclean women of the lower people, who has a horror of blood— no more, not much more! On the other hand, of course, from the very nature of an essentially priestly aristocracy it is clear enough how precisely here the opposition between different evaluations could early on become dangerously internalized and sharpened. And, in fact, they finally ripped open fissures between man and man, over which even an Achilles of the free spirit could not cross without a shudder.[1] From the beginning there has been something *unhealthy* about such priestly aristoc-racies and about the customary attitudes which govern in them, which turn away from action, sometimes brooding, sometimes exploding with emotion, as a result of which in the priests of almost all ages there have appeared almost unavoidably those debilitating intestinal illnesses and neurasthenia.[2] But what they themselves came up with as a remedy for this pathologi-cal disease—surely, we must assert that it has finally shown it-self, through its effects, even a hundred times more dangerous than the illness for which it was to provide relief. Human beings themselves are still sick from the after-effects of this priestly naïveté in healing! Let's think, for example, of certain forms of diet (avoiding meat), of fasting, of celibacy, of the flight "into the desert" (Weir-Mitchell's isolation,[3] but naturally without

---

1 Achilles is the warrior hero of Homer's *Iliad*. Achilles is half-divine and half-human, and his impetuous rage is the central theme of the epic poem, which dates from the eighth century BCE.

2 A term popularized during the nineteenth century to diagnose a syndrome of physical symptoms associated with nervous exhaustion brought on by the conditions of modernity.

3 Silas Weir Mitchell (1829–1914), American polymathic physician and writer, considered the founder of neurology, whose "rest cure" was a widely influential treatment for neurasthenia. In Nietzsche's time, "hysteria" was a catch-all diagnosis for mental illness and was considered primarily an affliction of women. Later the subject of Sigmund Freud's *Studies in Hysteria* (1895), in which hysteria is treated as the result of repressed emotions and desires.

the fattening-up cure and overeating which follow it and which constitute the most effective treatment for all hysteria induced by the ascetic ideal): consider also the whole metaphysic of the priests, so hostile to the senses, making men lazy and sophisticated, the way they hypnotize themselves in the manner of fakirs and Brahmins—Brahmanism employed as a crystal ball and *idée fixe* [French: fixed idea]—and finally the only too understandable and common dissatisfaction with its radical cure, with *nothingness* (or God—the desire for a *unio mystica* [Latin: mystical union] with God is the longing of the Buddhist for nothingness, *nirvana*[1]—and nothing more!). Among the priests, *everything* simply becomes more dangerous—not only the remedies and arts of healing, but also pride, vengeance, mental acuity, dissipation, love, thirst for power, virtue, and illness—although it's fair enough also to add that on the foundation of this *fundamentally dangerous* form of human existence, the priestly, for the first time the human being became, in general, *an interesting animal*, that here the human soul first attained *depth* in a higher sense and became *evil*—and, indeed, these are the two basic reasons for humanity's superiority, up to now, over other animals!

7

You will have already guessed how easily the priestly way of evaluating can split from the knightly-aristocratic and then continue to develop into its opposite. Such a development receives a special stimulus every time the priestly caste and the warrior caste confront each other jealously and are not willing to agree among themselves about the reward. The knightly-aristocratic judgments of value have as their basic assumption a powerful physicality, a blooming, rich, even overflowing health, together with those things required to maintain these qualities—war, adventure, hunting, dancing, war games, and, in general, everything which involves strong, free, and happy action. The priestly-noble method of evaluating has, as we saw, other preconditions: these make it difficult enough for them when it comes to war! As is well known, priests are the *most evil of enemies*—but why? Because they are the most powerless. From their powerlessness, their

---

1 Fakirs: Hindu ascetics; Brahmins: the highest caste of scholars comprising the ruling priesthood in Hinduism. In Buddhism "nirvana" denotes the ideal state achieved with the extinction of the individual will.

hate grows among them into something huge and terrifying, to the most spiritual and most poisonous manifestations. The really great haters in world history and also the cleverest haters have always been priests—in comparison with the spirit of priestly revenge all the remaining spirits are hardly worth considering at all. Human history would be a really stupid affair without the spirit that entered it from the powerless. Let us quickly consider the greatest example. Nothing on earth which has been done against "the nobility," "the powerful," "the masters," and "the possessors of power" is worth mentioning in comparison with what *the Jews* have done against them: the Jews, that priestly people, who knew how to get final satisfaction from their enemies and conquerors merely through a radical transformation of their values, that is, through an act of the *most spiritual revenge*. This was appropriate only to a priestly people with the most deeply suppressed priestly desire for revenge. In opposition to the aristocratic value equation (*good = noble = powerful = beautiful = fortunate = loved by god*), the Jews, with a consistency inspiring fear, dared to reverse things and to hang on to that with the teeth of the most profound hatred (the hate of powerlessness), that is, to "only those who suffer are good; the poor, the powerless, the low are the only good people; the suffering, those in need, the sick, the ugly are also the only pious people; only they are blessed by God; for them alone there is salvation.—By contrast, you privileged and powerful people, you are for all eternity the evil, the cruel, the lecherous, the insatiable, the godless; you will also be the unblessed, the cursed, and the damned for all eternity!" ... We know *who* inherited this Judaic transformation of values ... In connection with that huge and immeasurably disastrous initiative which the Jews launched with this most fundamental of all declarations of war, I recall the sentence I wrote at another time (in *Beyond Good and Evil*, page 118 [Section 195]) namely, that with the Jews *the slave rebellion in morality* begins: that rebellion which has a two-thousand-year-old history behind it and which we nowadays no longer even notice because it—has triumphed.[1]

---

1 Nietzsche's "slave rebellion in morality" is associated with Jesus, whose origins as a Jew, however inconvenient for many self-proclaimed defenders of Western culture—from Ernest Renan to Heinrich Himmler—is nonetheless consistent with the social status of Jews—as marginalized, colonized, oppressed, and often enslaved—in the ancient world. Throughout *The Genealogy* Nietzsche conflates Platonism, Judaism, and Christianity with an (*continued*)

But you fail to understand that? You have no eye for something that needed two millennia to emerge victorious? ... That's nothing to wonder at: all *lengthy* things are hard to see, to assess. However, *that* is what took place: out of the trunk of that tree of vengeance and hatred, of Jewish hatred—the deepest and most sublime hatred, that is, a hatred which creates ideals and transforms values, something whose like has never existed on earth— from that grew something just as incomparable, a *new love*, the most profound and most sublime of all the forms of love:—from what other trunk could it have even grown? ... However, one should not assume that this love arose essentially as the denial of that thirst for revenge, as the opposite of Jewish hatred! No. The reverse is the truth! This love grew out of that hatred, as its crown, as the victorious crown unfolding itself wider and wider in the purest brightness and radiant sunshine, the crown which, so to speak, was seeking in the kingdom of light and height the goal of that hate, aiming for victory, trophies, and seduction, with the same urgency with which the roots of that hatred were sinking down ever deeper and more greedily into everything profound and evil. This Jesus of Nazareth, the personified evangelist of love, this "Savior" bringing holiness and victory to the poor, to the sick, to the sinners—was he not that very seduction in its most sinister and most irresistible form, the seduction and detour to exactly those *Judaic* values and innovations in ideals? Didn't Israel attain, precisely with the detour of this "Savior," of this apparent enemy against and dissolver of Israel, the final goal of its sublime thirst for vengeance? Isn't it part of the secret black art of a truly *great* politics of revenge, a farsighted, underground, slowly expropriating, and premeditated revenge, that Israel itself had to disown and nail to the cross, like some mortal enemy, the tool essential to its revenge before all the world, so that "all the world," that is, all Israel's enemies, could then take this particular bait without a second thought? On the other hand, could

---

identical ethical doctrine (under historically different guises) that devalues life and the present moment in favor of a utopian transcendent realm. It is important to note that Nietzsche was not racially antisemitic, but he associated Judaism and its offshoot Christianity with a dangerous slave morality of quietism as opposed to active aristocracy. Nietzsche's first use of this phrase is found in *Beyond Good and Evil* (1886).

anyone, using the full subtlety of his mind, even imagine a *more dangerous* bait, something to match the enticing, intoxicating, narcotizing, corrupting power of that symbol of the "holy cross," that ghastly paradox of a "god on the cross," that mystery of an unimaginable and ultimate final cruelty and self-crucifixion of God *for the salvation of humankind?* ... At least it is certain that *sub hoc signo* [Latin: under this sign][1] Israel, with its vengeance and revaluation of the worth of all other previous values, has triumphed again and again over all other ideals, over all *nobler* ideals.

9

—"But what are you doing still talking about *nobler* ideals! Let's follow the facts: the people have triumphed—or 'the slaves,' or 'the rabble,' or 'the herd,' or whatever you want to call them—if this has taken place because of the Jews, then good for them! No people ever had a more world-historical mission. 'The masters' have been disposed of. The morality of the common man has prevailed. We may also take this victory as a blood poisoning (it did mix the races up together)—I don't deny that.[2] But this intoxication has undoubtedly *been successful.* The 'salvation' of the human race (namely, from 'the masters') is well under way. Everything is visibly turning Jewish or Christian or plebeian (what do the words matter!). The progress of this poison through the entire body of humanity seems irresistible, although its tempo and pace may seem from now on constantly slower, more delicate, less audible, and more circumspect—well, we have time enough ... From this point of view, does the church today still have *necessary* work to do, does it still have a right to exist at all? Or could we dispense with it? *Quaeritur* [Latin: that's a question to be asked]. It seems that it rather obstructs and hinders the progress of that poison, instead of speeding it up? Well, that just might be what makes the church useful ... Certainly the church is for all intents and purposes

---

1 Nietzsche revises the motto of emperor Constantine the Great (c. 272–337 CE), which he had inscribed on the cross ("in hoc signo vinces" [in this sign you will triumph]) in order to convert the cross into a symbol of subjugation rather than of victory.

2 Earnest theorizing on issues of race and blood was commonplace in the nineteenth and twentieth centuries. It forms the backdrop to the pseudo-science of eugenics, American compulsory sterilization programs, and the Nazi Holocaust.

something gross and vulgar, which a more delicate intelligence, a truly modern taste, resists. Shouldn't the church at least be something more sophisticated? ... Today it alienates more than it seduces.... Who among us would really be a free spirit if the church were not there? The church repels us, *not* its poison.... Apart from the church, we even love the poison...."—This is the epilogue of a "freethinker" to my speech, an honest animal, as he has richly revealed, and in addition a democratic one. He listened to me up to that point and could not bear to hear my silence—since for me at this juncture there is much to be silent about.

10

The slave revolt in morality begins when the *ressentiment*[1] itself becomes creative and gives birth to values: the *ressentiment* of those beings who are prevented from a genuine reaction, that is, something active, and who compensate for that with a merely imaginary vengeance. Whereas all noble morality grows out of a triumphant affirmation of one's own self, slave morality from the start says "No" to what is "outside," "other," "not itself." And *this* "No" is its creative act. This transformation of the glance which confers value—this *necessary* projection towards what is outer instead of back onto itself—that is inherent in *ressentiment*. In order to arise, slave morality always requires first an opposing world, a world outside itself. Psychologically speaking, it needs external stimuli in order to act at all—its action is basically reaction. The reverse is the case with the noble method of valuing: it acts and grows spontaneously. It seeks its opposite only to affirm its own self even more thankfully, with even more rejoicing—its negative concept of "low," "common," "bad" is merely a pale contrasting image after the fact in relation to its positive basic concept, thoroughly saturated with life and passion, "We are noble, good, beautiful, and happy!" When the noble way of evaluating makes a mistake and abuses reality, this happens with reference to the sphere which it does *not* know well enough, indeed, the sphere it has strongly resisted learning the truth about: under certain circumstances it misjudges the sphere it despises, the sphere of the common man, of the low people. On the other hand, even if we assume that the feeling

---

1 Nietzsche uses this French word to stand for the essence of slave morality, which constitutes the Jewish-Christian legacy of nihilism as opposed to the pagan-noble-aristocratic affirmation of life.

of contempt, of looking down, or of looking superior *falsifies* the image of the person despised, we should note that such distortion will fall short by a long way of the distortion with which the suppressed hatred and vengeance of the powerless man assaults his opponent—naturally, *in effigie* [Latin: as a representation]. In fact, contempt contains too much negligence, too much lack of concern, too much looking away and impatience mixed in with it, even too much of a personal feeling of joy, for it to be capable of converting its object into a truly distorted image and monster. We should not fail to hear the almost benevolent nuances which, for example, the Greek nobility places in all the words with which it separates itself from the lower people—how a constant form of pity, consideration, and forbearance is mixed in there, sweetening the words, to the point where almost all words referring to the common man finally remain as expressions for "unhappy" and "worthy of pity" (compare δειλός [deilos: cowardly], δείλαιος [deilaios: mean, low], πονηρός [poneros: oppressed by toil, wretched, base], μοχθηρός [mochtheros: suffering, wretched]—the last two basically designating the common man as a slave worker and beast of burden)—and how, on the other hand, for the Greek ear the words "bad," "low," and "unhappy" have never stopped echoing a single note, one tone color, in which "unhappy" predominates. This is the inheritance of the old, nobler, and aristocratic way of evaluating, which does not betray its principles even in contempt. (—Philologists should recall the sense in which οϊζυρος [oizyros: miserable, wretched], άνολβος [anolbos: unblessed, wretched, poor], τλήμων [tlemon: wretched, miserable], δυστυχεῖν [dystychein: unfortunate, unlucky] *and* ξυμφορά [xymphora: misfortune] were used). The "well born" simply *felt* they were "the happy ones"; they did not have to construct their happiness artificially first by looking at their enemies, or in some circumstances to talk themselves into it, *to lie to themselves into it* (the way all men of *ressentiment* habitually do). Similarly, they knew, as complete men overloaded with power and thus *necessarily* active, that they must not separate action from happiness—they considered being active necessarily associated with happiness (that's where the phrase εὖ πράττειν [eu prattein: prosper, succeed] derives its origin)—all this is very much the opposite of "happiness" at the level of the powerless and oppressed, those festering with poisonous and hostile feelings, among whom happiness comes out essentially as a narcotic, an anaesthetic, quiet, peace, "Sabbath," relaxing the soul, and stretching one's limbs, in short, as something *passive*. While the noble man lives for himself with trust and candor (γενναῖος [gennaios], meaning "of noble birth," stresses the nuance "upright" and also probably "naive"), the man of *ressentiment* is neither upright nor naive, nor honest and direct with himself. His soul *squints*. His spirit loves hiding places, secret paths, and back doors. Everything furtive attracts him as *his* world, *his* security, *his* refreshment. He understands about remaining silent, not forgetting, waiting, temporarily diminishing himself, humiliating himself. A race of such men of *ressentiment* will inevitably end up *cleverer* than any noble race. It will also value cleverness to a completely different extent, that is, as a condition of existence of the utmost importance; whereas, cleverness among noble men easily acquires a delicate aftertaste of luxury and sophistication about it:—here it is simply far less important than the complete functional certainty of the ruling *unconscious* instincts or even a certain lack of cleverness, something like brave recklessness, whether in the face of danger or of an enemy, or those wildly enthusiastic, sudden fits of anger, love, reverence, thankfulness, and vengeance, by which in all ages noble souls have recognized each other. The *ressentiment* of the noble man himself, if it comes over him, consumes and exhausts itself in an immediate reaction and therefore does not *poison*. On the other hand, in countless cases it just does not appear at all; whereas, in the case of all weak and powerless people it is unavoidable. Being unable to take one's enemies, one's misfortunes, even one's *bad deeds* seriously for any length of time—that is the mark of strong, complete natures, in whom there is a surplus of plastic, creative, healing power, as well as the power to make one forget (a good example for that from the modern world is Mirabeau, who had no memory of the insults and the maliciousness people directed at him and who therefore could not forgive, merely because he—forgot). Such a man with a single shrug simply throws off himself the many worms which eat into other men.[1] Only here is the real "*love* for one's enemy"[2] even possible—provided that it is at all possible on earth.—How much respect a noble man already has

---

1 Honoré Gabriel Riqueti, comte de Mirabeau (1749–91), French politician and writer at the time of the French Revolution and president of the National Assembly in 1791. Mirabeau was a controversial figure, vilified by many for his perceived willingness to compromise Jacobin ideals.

2 Nietzsche notes that Matthew 5:43–44 contains a distillation of the transformation of aristocratic values: "Ye have heard that it hath

for his enemies!—and such a respect is already a bridge to love....
In fact, he demands his enemy for himself, as his mark of honor.
Indeed, he has no enemy other than one in whom there is nothing to despise and a *great deal* to respect! By contrast, imagine for
yourself "the enemy" as a man of *ressentiment* conceives him—
and right here we have his action, his creation: he has conceptualized "the evil enemy," "*the evil one*," as, in fact, a fundamental
idea from which he now also thinks his way to a complementary
image and counterpart, a "good man"—himself! ...

11

We see exactly the opposite with the noble man, who conceives the
fundamental idea "good" in advance and spontaneously, that is,
from himself, and from there he first creates a picture of "bad" for
himself! This "bad" originating from the noble man and that "evil"
arising out of the stew pot of insatiable hatred—of these the first is
a later creation, an afterthought, a complementary color; by contrast, the second is the original, the beginning, the essential *act* in
the conception of a slave morality—although the two words "bad"
and "evil" both seem opposite to the same idea of "good," how
different they are! But it is *not* the same idea of "good." Instead, we
should ask *who* the "evil person" really is in the sense of the morality of *ressentiment*. The strict answer to that is as follows: *simply* the
"good person" of the other morality, the noble man, the powerful,
the ruling man, only colored over, only re-interpreted, only looked
at again through the poisonous eyes of *ressentiment*. Here there is
one thing we will be the last to deny: whoever has come to know
those "good men" only as enemies, has known them also as nothing but *evil enemies*, and the same people who are kept within such
strict limits by custom, honor, habit, gratitude, and even more by
mutual surveillance and jealousy *inter pares* [Latin: among equals]
and who, by contrast, demonstrate in relation to each other such
resourceful consideration, self-control, refinement, loyalty, pride,
and friendship—to the outside, where the strange world, the world
of what is foreign to them, begins, these men are not much better
than beasts of prey turned loose. Here they enjoy freedom from all
social constraints. In the wilderness they make up for the tension

---

been said, Thou shalt love thy neighbor, and hate thine enemy.—
But I say unto you, Love your enemies, bless them that curse you,
do good to them that hate you, and pray for them that despitefully
use you, and persecute you." See Appendix C2.

which a long fenced-in confinement within the peace of the community brings about. They go *back* to the innocent conscience of a beast of prey, as joyful monsters, who perhaps walk away from a dreadful sequence of murder, arson, rape, and torture with an exhilaration and spiritual equilibrium, as if they had merely pulled off a student prank, convinced that now the poets once again have something to sing about and praise for a long time to come. At the bottom of all these noble races we cannot fail to recognize the beast of prey, the *blond beast*[1] splendidly roaming around in its lust for loot and victory. This hidden basis from time to time needs to be discharged: the beast must come out again, must go back into the wilderness once more,—Roman, Arab, German, Japanese nobility, Homeric heroes, Scandinavian Vikings—in this need they are all alike. It is the noble races that left behind the concept of the "barbarian" in all their tracks, wherever they went. A consciousness of and even a pride in this fact still reveals itself in their highest culture (for example, when Pericles says to his Athenians, in that famous funeral speech, "our audacity has broken a way through to every land and sea, putting up permanent memorials to itself for good *and ill*"). This "audacity" of the noble races, mad, absurd, and sudden in the way it expresses itself, its unpredictability, even the improbability of its undertakings—Pericles[2] emphatically praises the ῥαθυμία [rathymia: frivolity] of the Athenians—their indifference to and contempt for safety, body, life, comfort, their fearsome cheerfulness and the depth of their joy in all destruction, in all the physical pleasures of victory and cruelty—all this was summed up for those who suffered from such audacity in the image of the "barbarian," of the "evil enemy," of something like the "Goth" or "Vandal."[3] The deep, icy mistrust which the

---

1 The "blond beast" is upheld by Nietzsche as the archetype of the strong, willful, healthy, proud, natural, life-affirming, aristocratic being who stands in direct contradiction to the civilized, life-denying, priest-guided peoples whom he identifies with slave morality.

2 Pericles (495–429 BCE), political leader and orator in Athens at the outbreak of the Peloponnesian War (431–404 BCE). He delivered his famous funeral oration at the end of the first year of the war.

3 The Goths were tribes from eastern Germany who attacked the Roman Empire in the third and fourth centuries. Later (as the Visigoths and Ostrogoths), following the collapse of the Roman Empire, they gained political dominance in parts of Europe. Vandals were eastern Germanic tribes, allied to the Goths, who also invaded the Roman Empire.

German evokes, as soon as he comes to power, once more again today—is still an after-effect of that unforgettable terror with which for centuries Europe confronted the rage of the blond Germanic beast (although there is hardly any idea linking the old Germanic tribes and we Germans, let alone any blood relationship).[1] Once before I have remarked on Hesiod's dilemma when he thought up his sequence of cultural periods and sought to express them as Gold, Silver, and Iron.[2] He didn't know what to do with the contradiction presented to him by the marvelous but, at the same time, so horrifying and violent world of Homer, other than to make two cultural ages out of one and then place one after the other—first the Age of Heroes and Demigods from Troy and Thebes, just as that world remained in the memories of the noble families who had their own ancestors in it, and then the Age of Iron as that same world appeared to the descendants of the downtrodden, exploited, ill-treated, and those carried off and sold—an age of iron, as mentioned: hard, cold, cruel, empty of feeling and scruples, with everything crushed and covered with blood.[3] Assuming as true what in any event is taken as "the truth" nowadays, that it is the *point of all culture* simply to breed a tame and civilized animal, a *domestic pet*, out of the beast of prey "man," then we would undoubtedly have to consider all those instincts of reaction and of *ressentiment* with whose help the noble races and all their ideals were finally disgraced and overpowered as the essential *instruments of culture*—though to do that would not yet be to claim that the *bearers* of these instincts also in themselves represented culture. Instead, the opposite would not only be probable—no! nowadays it is *visibly apparent!* These people carrying instincts of oppression and of a lust for revenge, the descendants of all European and non-European slavery, of all pre-Aryan populations in particular—they represent the regression

---

1 Typical of Nietzsche, he is dismissive of German nationalism, especially German assertions of racial superiority linked to heredity.

2 Hesiod (fl. c. 700 BCE), Greek poet who was the subject of Nietzsche's lecture "Homer's Contest," delivered at Basel in 1872, in which Hesiod is seen as the exponent of a purely human, if plebian culture, while the world represented in Homer, based on warfare and aristocratic values, is still dominated by the gods.

3 Nietzsche's point here is that Hesiod divided the last of his ages into two: the age of Gold, which was a Heroic Age, symbolized by the legendary heroes of Troy and Thebes; and an Iron Age, which was not a heroic and glorious period but one full of misery and suffering.

of mankind! These "instruments of culture" are a disgrace to humanity and more a reason to be suspicious of or a counterargument against "culture" in general! We may well be right when we hang onto our fear of the blond beast at the bottom of all noble races and keep up our guard. But who would not find it a hundred times better to fear, if he could at the same time admire, rather than *not* fear but in the process no longer be able to rid himself of the disgusting sight of the failures, the stunted, the emaciated, and the poisoned? And is not that *our* fate? Today what is it that constitutes our aversion to "man"?—For we *suffer* from man. There's no doubt of that. It is *not* a matter of fear. Rather it's the fact that we have nothing more to fear from man, that the maggot "man" is in the foreground swarming around, that the "tame man," the hopelessly mediocre and unedifying man, has already learned to feel that he is the goal, the pinnacle, the meaning of history, "the higher man,"—yes indeed, that he has a certain right to feel that about himself, insofar as he feels separate from the excessive number of failed, sick, tired, and spent people, who are nowadays beginning to make Europe stink, so that he senses that he is at least relatively successful, at least still capable of life, of at least saying "Yes" to life.

12

—At this point I won't suppress a sigh and a final confidence. What is it exactly that I find so totally unbearable? Something which I cannot deal with on my own, which makes me choke and feel faint? Bad air! Bad air! That something which has failed is coming close to me, that I have to smell the entrails of a failed soul! ... Apart from that, what can we not endure by way of need, deprivation, bad weather, infirmity, hardship, and loneliness? Basically, we can deal with all the other things, born as we are to an underground and struggling existence. We come back again and again into the light, we live over and over our golden hour of victory—and then we stand there, just as we were born, unbreakable, tense, ready for something new, for something even more difficult, more distant, like a bow which all troubles only serve to pull even tighter. But if there are heavenly goddesses who are our patrons, beyond good and evil,[1] then from time to time grant me a glimpse, just grant me a single glimpse at something perfect, something completely developed, happy, powerful, triumphant,

---

1 A reference to Nietzsche's work by this title published in 1886.

from which there is still something to fear! A glimpse of a man who justifies *the* human being, of a complementary and redeeming stroke-of-luck [*Glücksfall*] of a man, for whose sake we can hang onto *a faith in humanity*! ... For matters stand like this: the diminution and leveling of European man conceal *our* greatest danger, since we grow tired at the sight of him ... We see nothing today which wants to be greater. We suspect that things are still going down, down into something thinner, more good-natured, more prudent, more comfortable, more mediocre, more indifferent, more Chinese, more Christian—humanity, there is no doubt, is becoming constantly "better." ... Europe's fate lies right here—with the fear of man we also have lost the love for him, the reverence for him, the hope for him, indeed, our will to him. A glimpse at man nowadays makes us tired—what is contemporary nihilism, if it is not *that*? ... We are weary of *man*....

13

—But let's come back: the problem with the *other* origin of the "good," of the good man, as the person of *ressentiment* has imagined it for himself, demands its own conclusion.—That the lambs are upset about the great predatory birds is not strange, but the fact that these large birds of prey snatch away small lambs provides no reason for holding anything against them. And if the lambs say among themselves, "These predatory birds are evil, and whoever is least like a predatory bird and instead is like its opposite, a lamb—shouldn't that animal be good?" there is nothing to find fault with in this setting up of an ideal, except for the fact that the birds of prey will look down on them with a little mockery and perhaps say to themselves, "*We* are not at all annoyed with these good lambs. We even love them. Nothing is tastier than a tender lamb." To demand from strength that it does *not* express itself as strength, that it does *not* consist of a will to overpower, a will to throw down, a will to rule, a thirst for enemies and opposition and triumphs, is just as unreasonable as to demand from weakness that it express itself as strength. A quantum of force is simply such a quantum of drive, will, and action—rather, it is nothing but this very driving, willing, and acting itself—and it cannot appear as anything else except through the seduction of language (and the fundamental errors of reason petrified in it), which understands and misunderstands all action as conditioned by something which causes actions, by a "subject."[1] For, in just the same way as people separate lightning from its flash and take the latter as an *action*, as the effect of a subject called lightning, so popular morality separates strength from manifestations of strength, as if behind the strong person there were an indifferent substrate that is *free* to express strength or not. But there is no such substrate; there is no "being" behind the doing, acting, or becoming. "The doer" is merely fabricated and added into the action—the act is everything. People basically duplicate the action: when they see a lightning flash, that is an action-action [*ein Thun-Thun*]: they set up the same event first as the cause and then yet again as its effect. Natural scientists are no better when they say "Force moves, force causes," and so on—our entire scientific knowledge, for all its coolness and freedom from feelings, still remains exposed to the seduction of language and has not gotten rid of the changelings foisted on it, the "subjects" (the atom, for example, is such a changeling, like the Kantian "thing-in-itself"[2]): it's no wonder, then, that the repressed, secretly smoldering feelings of revenge and hate use this belief for their own purposes and even, in fact, maintain a faith in nothing more fervently than in the idea that *the strong person is free* to be weak and that the predatory bird is free to be a lamb:—in so doing, of course, they arrogate to themselves the right to *blame* the bird of prey for being a bird of prey.... When the oppressed, the downtrodden, and the violated say to each other, with the vengeful cunning of the powerless, "Let us be different from evil people, namely, good! And every person is good who does not oppress, who hurts no one, who does not attack, who does not retaliate, who hands revenge over to God, who keeps himself hidden, as we do, the person who avoids all evil and demands little from life in general, like us, the patient, humble, and upright"—what that amounts to, coolly expressed and without bias, is essentially nothing more than "We weak people are merely weak. It's good if we do not do anything *for which we are*

---

1 Grammatically, the part of a sentence ("the doer") that performs the action being described. In terms of epistemology, the subject is the basis for knowledge. For example, according to Schopenhauer, the knowing subject seeks release from the all-desiring will.

2 The "thing-in-itself" is Kant's term for irreducible reality. Not perceivable by the senses, its existence can be intellectually deduced only from appearances. In Nietzsche's time, thc atom had been postulated by Ernst Mach (1836–1916), but only as an idealized mental construct and not as an actual unit of matter.

not strong enough"—but this bitter state, this shrewdness of the lowest ranks, which even insects possess (when in great danger they act as if they were dead in order not to do "too much"), has, thanks to that counterfeiting and self-deception of powerlessness, dressed itself in the splendor of a self-denying, still, patient virtue, as if the weakness of the weak man himself—that means his *essence*, his actions, his entire single, inevitable, and irredeemable reality—is a voluntary achievement, something willed, chosen, an *action, something of merit*. This kind of man *has to* believe in the disinterested, freely choosing "subject" out of an instinct for self-preservation and self-affirmation, in which every falsehood is habitually sanctified. Hence, the subject (or, to use a more popular style, the *soul*) has up to now perhaps been the best principle for belief on earth, because for the majority of the dying, the weak, and the downtrodden of all sorts it makes possible that sublime self-deception that establishes weakness itself as freedom and their being like this or that as *a commendable act*.

14

Is there anyone who would like to take a little look down on and under that secret how man *fabricates ideals* on earth? Who has the courage for that? ... Come on, now! Here's an open glimpse into this dark workshop. Just wait a moment, my dear Mr. Curious Daredevil: your eye must first get used to this artificial flickering light.... So, enough! Now speak! What's going on down there? Speak up. Say what you see, man of the most dangerous curiosity—now *I'm* the one who's listening. —

—"I see nothing, but I hear all the more. It is a careful, crafty, light rumor-mongering and whispering from every nook and cranny. It seems to me that people are lying; a sugary mildness clings to every sound. Weakness is going to be falsified into *something of merit*. There's no doubt about it—things are just as you said."

—Keep talking!

—"And powerlessness that does not retaliate is being falsified into 'goodness,' anxious baseness into 'humility,' submission before those one hates to 'obedience' (of course, obedience to the one who, they say, commands this submission—they call him God). The inoffensiveness of the weak man—cowardice itself, in which he is rich, his standing at the door, his inevitable need to wait around—here acquires good names, like 'patience,' and is even called *the* virtue. That incapacity for revenge is called the lack of

desire for revenge, perhaps even forgiveness ('for *they* know not what they do[1]—only we know what *they* do!'). People are even talking about 'love for one's enemies'—and sweating as they say it."
—Keep talking!

—"They are miserable—there's no doubt about that—all these rumor-mongers and counterfeiters in the corners, although crouched down beside each other in the warmth—but they are telling me that their misery is God's choice, His sign, that one beats the dog one loves the most, that this misery may perhaps be a preparation, a test, an education, perhaps it is even more— something that will one day be requited and paid out with huge interest in gold, no, in happiness. They call that 'blessedness'."
—Go on!

—"Now they are letting me know that they are not only better than the powerful, the masters of the earth, whose spit they have to lick (*not* out of fear, certainly not out of fear, but because God commands that they honor all those in authority)—that they are not only better than these, but also 'better off,' or at any rate will one day have it better. But enough! Enough! I can't take it anymore. Bad air! Bad air! This workshop where man *fabricates ideals*—it seems to me it stinks of nothing but lies."

—No! Just one minute more! So far you haven't said anything about the masterpiece of these black magicians who make whiteness, milk, and innocence out of every blackness:—have you not noticed the perfection of their *raffinement* [French: sophistication], their most daring, most refined, most imaginative, and most fallacious artistic attempt? Pay attention! These cellar animals full of vengeance and hatred—what exactly are they making out of that vengeance and hatred? Have you ever heard these words? If you heard only their words, would you suspect that you were completely among men of *ressentiment*? ...

—"I understand. Once again, I'll open my ears (oh! oh! oh! and *hold* my nose). Now I'm hearing for the first time what they've been saying so often: 'We good men—*we are the righteous*'— what they demand they don't call repayment but 'the triumph of *righteousness*.' What they hate is not their enemy. No! They hate '*injustice*,' 'godlessness.' What they believe and hope for is not a hope for revenge, the intoxication of sweet vengeance (something Homer has already called 'sweeter than honey'), but the victory of God, the *righteous* God, over the godless. What

---

1 Luke 23:24: "Then said Jesus, Father, forgive them; for they know not what they do."

remains for them to love on earth is not their brothers in hatred but their 'brothers in love,' as they say, all the good and righteous people on the earth."

—And what do they call what serves them as a consolation for all the suffering of life—the phantasmagoria of future blessedness which they are waiting for?

—"What's that? Am I hearing correctly? They call that 'the last judgment,' the coming of *their* kingdom, the coming of 'God's kingdom'—but *in the meanwhile* they live 'in faith,' 'in love,' 'in hope.'"

—Enough! Enough!

15

In belief in what? In love with what? In hope for what?—There's no doubt that these weak people—at some time or another *they* also want to be the strong people, some day *their* "kingdom" is to arrive—they call it simply "the kingdom of God," as I mentioned. People are indeed so humble about everything! Only to experience *that*, one has to live a long time, beyond death—in fact, people must have an eternal life, so they can also win eternal recompense in the "kingdom of God" for that earthly life "in faith, in love, in hope." Recompense for what? Recompense through what? ... In my view, Dante was grossly in error when, with an ingenuousness inspiring terror, he set that inscription over the gateway into his hell: "Eternal love also created me."[1] Over the gateway into the Christian paradise and its "eternal blessedness" it would, in any event, be more fitting to let the inscription stand "Eternal *hate* also created me"—provided it's all right to set a truth over the gateway to a lie! For *what* is the bliss of that paradise? ... Perhaps we might have guessed that already, but it is better for it to be expressly described for us by an authority we cannot underestimate in such matters, Thomas Aquinas,[2] the great teacher and saint: "In the

---

1 Dante Alighieri (c. 1265–1321), Florentine poet and author of *The Divine Comedy* (c. 1308–20). The phrase Nietzsche quotes is from the first book of *The Inferno* (iii. 5–6). It is engraved above the entrance to hell: "Feccemilia divina potestate / La somma sapienzae 'l primo amore."

2 Thomas Aquinas (1225–74), Catholic saint and Scholastic (dialectical) theologian. Nietzsche quotes the original Latin from *Summa theologicae*, III, *Supplementum*, Q. 94, Art. I: "Beati in regno coelesti videbunt poenas damnatorum, ut beatitudo illis magis complaceat."

kingdom of heaven" he says as gently as a lamb, "the blessed will see the punishment of the damned, *so that they will derive all the more pleasure from their heavenly bliss.*" Or do you want to hear that message in a stronger tone, for example, from the mouth of a triumphant father of the church, who warns his Christians against the cruel sensuality of the public spectacles.[1] But why? "Faith, in fact, offers much more to us," he says (in *de Spectaculis* [*On Spectacles*] c. 29 ff), "something *much stronger.* Thanks to the redemption, very different joys are ours to command; in place of the athletes, we have our martyrs. If we want blood, well, we have the blood of Christ ... But what awaits us on the day of His coming again, of His triumph!"—and now he takes off, the rapturous visionary: "However, there are other spectacles—that last eternal day of judgment, ignored and derided by nations, when after so many years the old age of the world and all the many things they produced will be burned in a single fire. What a broad spectacle then appears! *How I will be lost in admiration! How I will laugh! How I will rejoice! How I will exult,* as I see so many great *kings* who by public report were accepted into heaven groaning in the deepest darkness alongside those very men who testified on their behalf, along with Jove himself! They will include governors of provinces who persecuted the name of our Lord melting in flames fiercer than those with which they proudly raged against the Christians! And then those wise philosophers who convinced their disciples that nothing was of any concern to God and who claimed either that there is no such thing as a soul or that our souls would not return to their original bodies are shamed before those very disciples as they burn in the conflagration with them! And the poets, too, shaking with fear, not in front of the tribunal of Rhadamanthus or Minos, but of the Christ they did not anticipate![2] Then it will be easier to hear the tragic actors, because their voices will be more resonant in their own calamity" (better voices since they will be screaming in even greater terror). "The comic actors will then be easy to recognize, for the fire will make them much more agile. Then

---

1 Born in Roman Africa, the "triumphant father of the church" is Tertullian (c. 155–240 CE), a fierce Christian apologist and energetic fighter against heresies. The long passage Nietzsche quotes is from Tertullian's *On Spectacles*, as translated by Alexander Roberts and James Donaldson in 1869.

2 The brothers Rhadamanthus and Minos are judges in the pagan underworld.

the charioteer will be on show, all red in a wheel of fire, and the athletes will be visible, thrown, not in the gymnasium, but into the flames, unless I have no wish to look at them then, so that I can more readily cast an *insatiable* gaze on those who raged against our Lord.[1] 'This is the man,' I will say, 'the son of a workman or a prostitute'" (in everything that follows and especially in the well-known description of the mother of Jesus from the Talmud,[2] Tertullian from this point on is referring to the Jews) "the destroyer of the Sabbath, the Samaritan possessed by the devil. He is the man whom you bought from Judas, the man who was beaten with a reed and with fists, reviled with spit, who was given gall and vinegar to drink. He is the man whom his disciples took away in secret, so that it could be said that he was resurrected, or whom the gardener took away, so that the crowd of visitors would not harm his lettuce.' What praetor or consul or quaestor[3] or priest will from his own generosity grant you this so that you may see such sights, *so that you can exult in such things*? And yet we already have these things to a certain extent *truly* represented to us by the imagining spirit. Besides, what sorts of things has the eye not seen or the ear not heard and what sorts of things have not arisen in the human heart? (1. Cor. 2, 9). I believe these are more pleasing than the racetrack and the circus and both enclosures" (the first and fourth tier of seats or, according to others, the comic and tragic stages).[4]

---

1 Nietzsche's Latin quotation of Tertullian in this sentence contains a slight misquote: *"vivos"* (living) rather than *"visos"* (seen). The English text above uses *visos* (Tertullian's word).

2 A post-biblical collection of writings and teachings in the Jewish tradition.

3 "Praetor," "consul," and "quaestor" are Roman official titles referring to holders of office involving legal duties.

4 Nietzsche quotes the Latin and inserts some of his own comments, as follows: "At enim supersunt alia spectacula, ille ultimus et perpetuus judicii dies, ille nationibus insperatus, ille derisus, cum tanta saeculi vetustas et tot eius nativitates uno igne haurientur. Quae tunc spectaculi latitudo! Quid admirer! Quid rideam! Ubi gaudeam! Ubi exultem, spectans tot et tantos reges, qui in coelum recepti nuntiabantur, cum ipso Jove et ipsis suis testibus in imis tenebris congemescentes! Item praesides" (die Provinzialstatthalter) "persecutores dominici nominis saevioribus quam ipsi flammis saevierunt insultantibus contra Christianos liques (*continued*)

Perfidem[1] [Latin: truly]: that's how it's written.

16

Let's bring this to a conclusion. The two *opposing* values "good and bad" and "good and evil" have fought a fearful battle on earth for thousands of years. And if it's true that the second value has for a long time had the upper hand, even now there is still no lack of places where the battle goes on without a final decision. We could even say that in the intervening time the battle has been constantly drawn to greater heights and, in the process, to constantly greater depths and has become constantly more spiritual, so that nowadays there is perhaps no more decisive mark of a *"higher nature,"* a more spiritual nature, than that it is split in that sense and is

---

centes! Quos praeterea sapientes illos philosophos coram discipulis suis una conflagrantibus erubescentes, quibus nihil ad deum pertinere suadebant, quibus animas aut nullas aut non in pristina corpora redituras affirmabant! Etiam poetas non ad Rhadamanti nec ad Minois, sed ad inopinati Christi tribunal palpitantes! Tunc magis tragoedi audiendi, magis scilicet vocales" (besser bei Stimme, noch ärgere Schreier) "in sua propria calamitate; tunc histriones cognoscendi, solutiores multo per ignem; tunc spectandus auriga in flammea rota totus rubens, tunc xystici contemplandi non in gymnasiis, sed in igne jaculati, nisi quod ne tunc quidem illos velim vivos, ut qui malim ad eos potius conspectum insatiabilem conferre, qui in dominum desaevierunt. 'Hic est ille,' dicam, 'fabri aut quaestuariae filius'" (wie alles Folgende und insbesondere auch diese aus dem Talmud bekannte Bezeichnung der Mutter Jesu zeigt, meint Tertullian von hier ab die Juden), "'sabbati destructor, Samarites et daemonium habens. Hic est, quem a Juda redemistis, hic est ille arundine et colaphis diverberatus, sputamentis dedecoratus, felle et aceto potatus. Hic est, quem clam discentes subripuerunt, ut resurrexisse dicatur vel hortulanus detraxit, ne lactucae suae frequentia commeantium laederentur.' Ut talia spectes, ut talibus exultes, quis tibi praetor aut consul aut quaestor aut sacerdos de sua liberalitate praestabit? Et tamen haec jam habemus quodammodo per fidem spiritu imaginante repraesentata. Ceterum qualia illa sunt, quae nec oculus vidit nec auris audivit nec in cor hominis ascenderunt?" (1. Cor. 2, 9.) "Credo circo et utraque cavea" (erster und vierter Rang oder, nach anderen, komische und tragische Bühne) "et omni stadio gratiora."

1 Nietzsche is punning here, as *perfid* in German means "perfidious."

truly still a battleground for those opposites. The symbol of this battle, written in a script which has remained legible through all human history up to the present, is called "Rome against Judea, Judea against Rome." To this point there has been no greater event than *this* war, *this* posing of a question, *this* contradiction between deadly enemies. Rome felt that the Jew was like something contrary to nature itself, its monstrous polar opposite, as it were. In Rome the Jew was considered "*convicted* of hatred against the entire human race."[1] And that view was correct, to the extent that we are right to link the health and the future of the human race to the unconditional rule of aristocratic values, to Roman values. By contrast, how did the Jews feel about Rome? We can guess that from a thousand signs, but it is sufficient to treat ourselves again to the Apocalypse of John, that wildest of all written outbursts which vengeance has on its conscience. (Incidentally, we must not underestimate the deep consistency of the Christian instinct when it ascribed this particular book of hate to the name of the disciple of love, the same man to whom it attributed that enthusiastic amorous gospel—: there is some truth to this, no matter how much literary counterfeiting[2] may have been necessary for this purpose). The Romans were indeed strong and noble men, stronger and nobler than any people who had lived on earth up until then or even than any people who had ever been dreamed up. Everything they left as remains, every inscription, is delightful, provided that we can guess *what* is doing the writing there. By contrast, the Jews were *par excellence* that priestly people of *ressentiment*, who possessed an unparalleled genius for popular morality. Just compare people with related talents—say, the Chinese or the Germans—with the Jews, in order to understand which is ranked first and which is ranked fifth. Which of them has *proved victorious* for the time being, Rome or Judea? Surely there's not the slightest doubt. Just think of who it is people bow down to today in Rome itself as the personification of all the highest values—and not only in Rome, but in almost half the earth, all the places where people have become merely tame or want to become tame—in front of *three Jews*, as we know, and *one Jewess* (in front of Jesus of Nazareth, the fisherman Peter, the carpet maker Paul, and the mother of the first-mentioned Jesus, named Mary). This is very remarkable: without doubt Rome has been conquered. It

---

1 Tacitus, *Annals*, xv, 14.
2 Nietzsche alludes to the dubious conflation of the authors of the Gospel of John and the Book of Revelation into a unitary figure.

is true that in the Renaissance there was an incredibly brilliant reawakening of the classical ideal, of the noble way of evaluating everything. Rome itself behaved like someone who had woken up from a coma induced by the pressure of the new Jewish Rome built over it, which looked like an ecumenical synagogue and was called "Church." But Judea immediately triumphed again, thanks to that thoroughly vulgar (German and English) movement of *ressentiment* we call the Reformation, together with what had to follow as a result, the re-establishment of the church—as well as the re-establishment of the old grave-like tranquility of classical Rome. In what is an even more decisive and deeper sense than that, Judea once again was victorious over the classical ideal with the French Revolution. The last political nobility which there was in Europe, in seventeenth- and eighteenth-century *France*, broke apart under the instincts of popular *ressentiment*—never on earth has there been heard a greater rejoicing, a noisier enthusiasm! It's true that in the midst of all this the most dreadful and most unexpected events took place: the old ideal itself stepped *physically* and with unheard of splendor before the eyes and the conscience of humanity—and once again stronger, simpler, and more urgently than ever rang out, in opposition to the old lying slogan of *ressentiment* about the *privileged rights of the majority*, in opposition to that will for a low condition, for abasement, for equality, for the decline and twilight of humankind—in opposition to all that there rang out the fearsome and delightful counter-slogan about the *privilege of the very few*! As a last signpost to a *different* road, Napoleon appeared, that most singular and late-born man there ever was, and in him the problem of the *noble ideal itself* was made flesh—we should consider well *what* a problem that is: Napoleon, this synthesis of *monster* [*Unmensch*] and *superman* [*Übermensch*] ...[1]

---

1 Napoléon Bonaparte (1769–1821), Corsican military officer who came to prominence during the French Revolution and the wars that followed. First Consul (1799–1804) and then Emperor of France (1804–14, 1815), he was a secularizing and egalitarian reformer of laws and the scourge of tyrants throughout Europe. Nietzsche considers the appearance of Napoléon as a return to the predatory, aristocratic, noble morality of the classical period which had been suppressed by medieval Christianity and, following the Renaissance, the reimposition of the slave morality, first by the Protestant Reformation and then by the democratizing influence of the French Revolution.

17

—Did that end it? Was that greatest of all oppositions of ideals thus set *ad acta* [Latin: aside] for all time? Or was it merely postponed, postponed indefinitely? ... Someday would there not have to be an even more fearful blaze from the old fire, one which would take much longer to prepare? More than that: would this not be exactly *what* we should hope for with all our strength? Even will it? Even demand it? Anyone who, like my readers, begins to reflect on these points, to think further, will have difficulty coming to a quick conclusion—reason enough for me to come to a conclusion myself, provided that it has been sufficiently clear for a long time what I *want*, precisely what I want with that dangerous slogan which is written on the body of my last book: *"Beyond Good and Evil"* ... At least this does *not* mean "Beyond Good and Bad."—

Note

I am taking the opportunity provided to me by this essay publicly and formally to state a desire which I have expressed up to now only in occasional conversations with scholars, namely, that some faculty of philosophy might set up a series of award-winning academic essays in order to serve the advancement of studies into the *history of morality*. Perhaps this book could serve to provide a forceful push in precisely such a direction. Bearing in mind a possibility of this sort, let me propose the following question—it merits the attention of philologists and historians as much as of truly professional philosophical scholars:
What suggestions does the scientific study of language, especially etymological research, provide for the history of the development of moral concepts?
—On the other hand, it is, of course, just as necessary to attract the participation of physiologists and doctors to these problems (of the *value* of all methods of evaluating up to now). Also, for this task it might be left to the professional philosophers in this particular case to become advocates and mediators, after they have completely succeeded in converting the relationships between philosophy, physiology, and medicine, originally so aloof and so mistrusting, into the friendliest and most fruitful exchange. In fact, all the tables of value, all examples of "thou shalt" that history or ethnological research knows about, need, first and foremost, illumination and interpretation

from *physiology*[1]—at any rate before one from psychology. All of them similarly await a critique from the point of view of medical science. The question "What is this or that table of values and 'morality' *worth*?" needs to be viewed from the most varied perspectives. For we cannot analyze the question "Value *for what*?" too finely. Something, for example, that would have an apparent value with respect to the longest possible capacity for the survival of a race (or to an increase in its power to adapt to a certain climate or to the preservation of the greatest number) would have nothing like the same value, if the issue were one of developing a stronger type. The well-being of the greatest number[2] and the well-being of the smallest number are opposing viewpoints where values are concerned. We wish to leave it to the naïveté of English biologists to take the first as already the one of *inherently* higher value.... *All* the sciences from now on have to do the preparatory work for the future job of the philosopher, understanding that the philosopher's task is to solve the *problem of value*, that he has to determine the *rank order of values*.

---

1 In addition to etymology, physiology, the study of the body and its functions, is one of the chief methodological tools employed by Nietzsche in *The Genealogy* as when, for example, he critiques the slave morality by appealing to the body as well as history for normative reference points.

2 This phrase serves as one of the fundamental axioms associated with the English philosopher and social reformer Jeremy Bentham (1748–1832), and with utilitarianism generally.

SECOND ESSAY

GUILT, BAD CONSCIENCE, AND RELATED MATTERS

1

To breed an animal that *is entitled to make promises*—is that not precisely the paradoxical task nature has set itself where human beings are concerned? Isn't that the real problem *of* human beings? ... The fact that this problem has to a great extent been solved must seem all the more astonishing to a person who knows how to appreciate fully the power which works against this promise-making, namely *forgetfulness*. Forgetfulness is not merely a *vis interiae* [Latin: force of inertia], as superficial people think. Is it much rather an active capability to repress, something positive in the strongest sense, to which we can ascribe the fact that while we are digesting what we alone live through and experience and absorb into ourselves (we could call the process mental ingestion [*Einverseelung*]), we are conscious of what is going on as little as we are with the entire thousand-fold process which our bodily nourishment goes through (so-called physical ingestion [*Einverleibung*]).[1] The doors and windows of consciousness are shut temporarily; they remain undisturbed by the noise and struggle with which the underworld of our functional organs keeps working for and against one another; a little stillness, a little *tabula rasa*[2] [Latin: blank slate] of the consciousness, so that there will again be room for something new, above all, for the nobler functions and officials, for ruling, thinking ahead, determining what to do (for our organism is arranged as an oligarchy)—that is, as I said, the use of active forgetfulness, a porter at the door, so to speak, a custodian of psychic order, quiet, etiquette. From that we can see at once how, if forgetfulness were not present, there could be no happiness, no cheerfulness, no hoping, no pride, no *present*. The man in whom this repression apparatus is harmed and not working properly we can compare

---

1 *Einverseelung*: Nietzsche's neologism which is meant to mirror the previously existing word *Einverleibung* (physical ingestion or assimilation).

2 A concept first employed by the English philosopher John Locke to describe the human mind at birth as not containing any innate ideas and that all knowledge is the product of experience.

to a dyspeptic (and not just compare)—he is "finished" with nothing…. Now, this particular animal, which is necessarily forgetful, in which forgetfulness is present as a force, as a form of *strong* health, has had an opposing capability bred into it, a memory, with the help of which, in certain cases, forgetfulness will cease to function—that is, for those cases where promises are to be made. This is in no way a merely passive inability ever to be rid of an impression once it has been etched into the mind, nor is it merely indigestion over a word one has pledged at a particular time and which one can no longer be over and done with. No, it's an active *wish* not to be free of the matter again, an ongoing and continuing desire for what one willed at a particular time, a real *memory of one's will*, so that between the original "I will," "I will do," and the actual discharge of the will, its *action*, a world of strange new things, circumstances, even acts of the will can be interposed without a second thought and not break this long chain of the will. But how much all that presupposes! In order to organize the future in this manner, human beings must have first learned to separate necessary events from chance events, to think in terms of cause and effect, to see distant events as if they were present, to anticipate them, to set goals and the means to reach them with certainty, to develop a capability for figures and calculations in general—and for that to occur, a human being must *necessarily* have first himself become *something one could predict, something bound by regular rules*, even in the way he imagined himself to himself, so that finally he is able to act like someone who makes promises—he can make himself into a pledge *for the future*!

2

Precisely that development is the long history of the origin of *responsibility*. That task of breeding an animal which is permitted to make promises contains within it, as we have already grasped, as a condition and prerequisite, the more precise task of first *making* a human being necessarily uniform to some extent, one among others like him, regular and consequently predictable. The immense task involved in this, what I have called the "morality of custom" (cf. *The Dawn* 9, 14, 16)—the essential work of a man on his own self in the longest-lasting age of the human race, his entire *pre-historical* work, derives its meaning, its grand justification, from the following point, no matter how much hardship, tyranny, monotony, and idiocy it also manifested: with the help of the morality of custom and the social strait jacket, the human being *was made* truly predictable. Let's position ourselves, by contrast, at the end of this immense process, in the place where the tree at last yields its fruit, where society and the morality of custom finally bring to light *the end for which* they were simply the means: then we find, as the ripest fruit on that tree, the *sovereign individual*, something which resembles only itself, which has broken loose again from the morality of custom, the autonomous individual beyond morality (for "autonomous" and "moral" are mutually exclusive terms), in short, the human being who possesses his own independent and enduring will, who is *entitled to make promises*—and in him a consciousness quivering in every muscle, proud of *what* has finally been achieved and has become a living embodiment in him, a real consciousness of power and freedom, a feeling of completion for human beings generally. This man who has become free, who really *is entitled* to make promises, this master of *free* will, this sovereign—how is he not to realize the superiority he enjoys over everything which is not permitted to make a promise and make pledges on its own behalf, knowing how much trust, how much fear, and how much respect he creates—he *"is worthy"* of all three—and how, with this mastery over himself, he has necessarily been given in addition mastery over his circumstances, over nature, and over all less reliable creatures with a shorter will? The "free" man, the owner of an enduring unbreakable will, by possessing this, also acquires his own *standard of value*: he looks out from himself at others and confers respect or contempt. And just as it will be necessary for him to honor those like him, the strong and dependable (who *are entitled* to make promises)—in other words, everyone who makes promises like a sovereign, seriously, rarely, and slowly, who is sparing with his trust, who *honors* another when he does trust, who gives his word as something reliable, because he knows he is strong enough to remain upright even when opposed by misfortune, even when "opposed by fate"—in just the same way it will be necessary for him to keep his foot ready to kick the scrawny unreliable men, who make promises without being entitled to, and to hold his cane ready for the liar, who breaks his word in the very moment it comes out of his mouth. The proud knowledge of the extraordinary privilege of *responsibility*, the consciousness of this rare freedom, of this power over oneself and destiny, has become internalized into the deepest parts of him and grown instinctual, has become an instinct, a dominating instinct:—what will he call it, this dominating instinct, assuming that he finds he needs a word for it? There's no doubt: the sovereign man calls this instinct his *conscience*.

3

His conscience? ... To begin with, we can conjecture that the idea "conscience," which we are encountering here in its highest, almost perplexing form, has a long history and changing developmental process behind it already. To be entitled to pledge one's word, and to do it with pride, and also *to be permitted to say* "*Yes*" to oneself—that is a ripe fruit, as I have mentioned, but it is also a *late* fruit:—for what a long stretch of time this fruit must have hung tart and sour on the tree! And for an even much longer time it was impossible to see any such fruit—no one could have promised it would appear, even if everything about the tree was certainly getting ready for it and growing in that very direction!—"How does one create a memory for the human animal? How does one stamp something like that into this partly dull, partly flickering, momentary understanding, this living embodiment of forgetfulness, so that it stays current?" ... This ancient problem, as you can imagine, was not resolved right away with tender answers and methods. Indeed, there is perhaps nothing more fearful and more terrible in the entire prehistory of human beings than the *technique for developing his memory*. "We burn something in so that it remains in the memory. Only something which never ceases *to cause pain* remains in the memory"—that is a leading principle of the most ancient (unfortunately also the longest) psychology on earth. We might even say that everywhere on earth nowadays where there is still solemnity, seriousness, mystery, and gloomy colors in the lives of men and people, something of that terror *continues its work*, the fear with which in earlier times everywhere on earth people made promises, pledged their word, made a vow. The past, the longest, deepest, most severe past, breathes on us and surfaces in us when we become "solemn." When the human being considered it necessary to make a memory for himself, it never happened without blood, martyrs, and sacrifices, the most terrible sacrifices and pledges (among them the sacrifice of the first born), the most repulsive self-mutilations (for example, castration), the cruelest forms of ritual in all the religious cults (and all religions are in their deepest foundations systems of cruelty)—all that originates in that instinct which discovered in pain the most powerful means of helping to develop the memory. In a certain sense all asceticism belongs here: a couple of ideas are to be made indissoluble, omnipresent, unforgettable, "fixed," in order to hypnotize the entire nervous and intellectual system through these "fixed ideas"—and the ascetic procedures and forms of life are the means whereby these ideas are freed from jostling around with all the other ideas, in order to make them "unforgettable." The worse humanity's "memory" was, the more terrible its customs have always appeared. The harshness of the laws of punishment, in particular, provide a standard for measuring how much trouble people went to in order to triumph over forgetfulness and to maintain a *present awareness* of a few primitive demands of social living together for this slave of momentary feelings and desires. We Germans certainly do not think of ourselves as an especially cruel and hard-hearted people, even less as particularly careless people who live only in the present. But just take a look at our old penal code in order to understand how much trouble it takes on this earth to breed a "People of Thinkers" (by that I mean *the* European people among whom today we still find a maximum of trust, seriousness, tastelessness, and practicality, and who, with these characteristics, have a right to breed all sorts of European mandarins). These Germans have used terrible means to make themselves a memory in order to attain mastery over their vulgar basic instincts and their brutal crudity: think of the old German punishments, for example, stoning (—the legend even lets the mill stone fall on the head of the guilty person), breaking on the wheel (the most characteristic invention and specialty of the German genius in the realm of punishment!), impaling on a stake, ripping people apart or stamping them to death with horses ("quartering"), boiling the criminal in oil or wine (still done in the fourteenth and fifteenth centuries), the well-loved practice of flaying ("cutting flesh off in strips"), carving flesh out of the chest, and probably covering the offender with honey and leaving him to the flies in the burning sun. With the help of such images and procedures people finally retained five or six "I will nots" in the memory, and, so far as these precepts were concerned, they gave *their word* in order to live with the advantages of society—and it's true! With the assistance of this sort of memory people finally came to "reason"!—Ah, reason, seriousness, mastery over emotions, this whole gloomy business called reflection, all these privileges and showpieces of human beings: how expensive they were! How much blood and horror is at the bottom of all "good things"! ...

But then how did that other "gloomy business," the consciousness of guilt, the whole "bad conscience" come into the world?—And with this we turn back to our genealogists of morality. I'll say it once more—or have I not said anything about it yet?—they are useless. With their own merely "modern" experience extending through only a brief period [fünf Spannen lange], with no knowledge of and no desire to know the past, even less a historical instinct, a "second sight"—something necessary at this very point—they nonetheless pursue the history of morality. That must justifiably produce results which have a less than tenuous relationship to the truth. Have these genealogists of morality up to now allowed themselves to dream, even remotely, that, for instance, that major moral principle of "guilt" [Schuld] derived its origin from the very materialistic idea of "debt" [Schulden]? Or that punishment developed as a repayment, completely without reference to any assumption about freedom or lack of freedom of the will?—and did so, by contrast, to the point where it always first required a high degree of human development so that the animal "man" began to make those much more primitive distinctions between "intentional," "negligent," "accidental," "responsible," and their opposites and bring them to bear when meting out punishment? That idea, nowadays so trite, apparently so natural, so unavoidable, which has even had to serve as the explanation how the feeling of justice in general came into existence on earth, "The criminal deserves punishment because he could have acted otherwise," this idea is, in fact, an extremely late achievement, indeed, a sophisticated form of human judgment and decision making. Anyone who moves this idea back to the beginnings is sticking his coarse fingers inappropriately into the psychology of older humanity. For the most extensive period of human history, punishment was certainly not meted out because people held the instigator of evil responsible for his actions, and thus it was not assumed that only the guilty party should be punished:—it was much more as it still is now when parents punish their children out of anger over some harm they have suffered, anger vented on the perpetrator—but anger restrained and modified through the idea that every injury has some equivalent and that compensation for it could, in fact, be paid out, even if that is through the pain of the perpetrator. Where did this primitive, deeply rooted, and perhaps by now ineradicable idea derive its power, the idea of an equivalence between punishment and pain? I have already given away the answer: in the contractual relationship between *creditor* and *debtor*, which is, in general, as ancient as the idea of "legal subject" and which, for its part, refers back to the basic forms of buying, selling, bartering, trading, and exchanging goods.

5

It's true that recalling this contractual relationship arouses, as we might initially expect from what I have observed above, all sorts of suspicion of and opposition to older humanity, which established or allowed it. It's at this particular moment that people *make promises*. At this very point the pertinent issue is to *create* a memory for the person who makes a promise, so that precisely here, we can surmise, there will exist a place for harshness, cruelty, and pain. In order to inspire trust in his promise to pay back, in order to give his promise a guarantee of its seriousness and sanctity, in order to impress on his own conscience the idea of paying back as a duty, an obligation, the debtor, by virtue of a contract, pledges to the creditor, in the event that he does not pay, something else that he still "owns," something else over which he still exercises power, for example, his body or his woman or his freedom or even his life (or, under certain religious conditions, even his blessedness, the salvation of his soul, finally even his peace in the grave, as was the case in Egypt, where the dead body of the debtor even in the tomb found no peace from the creditor—and among the Egyptians, in particular, such peace certainly mattered). That means that the creditor could inflict all kinds of ignominy and torture on the body of the debtor, for instance, slice off the body as much as seemed appropriate for the size of the debt:—and this point of view early on and everywhere gave rise to precise, sometimes horrific estimates going into the smallest detail, *legally* established estimates about individual limbs and body parts. I consider it already a step forward, as evidence of a freer conception of the law, something which calculates more grandly, a *more Roman* idea of justice, when Rome's Twelve Tables of Laws decreed it was all the same, no matter how much or how little the creditor cut off in such cases: *"let it not be thought a crime if they cut off more or less."*[1] Let us clarify for

---

1 In 450 BCE the Roman senate enacted a new set of laws that were inscribed on twelve bronze tablets. Nietzsche quotes from the sixth paragraph of the third tablet: "si plus minusve secuerunt, ne fraude esto."

ourselves the logic of this whole method of compensation—it is weird enough. The equivalency is given in this way: instead of an advantage making up directly for the harm (hence, instead of compensation in gold, land, possessions of some sort or another), the creditor is given a kind of *pleasure* as repayment and compensation—the pleasure of being allowed to discharge his power on a powerless person without having to think about it, the delight in *"de faire le mal pour le plaisir de le faire"* [French: doing evil for the pleasure of doing it],[1] the enjoyment of violation. This enjoyment is more highly prized the lower and baser the creditor stands in the social order, and it can easily seem to him a delicious mouthful, in fact, a foretaste of a higher rank. By means of the "punishment" of the debtor, the creditor participates in a *right belonging to the masters*. Finally, he also for once comes to the lofty feeling of despising a being as someone "beneath him," as someone he is entitled to mistreat—or at least, in the event that the real force of punishment, of executing punishment, has already been transferred to the "authorities," the feeling of *seeing* the debtor despised and mistreated. The compensation thus consists of an order for and a right to cruelty.

6

In *this* area, that is, in the laws of obligation, the world of the moral concepts "guilt," "conscience," "duty," and "sanctity of obligation" has its origin—its beginning, like the beginning of everything great on earth, was watered thoroughly and for a long time with blood. And can we not add that this world deep down has never again been completely free of a certain smell of blood and torture—(not even with old Kant whose categorical imperative stinks of cruelty[2])? In addition, here that weird knot linking the ideas of "guilt and suffering," which perhaps has become impossible to undo, was first knit together. Let me pose the question once more: to what extent can suffering be a compensation for "debts"? To the extent that *making* someone suffer provides the highest degree of pleasure, to the extent that the person hurt by the debt, in exchange for the injury as well as for the distress

---

1 Nietzsche quotes from Prosper Mérimée, *Lettres d'une inconnue* (1874).

2 Kant's improvement on the golden rule, the "categorial imperative," states: Act as you would wish other rational people to behave, as if it were a universal law.

caused by the injury, got an extraordinary offsetting pleasure: *creating* suffering—a real *celebration*, something that, as I've said, was valued all the more, the greater it contradicted the rank and social position of the creditor. I have been speculating here, for it's difficult to see through to the foundations of such subterranean things, quite apart from the fact that it's embarrassing. And anyone who crudely throws into the middle of all this the idea of "revenge" has buried and dimmed his insights rather than illuminated them (—revenge itself, in fact, simply takes us back to the same problem: "How can making someone suffer give us a feeling of satisfaction?"). It seems to me that the delicacy and, even more, the *Tartufferie* [French: hypocrisy] of tame house pets (I mean modern man, I mean us) resist imagining with all our power how much *cruelty* contributes to the great celebratory joy of older humanity, as, in fact, an ingredient mixed into almost all their enjoyments and, from another perspective, how naive, how innocent, their need for cruelty appears, how they fundamentally think of its particular "disinterested malice" (or to use Spinoza's words, the *sympathia malevolens* [Latin: malevolent sympathy]) as a *normal* human characteristic:—and hence as something to which their conscience says a heartfelt *Yes!* A more deeply penetrating eye might still notice, even today, enough of this most ancient and most fundamental celebratory human joy. In *Beyond Good and Evil*, 229 (even earlier in *The Dawn*, 18, 77, 113), I pointed a cautious finger at the constantly growing spiritualization [*Vergeisterung*] and "deification" [*Vergöttlichung*] of cruelty, which runs through the entire history of higher culture (and, in a significant sense, even constitutes that culture). In any case, it's not so long ago that people wouldn't think of an aristocratic wedding and folk festival in the grandest style without executions, tortures, or something like an *auto-da-fé* [Portuguese: act of faith],[1] and similarly no noble household lacked creatures on whom people could vent their malice and cruel taunts without a second thought (—remember, for instance, Don Quixote at the court of the duchess; today we read all of *Don Quixote* with a bitter taste on the tongue; it's almost an ordeal.[2] In so doing, we would become very foreign, very obscure to the author and his contemporaries—they read it with a fully clear conscience

---

1 The Spanish Inquisition's condemnation of heretics to be burned at the stake.

2 In Part II of Cervantes's novel (published in 1615), the eponymous protagonist is ridiculed while a guest of nobility.

as the most cheerful of books. They almost died laughing at it). Watching suffering makes people feel good; creating suffering makes them feel even better—that's a harsh principle, but an old, powerful, and human, all-too-human major principle, which, by the way, even the apes might perhaps agree with as well. For people say that, in thinking up bizarre cruelties, the apes already anticipate a great many human actions and are, as it were, an "audition." Without cruelty there is no celebration: that's what the oldest and longest human history teaches us—and with punishment, too, there is so much *celebration*!

7

With these ideas, by the way, I have no desire whatsoever to give our pessimists grist for their discordant mills grating with weariness of life. On the contrary, I want to state very clearly that in that period when human beings had not yet become ashamed of their cruelty, life on earth was happier than it is today, now that we have our pessimists. The darkening of heaven over men's heads has always increased alarmingly in proportion to the growth of human beings' shame *before human beings*. The tired, pessimistic look, the mistrust of the riddle of life, the icy denial stemming from disgust with life—these are not the signs of the *wickedest* eras of human beings. It's much more the case that they first come to light as the swamp plants they are when the swamp to which they belong is there—I mean the sickly mollycoddling and moralizing, thanks to which the animal "man" finally learns to feel shame about all his instincts. On his way to becoming an "angel" (not to use a harsher word here), man cultivated for himself that upset stomach and that furry tongue which not only made the joy and innocence of the animal repulsive but also made life itself distasteful:—so that now and then he stands there before himself, holds his nose, and with Pope Innocent III · disapproves and makes a catalog of his nastiness ("conceived in filth, disgustingly nourished in his mother's body, developed out of evil material stuff, stinking horribly, a secretion of spit, urine, and excrement").[1] Now, when suffering always has to march out as the first among the arguments *against* existence, as its most serious question mark, it's good for us to remember the times

---

1 Innocent III (1161–1216), Roman Catholic pope during the heyday of the medieval Church (1198–1216) and author of *De miseria humanae conditionis* (*The Misery of the Human Condition*) (1195),

when people judged things the other way around, because they couldn't do without *making* people suffer and saw a first-class magic in it, a really tempting enticement *for* living. Perhaps, and let me say this as a consolation for the delicate, at that time pain did not yet hurt as much as it does nowadays. That at least could be the conclusion of a doctor who had treated a Negro (taking the latter as a representative of pre-historical man) for a bad case of inner inflammation, which drives the European, even one with the best constitution, almost to despair, but which does *not* have the same effect on the Negro.[1] (The graph of the human sensitivity to pain seems in fact to sink down remarkably and almost immediately after one has moved beyond the first ten thousand or ten million of the top members of the higher culture. And I personally have no doubt that, in comparison with one painful night of a single hysterical well-educated female, the total suffering of all animals which up to now have been interrogated by the knife in search of scientific answers is simply not worth considering). Perhaps it is even permissible to concede the possibility that that pleasure in cruelty does not really need to have died out. It would only require a certain sublimation [*Sublimierung*][2] and refinement, in proportion to the way pain hurts more nowadays; in other words, it would have to appear translated into the imaginative and spiritual and embellished with nothing but names so unobjectionable that they arouse no suspicion in even the most delicate hypocritical conscience ("tragic pity" is one such name; another is *"les nostalgies de la croix"* [French: nostalgias for the cross]). What truly enrages people about suffering is not the suffering itself, but the meaninglessness of suffering. But neither for the Christian, who has interpreted into suffering an entire secret machinery for salvation, nor for the naive men of older times, who understood how to interpret all suffering in relation to the spectator or to the person inflicting the suffering, was there

---

whose disgust at the human body and its processes Nietzsche quotes from here as a cardinal example of the "nay-saying" to life that he associates with Christian slave morality.

1 Implicit in Nietzsche's use of racist terms and his outlook on people of African descent is the common but spurious belief in his time, even among the highly educated, that white Europeans and Black Africans had separate evolutionary lineages.

2 Nietzsche articulates, in advance of Freud, the idea of sublimation of instinctive drives as the prerequisite for and foundation of culture.

generally any such *meaningless* suffering. In order for the hidden, undiscovered, unwitnessed suffering to be removed from the world and for people to be able to deny it honestly, they were then almost compelled to invent gods and intermediate beings at all levels, high and low—briefly put, something that also roamed in hidden places, that also looked into the darkness, and that would not readily permit an interesting painful spectacle to escape its attention. For with the help of such inventions life then understood and has always understood how to justify itself by a trick, how to justify its "evil." Nowadays perhaps it requires other helpful inventions for that purpose (for example, life as riddle, life as a problem of knowledge). "Every evil a glimpse of which edifies a god is justified": that's how the pre-historical logic of feeling rang out—and was that really confined only to prehistory? The gods conceived of as friends of *cruel* spectacle—O how widely this primitive idea still rises up even within our European humanity! We might well seek advice from, say, Calvin and Luther on this point.[1] At any rate it is certain that even the *Greeks* knew of no more acceptable snack to offer their gods to make them happy than the joys of cruelty. With what sort of expression, do you think, did Homer allow his gods to look down on the fates of men? What final sense was there basically in the Trojan War and similar tragic terrors? We cannot entertain the slightest doubts about this: they were intended as *celebrations* for the gods: and, to the extent that the poet is in these matters more "godlike" than other men, as festivals for the poets as well…. Later the Greek moral philosophers in the same way imagined the eyes of god no differently, still looking down on the moral struggles, on heroism and the self-mutilation of the virtuous: the "Hercules of duty" was on a stage, and he knew he was there.[2] Without someone watching, virtue for this race of actors was something entirely inconceivable. Surely such a daring and fateful philosophical invention, first made for Europe at that time, the invention of the "free will," of the absolutely spontaneous nature of human beings in matters of good and evil, was created above all to justify the idea that the interest of gods in men, in human virtue, *could never run out*? On this earthly stage there was never to be any lack

---

1 Nietzsche recalls that both leading Protestant reformers, John Calvin (1509–64) and Martin Luther (1483–1546), authorized violence as a means of extending the power of the Reformation.

2 As recorded in Xenophon's *Memorabilia* (after 371 BCE), Hercules stoically chooses virtue over pleasure.

of really new things, really unheard-of suspense, complications, and catastrophes. A world conceived of as perfectly deterministic would have been predictable to the gods and therefore also soon boring for them—reason enough for these *friends of the gods*, the philosophers, not to ascribe such a deterministic world to their gods! All of ancient humanity is full of sensitive consideration for "the spectator," for a truly public, truly visible world, which did not know how to imagine happiness without dramatic performances and festivals. And, as I have already said, in great *punishment* there is also so much celebration!

8

To resume the path of our enquiry, the feeling of guilt, of personal obligation has, as we saw, its origin in the oldest and most primitive personal relationship there is, in the relationship between seller and buyer, creditor and debtor. Here for the first time one person moved up against another person, here an individual *measured himself* against another individual. We have found no *civilization* still at such a low level that something of this relationship is not already perceptible. To set prices, to measure values, to think up equivalencies, to exchange things—that preoccupied man's very first thinking to such a degree that in a certain sense it's what thinking *itself* is. Here the oldest form of astuteness was bred; here, too, we can assume are the first beginnings of man's pride, his feeling of pre-eminence in relation to other animals. Perhaps our word "man" (*manas* [Sanskrit: consciousness]) continues to express directly something of *this* feeling of the self: the human being describes himself as a being which assesses values, which values and measures, as the "inherently calculating animal." Selling and buying, together with their psychological attributes, are even older than the beginnings of any form of social organizations and groupings; out of the most rudimentary form of personal legal rights the budding feeling of exchange, contract, guilt, law, duty, and compensation was instead first *transferred* to the crudest and earliest social structures (in their relationships with similar social structures), along with the habit of comparing power with power, of measuring, of calculating. The eye was now adjusted to this perspective, and with that awkward consistency characteristic of thinking in more ancient human beings, hard to get started but then inexorably moving forward in the same direction, people soon reached the great generalization: "Each thing has its price, *everything* can be paid off"—the oldest and most naive moral principle of *justice*, the beginning of all "good nature," all "fairness," all "good will," all "objectivity" on earth. Justice at this first stage is good will among those approximately equal in power to come to terms with each other, to "come to an agreement" again with each other by compensation—and in relation to those less powerful, to *compel* them to arrive at some settlement among themselves.—

9

Always measured by the standard of prehistory (a prehistory which, by the way, is present at all times or is capable of returning), the community also stands in relation to its members in that important basic relationship of the creditor to his debtor. People live in a community. They enjoy the advantages of a community (and what advantages they are! Nowadays we sometimes underestimate them); they live protected, cared for, in peace and trust, without worries concerning certain injuries and enmities from which the man *outside* the community, the "man without peace," is excluded—a German understands what "misery" [*Elend*] or *êlend* [Middle High German: other country] originally means—and how people pledged themselves to and entered into obligations with the community bearing in mind precisely these injuries and enmities. What will happen with *an exception* to this case? The community, the defrauded creditor, will see that it gets paid as well as it can—on that people can rely. The issue here is least of all the immediate damage which the offender has caused. Setting this to one side, the criminal [*Verbrecher*] is above all a "breaker" [*Brecher*], a breaker of contracts and a breaker of his word *against the totality*, with respect to all the good features and advantages of the communal life in which, up to that point, he has had a share. The lawbreaker is a debtor who does not merely not pay back the benefits and advances given to him, but who even attacks his creditor. So, from this point on not only does he forfeit, as is reasonable, all these good things and benefits—but he is also now reminded *what these good things are all about*. The anger of the injured creditor, the community, gives him back again to the wild outlawed condition, from which he was earlier protected. It pushes him away from itself—and now every form of hostility can vent itself on him. At this stage of cultural behavior "punishment" is simply the image, the *mimus* [Latin], of the normal conduct towards the hated, disarmed enemy who has been thrown down, who has forfeited not only all legal rights and protection but also all mercy; hence it is a case of the rights of war and the victory celebration of *Vae Victis* [Latin: woe to the conquered][1] in all its ruthlessness and cruelty:—which accounts for the fact that war itself (including the warlike cult of sacrifice) has given us all the *forms* in which punishment has appeared in history.

10

As it acquires more power, a community no longer considers the crimes of the single individual so serious, because it no longer is entitled to consider him as dangerous and unsettling for the existence of the totality as much as it did before. The wrongdoer is no longer "outlawed" and thrown out, and the common anger is no longer permitted to vent itself on him without restraint to the same extent as earlier—instead the wrongdoer from now on is carefully protected by the community against this anger, especially from that of the immediately injured person, and is taken into protective custody. The compromise with the anger of those particularly affected by the wrong doing, and thus the effort to localize the case and to avert a wider or even a general participation and unrest, the attempts to find equivalents and to settle the whole business (the *compositio*),[2] above all the desire, appearing with ever-increasing clarity, to consider every crime as, in some sense or other, *capable of being paid off*, and thus, at least to a certain extent, to *separate* the criminal and his crime from each other—those are the characteristics stamped more and more clearly on the further development of criminal law. If the power and the self-confidence of a community keep growing, the criminal law also grows constantly milder. Every weakening and deeper jeopardizing of the community brings its harsher forms of criminal law to light once again. The "creditor" has always become proportionally more humane as he has become richer. Finally, the *amount* of his wealth even becomes measured by how much damage he can sustain without suffering from it. It would not be impossible to imagine a society with a *consciousness of its own power* which allowed itself the most privileged luxury which it can have—letting its criminals *go without punishment*. "Why should I really bother about my parasites?"

---

1 Nietzsche quotes Livy's history of Rome, *Ab urbe condita* (*From the Founding of the City*), v.x/viii.9.

2 Roman legal term referring to a mutually acceptable outcome of a case.

it could then say. "May they live and prosper; for that I am still sufficiently strong!" ... Justice, which started with "Everything is capable of being paid for; everything must be paid off" ends at that point, by shutting its eyes and letting the person incapable of payment go free—it ends, as every good thing on earth ends, *by doing away with itself.* This self-negation of justice: we know what a beautiful name it calls itself—*mercy.* It goes without saying that mercy remains the privilege of the most powerful man, or even better, his beyond the law.

11

A critical comment here about a recently published attempt to find the origin of justice in a completely different place—that is, in *ressentiment.* But first a word in the ear of the psychologists, provided that they have any desire to study *ressentiment* itself up close for once: this plant grows most beautifully nowadays among anarchists and anti-Semites; in addition, it blooms, as it always has, in hidden places, like the violet, although it has a different fragrance.[1] And since like always has to emerge necessarily from like, it is not surprising to see attempts coming forward again from just such circles, as they have already done many times before—see above, Section 14 [*First Essay*]—to sanctify *revenge* under the name of *justice*—as if justice were basically only a further development of a feeling of being injured—and to bring belated honor to reactive emotions generally, all of them, using the idea of revenge. With this last point I personally take the least offense. It even seems to me a *service,* so far as the entire biological problem is concerned (in connection with which the worth of those emotions has been underestimated up to now). The only thing I am calling attention to is the fact that it is the very spirit of *ressentiment* out of which this new emphasis on scientific fairness grows (which favors hate, envy, resentment, suspicion, rancor, and revenge). This "scientific fairness," that is, ceases immediately and gives way to tones of mortal enmity and prejudice as soon as it deals with another group of emotions which, it strikes me, have a much higher biological worth than those reactive ones and which therefore have earned the right to be *scientifically* assessed and respected first—namely, the truly *active* emotions, like desire for mastery, acquisitiveness, and so on (E. Dühring, *The Value of Life: A Course in Philosophy,*

---

1 Nietzsche consistently condemns antisemitism, which he considers a typically modern expression of *ressentiment.*

the whole book really).[1] So much against this tendency in general. But in connection with Dühring's single principle that we have to seek the homeland of justice in the land of the reactive feeling, we must, for love of the truth, rudely turn this around by setting out a different principle: the *last* territory to be conquered by the spirit of justice is the land of the reactive emotions! If it is truly the case that the just man remains just even towards someone who has injured him (and not merely cold, moderate, strange, indifferent: being just is always a *positive* attitude), if under the sudden attack of personal injury, ridicule, and suspicion, the gaze of the lofty, clear objectivity of the just and *judging* eye, as profound as it is benevolent, does not itself grow dark, well, that's a piece of perfection and the highest mastery on earth—even something that it would be wise for people not to expect here; in any event, they should not *believe* in it too easily. It's certainly true that, on average, among the most just people themselves even a small dose of hostility, malice, and insinuation is enough to make them see red and chase fairness *out of* their eyes. The active, aggressive, over-reaching human being is still placed a hundred steps closer to justice than the reactive person. For him it is simply not necessary in the slightest to estimate an object falsely and with bias, the way the reactive man does and must do. Thus, as a matter of fact, at all times the aggressive human being, as the stronger, braver, more noble man, has had on his side a *better* conscience as well as a *more independent* eye; by contrast, we can already guess who generally has the invention of "bad conscience" on his conscience—the man of *ressentiment!* Finally, let's look around in history: up to now in what area has the whole implementation of law in general as well as the essential need for law been at home on earth? Could it be in the area of the reactive human beings? That is entirely wrong. It is much more the case that it's been at home with the active, strong, spontaneous, and aggressive men. Historically considered, the law on earth—let me say this to the annoyance of the above-mentioned agitator (who once even confessed about himself "The doctrine of revenge runs through all my work and efforts as the red thread of justice")[2]—represents that very struggle *against* the

---

1 Eugen Karl Dühring (1833–1921), German philosopher, economist, and self-proclaimed founder of modern antisemitism. Author of *The Replacement of Religion through Perfection and the Elimination of Judaism through the Modern Spirit of Peoples* (1882).
2 Nietzsche quotes from Dühring's autobiography, *The Cause, My Life and Enemies* (1882).

reactive feelings, the war with them on the part of active and aggressive powers, which have partly used up their strength to put a halt to or to restrain the excess of reactive pathos and to compel some settlement with it. Wherever justice is practiced, wherever justice is upheld, we see a stronger power in relation to a weaker power standing beneath it (whether with groups or individuals), seeking ways to bring an end among the latter to the senseless rage of *ressentiment*, partly by dragging the object of *ressentiment* out of the hands of revenge, partly by setting in the place of revenge a battle against the enemies of peace and order, partly by coming up with compensation, proposing it, under certain circumstances making it compulsory, partly by establishing certain equivalents for injuries as a norm, into which from now on *ressentiment* is directed once and for all. The most decisive factor, however, which the highest power carries out and sets in place against the superior numbers of the feelings of hostility and animosity—something that power always does as soon as it is somehow strong enough to do it—is to set up *law*, the imperative explanation of those things which, in its own eyes, are generally considered allowed and legal and things which are considered forbidden and illegal, while after the establishment of the law, the authorities treat attacks and arbitrary acts of individuals or entire groups as an outrage against the law, as rebellion against the highest power itself, and they steer the feeling of those beneath them away from the immediate damage caused by such outrages and thus, in the long run, achieve the reverse of what all revenge desires, which sees only the viewpoint of the injured party and considers only that valid. From now on, the eye becomes trained to evaluate actions always *impersonally*, even the eye of the harmed party itself (although this would be the very last thing to occur, as I have remarked earlier).—Consequently, only with the setting up of the law is there a "just" and "unjust" (and *not*, as Dühring will have it, from the time of the injurious action). To talk of just and unjust *in themselves* has no sense whatsoever; it's obvious that in themselves harming, oppressing, exploiting, destroying cannot be "unjust," inasmuch as life *essentially* works that way, that is, in its basic functions it harms, oppresses, exploits, and destroys, and cannot be conceived at all without this character. We have to acknowledge something even more disturbing: the fact that from the highest biological standpoint, conditions of justice must always be only *exceptional conditions*, partial restrictions on the basic will to live, which is set on power; they are subordinate to the total purpose of this will as individual means, that is, as means to create *larger* units of power. A legal system conceived of as sovereign and universal, not as a means in the struggle of power complexes, but as a means *against* all struggles in general, something along the lines of Dühring's communist cliché in which each will must be considered as equal to every will, that would be a principle *hostile to life*, a destroyer and dissolver of human beings, an assassination attempt on the future of human beings, a sign of exhaustion, a secret path to nothingness.—

12

Here one more word concerning the origin and purpose of punishment—two problems which are separate or should be separate. Unfortunately, people normally throw them together into one. How do the previous genealogists of morality deal with this issue? Naively—the way they have always worked. They find some "purpose" or other for punishment, for example, revenge or deterrence, then in a simple way set this purpose at the beginning as the *causa fiendi* [Latin: origin] of punishment and—they're finished. The "purpose in law," however, is the very last idea we should use in the history of the emergence of law. It is much rather the case that for all forms of history there is no more important principle than that one which we reach with such difficulty but which we also really *should reach*—namely that what causes a particular thing to arise and the final utility of that thing, its actual use and arrangement in a system of purposes, are separate *toto coelo* [Latin: by all the heavens, i.e., absolutely] from each other, that something existing, which has somehow come to its present state, will again and again be interpreted by the higher power over it from a new perspective, appropriated in a new way, reorganized for and redirected to new uses, that all events in the organic world involve *overpowering, acquiring mastery* and that, in turn, all overpowering and acquiring mastery involve a new interpretation, a readjustment, in which the "sense" and "purpose" up to then must necessarily be obscured or entirely erased. No matter how well we have understood the *usefulness* of some physiological organ or other (or a legal institution, a social custom, a political practice, some style in the arts or in a religious cult), we have still not, in that process, grasped anything about its origin—no matter how uncomfortable and unpleasant this may sound in elderly ears. From time immemorial people have believed that in demonstrable purposes, in the usefulness of a thing, a form, or an institution, they could also understand the reason it came into existence—the eye as something made to see, the hand as something made to grasp. So, people also imagined punishment as invented to punish. But all purposes, all uses, are only *signs* that a will to power[1] has become master over something with less power and has stamped on it its own meaning of some function, and the entire history of a "thing," an organ, a practice can by this process be seen as a continuing chain of signs of constantly new interpretations and adjustments, whose causes do not even need to be connected to each other—in some circumstances they rather follow and take over from each other by chance. Consequently, the "development" of a thing, a practice, or an organ has nothing to do with its *progressus* [Latin: progress] towards a single goal, even less is it the logical and shortest *progressus* reached with the least expenditure of power and resources—but rather the sequence of more or less profound, more or less mutually independent processes of overpowering which take place on that thing, together with the resistance which arises against that overpowering each time, the changes of form which have been attempted for the purpose of defense and reaction, as well as the results of successful counter-measures. Form is fluid; the "meaning," however, is even more so.... Even within each individual organism things are no different: with every essential growth in the totality, the "meaning" of the individual organ also shifts[2]—in certain circumstances its partial destruction, a reduction of its numbers (for example, through the obliteration of intermediate structures) can be a sign of growing power and perfection. What I wanted to say is this: the partial *loss of utility*, decline, and degeneration, the loss of meaning, and purposiveness, in short, death, also belong to the conditions of a real *progressus*, which always appears in the form of a will and a way to a *greater power* and always establishes itself at the expense of a huge number of smaller powers. The size of a "step forward" can even *be estimated* by a measure of everything that had to be sacrificed to it. The humanity as mass sacrificed for the benefit of a single *stronger* species of man—that *would be* a step forward.... I emphasize this major point of view

1 Perhaps the key idea in Nietzsche's work: the drive to dominate and assimilate everything within its grasp, which characterizes all life forms, even in instances where self-interest seems opposed to such impulses and actions.

2 Nietzsche's argument that the body is subject to change challenges his earlier assertion of the body's status as an unchanging, normative ground.

about historical methodology all the more since it basically runs counter to the very instinct which presently rules and to contemporary taste, which would rather still go along with the absolute contingency, even the mechanical meaninglessness, of all events rather than with the theory of a *will to power* playing itself out in everything that happens. The democratic idiosyncrasy of being hostile to everything which rules and wants to rule, the modern *hatred of rulers* [*Misarchismus*] (to make up a bad word for a bad thing)[1] has gradually transformed itself into and dressed itself up as something spiritual, of the highest spirituality, to such an extent that nowadays step by step it is already infiltrating the strictest, apparently most objective scientific research, and *is allowed* to infiltrate it. Indeed, it seems to me already to have attained mastery over all of physiology and the understanding of life, to their detriment, as is obvious, because it has conjured away from them their fundamental concept, that of real *activity*. By contrast, under the pressure of this idiosyncrasy we push "adaptation" into the foreground, that is, a second-order activity, a mere reactivity; in fact, people have defined life itself as an always purposeful inner adaptation to external circumstances (Herbert Spencer). But that simply misjudges the essence of life, its *will to power*. That overlooks the first priority of the spontaneous, aggressive, over-reaching, re-interpreting, re-directing, and shaping powers, after whose effects the "adaptation" then follows. Thus, the governing role of the highest functions in an organism itself, the ones in which the will for living appear active and creative, are denied. People should remember the criticism Huxley directed at Spencer for his "administrative nihilism."[2] But the issue here concerns much *more* than "administration" ...

13

Returning to the business at hand, that is, to *punishment*, we have to differentiate between two aspects of it: first its relative *duration*, the way it is carried out, the action, the "drama," a certain strict sequence of procedures and, on the other hand, its *fluidity*, the meaning, the purpose, the expectation linked to the implementation of such procedures. In this matter, we can

---

1 A Nietzschean neologism meaning hatred of power or mastery.
2 Spencer advanced the idea of evolution as a progressive force in society. Thomas Henry Huxley (1825–95), leading British biologist and champion of Darwinism.

here assume, without further comment, *per analogium* [Latin: by analogy], in accordance with the major viewpoints about the historical method we have just established, that the procedure itself will be somewhat older and earlier than its use as a punishment, that the latter was only first *injected* and interpreted into the procedure (which had been present for a long time but was a custom with a different meaning), in short, that it was *not* what our naive genealogists of morality and law up to now have assumed, who collectively imagined that the procedure *was invented* for the purpose of punishment, just as people earlier thought that the hand was invented for the purpose of grasping. Now, so far as that other element in punishment is concerned, the fluid element, its "meaning," in a very late cultural state (for example in contemporary Europe) the idea of "punishment" actually presents not simply one meaning but a whole synthesis of "meanings." The history of punishment up to now, in general, the history of its use for different purposes, finally crystallizes into a sort of unity, which is difficult to untangle, difficult to analyze, and, it must be stressed, totally *incapable of definition*. (Today it is impossible to say clearly *why* we really punish; all ideas in which an entire process is semiotically summarized elude definition. Only something which has no history is capable of being defined).[1] At an earlier stage, by contrast, that synthesis of "meanings" still appears easier to untangle, as well as even easier to adjust. We can still see how in every individual case the elements in the synthesis alter their valence and rearrange themselves accordingly, so that soon this or that element steps forward and dominates at the expense of the rest; indeed, under certain circumstances one element (say, the purpose of deterrence) appears to rise above all the other elements. In order to give at least an idea of how uncertain, how belated, how accidental "the meaning" of punishment is and how one and the same procedure can be used, interpreted, or adjusted for fundamentally different purposes, let me offer here an example which presented itself to me on the basis of relatively little random material: punishment as a way of rendering someone harmless, as a prevention from further harm; punishment as compensation for the damage to the person injured, in some form or other (also in the form of emotional

---

1 If words and language are ultimately unreliable and therefore escape stable definition, one might reasonably ask how Nietzsche's etymological method in *The Genealogy* can be considered a trustworthy tool for recapturing the origin of ethics in language praxis.

compensation); punishment as isolation of some upset to an even balance in order to avert a wider outbreak of the disturbance; punishment as way of inspiring fear of those who determine and carry out punishment; punishment as a sort of compensation for the advantages which the law breaker has enjoyed up until that time (for example, when he is made useful as a slave working in the mines); punishment as a cutting out of a degenerate element (in some circumstances an entire branch, as in Chinese law, and thus a means to keep the race pure or to sustain a social type); punishment as festival, that is, as the violation and humiliation of some enemy one has finally thrown down; punishment as a way of making a conscience, whether for the man who suffers the punishment—so-called "reform"—or whether for those who witness the punishment being carried out; punishment as the payment of an honorarium, set as a condition by those in power, which protects the wrongdoer from the excesses of revenge; punishment as a compromise with the natural condition of revenge, insofar as the latter is still upheld and assumed as a privilege by powerful families; punishment as a declaration of war and a war measure against an enemy to peace, law, order, and authority, which people fight with the very measures war makes available, as something dangerous to the community, as a breach of contract with respect to its conditions, as a rebel, traitor, and breaker of the peace.

14

Of course, this list is not complete. Obviously, punishment is overloaded with all sorts of useful purposes, all the more reason why people can infer from it an *alleged* utility, which, in the popular consciousness at least, is considered its most essential one—faith in punishment, which nowadays for several reasons is getting shaky, still finds its most powerful support in precisely that. Punishment is supposed to be valuable in waking the *feeling of guilt* in the guilty party. In punishment people are looking for the actual *instrument* [English in original] for that psychic reaction called "bad conscience," "pangs of conscience." But in doing this, people are misappropriating reality and psychology, even for today, and how much more for the longest history of man, his prehistory! Real pangs of conscience are something extremely rare, especially among criminals and prisoners. Prisons and penitentiaries are *not* breeding grounds in which this species of gnawing worm particularly likes to thrive:—on that point all conscientious observers agree, in many cases delivering such a judgment with sufficient unwillingness, going against their own desires. In general, punishment makes people hard and cold. It concentrates. It sharpens the feeling of estrangement; it strengthens powers of resistance. If it comes about that punishment shatters a man's energy and brings on a wretched prostration and self-abasement, such a consequence is surely even less pleasant than the typical result of punishment, characteristically a dry, gloomy seriousness. However, if we consider those thousands of years *before* the history of humanity, without a second thought we can conclude that the very development of a feeling of guilt was most powerfully *hindered* by punishment—at least with respect to the victims onto whom this force of punishment was vented. For let us not underestimate just how much the criminal is prevented by the very sight of judicial and executive procedures themselves from sensing that his act, the nature of his action, is something *inherently* reprehensible, for he sees exactly the same kind of actions committed in the service of justice, then applauded and practiced in good conscience, like espionage, lying, bribery, entrapment, the whole tricky and sly art of the police and prosecution, as it manifests itself in the various kinds of punishment—the robbery, oppression, abuse, imprisonment, torture, murder, all done, moreover, as a matter of principle, without even any emotional involvement as an excuse—all these actions are in no way rejected or condemned *in themselves* by his judges, but only in particular respects when used for certain purposes. "Bad conscience," this most creepy and most interesting plant among our earthly vegetation, did *not* grow in this soil—in fact, for the longest period in the past *nothing* about dealing with a "guilty party" penetrated the consciousness of judges or even those doing the punishing. By contrast, they were dealing with someone who had caused harm, with an irresponsible piece of fate. And even the man on whom punishment later fell, once again like a piece of fate, experienced in that no "inner pain," other than what might have come from the sudden arrival of something unpredictable, a terrible natural event, a falling, crushing boulder against which there is no way to fight any more.

15

At one point Spinoza became aware of this issue in an incriminating way (something which irritates his interpreters, like Kuno Fischer,[1] who really *go to great lengths* to misunderstand him on this matter), when one afternoon, he came up against some memory or other (who knows what?) and pondered the question about what, as far as he was concerned, was left of the celebrated *morsus conscientiae* [Latin: the bite of conscience]—for him, the man who had expelled good and evil into human fantasies and had irascibly defended the honor of his "free" God against those blasphemers who claimed that in everything God worked *sub ratione boni* [Latin: from the perspective of the good] ("but that means that God would be subordinate to Fate, a claim which, in truth, would be the greatest of all contradictions"). For Spinoza the world had gone back again into that state of innocence in which it had existed before the invention of bad conscience. So with that what, then, had become of the *morsus conscientiae*? "The opposite of *gaudium* [Latin: joy]," Spinoza finally told himself "is sorrow, accompanied by the image of something over and done with which happened contrary to all expectation" (*Ethics* III, Proposition XVIII, Schol. I. II). In a manner *no different from Spinoza's*, those instigating evil who incurred punishment have for thousands of years felt, so far as their "crime" is concerned, "Something has unexpectedly gone awry here," *not* "I should not have done that"—they submitted to their punishment as people submit to a sickness or some bad luck or death, with that brave fatalism free of revolt which, for example, even today gives the Russians an advantage over us westerners in coping with life. If back then there was some criticism of the act, such criticism came from prudence: without question we must seek the essential *effect* of punishment above all in an increase of prudence, in an extension of memory, in a will to go to work from now on more carefully, more mistrustfully, more secretly, with the awareness that we are in many things definitely too weak, in a kind of improved ability to judge ourselves. In general, what can be achieved through punishment, in human beings and animals,

---

1 Kuno Fischer (1824–1907), professor of German philosophy at Heidelberg, noted for categorizing all modern philosophers as either empiricists or rationalists. Nietzsche disagreed with Fischer's identification of Spinoza (a rationalist) regarding his so-called pantheism.

is an increase in fear, a honing of prudence, and control over desires. In the process, punishment *tames* human beings, but it does not make them "better"—people could with more justification assert the opposite. (Popular wisdom says, "Injury makes people prudent," but to the extent that it makes them prudent, it also makes them bad. Fortunately, often enough it makes people stupid).

16

At this point, I can no longer avoid setting out, in an initial, provisional statement, my own hypothesis about the origin of "bad conscience." It is not easy to get people to attend to it, and it requires them to consider it at length, to guard it, and to sleep on it. I consider bad conscience the profound illness which human beings had to come down with under the pressure of that most fundamental of all the changes which they ever experienced— that change when they finally found themselves locked within the confines of society and peace. Just like the things water animals must have gone through when they were forced either to become land animals or to die off, so events must have played themselves out with this half-beast so happily adapted to the wilderness, war, wandering around, adventure—suddenly all its instincts were devalued and "disengaged." From this point on, these animals were to go on foot and "carry themselves"; whereas previously they had been supported by the water. A terrible heaviness weighed them down. In performing the simplest things, they felt ungainly. In dealing with this new unknown world, they no longer had their old leaders, the ruling unconscious drives which guided them safely—these unfortunate creatures were reduced to thinking, inferring, calculating, bringing together cause and effect, reduced to their "consciousness," their most impoverished and error-prone organ! I believe that never on earth has there been such a feeling of misery, such a leaden discomfort—while at the same time those old instincts had not all of a sudden stopped imposing their demands! Only it was difficult and seldom possible to do their bidding. For the most part, they had to find new and, as it were, underground satisfactions for themselves. All instincts which are not discharged to the outside *are turned back inside*—this is what I call the *internalization [Verinnerlichung]* of man. From this first grows in man what people later call his "soul." The entire inner world, originally as thin as if stretched between two layers of skin, expanded and extended itself, acquired depth, width, and height, to the extent that what a person discharged out into the world was *obstructed*. Those frightening fortifications with which the organization of the state protected itself against the old instincts for freedom—punishments belong above all to these fortifications—brought it about that all those instincts of the wild, free, roaming man turned themselves backwards, *against man himself*. Enmity, cruelty, joy in pursuit, in attack, in change, in destruction—all those turned themselves against the possessors of such instincts. *That* is the origin of "bad conscience." The man who, because of a lack of external enemies and opposition, was forced into an oppressive narrowness and regularity of custom impatiently tore himself apart, persecuted himself, gnawed away at himself, grew upset, and did himself damage—this animal which scraped itself raw against the bars of its cage, which people want to "tame," this impoverished creature, consumed with longing for the wild, which had to create out of its own self an adventure, a torture chamber, an uncertain and dangerous wilderness—this fool, this yearning and puzzled prisoner, became the inventor of "bad conscience." But with him was introduced the greatest and weirdest illness, from which humanity up to the present time has not recovered, the suffering of man *from man, from himself*, a consequence of the forcible separation from his animal past, a leap and, so to speak, a fall into new situations and living conditions, a declaration of war against the old instincts, on which, up to that point, his power, joy, and ability to inspire fear had been based. Let us at once add that, on the other hand, the fact that there was on earth an animal soul turned against itself, taking sides against itself, meant there was something so new, profound, unheard of, enigmatic, contradictory, and *full of the future*, that with it the picture of the earth was fundamentally changed. In fact, it required divine spectators to appreciate the dramatic performance which then began and whose conclusion is by no means yet in sight—a spectacle too fine, too wonderful, too paradoxical, to be allowed to play itself out senselessly and unobserved on some ridiculous star or other! Since then, man has been included *among* the most unexpected and most thrillingly lucky rolls of the dice in the game played by Heraclitus' "great child," whether he's called Zeus or chance.[1] For himself he arouses a certain interest,

---

1 Heraclitus (c. 535–475 BCE), pre-Socratic philosopher analyzed by Nietzsche in *Philosophy in the Tragic Age of the Greeks*, a book that was drafted in 1873 but remained incomplete at his *(continued)*

a tension, a hope, almost a certainty, as if something is announcing itself with him, something is preparing itself, as if the human being were not the goal but only a way, an episode, a bridge, a great promise ...

17

Inherent in this hypothesis about the origin of bad conscience is, firstly, the assumption that the change was not gradual or voluntary and did not manifest itself as an organic growth into new conditions, but as a break, a leap, something forced, an irrefutable disaster, against which there was no struggle, nor even any *ressentiment*. Secondly, however, it assumes that the adaptation of a populace hitherto unchecked and shapeless into a fixed form, just as it was initiated by an act of violence, was carried to its conclusion by nothing but acts of violence—that consequently the oldest "State" emerged as a terrible tyranny, as an oppressive and inconsiderate machinery, and continued working until such raw materials of people and half-animals finally were not only thoroughly kneaded and submissive but also *given a shape*. I used the word "State": it is self-evident who is meant by that term—some pack of blond predatory animals, a race of conquerors and masters, which, organized for war and with the power to organize, without thinking about it, sets its terrifying paws on a subordinate population which may perhaps be vast in numbers but is still without any form, is still wandering about. That is, in fact, the way the "State" begins on earth. I believe that fantasy has been done away with which sees the beginning of the state in a "contract."[1] The man who can command, who is by nature a "master," who comes forward with violence in his actions and gestures—what has he to do with making contracts! We do not negotiate with such beings. They come like fate, without cause, reason, consideration, or pretext. They are present as lightning

---

death. Intuitive and self-contradictory, Heraclitus teaches that existence is predicated upon continuous strife between opposing qualities. Here Nietzsche alludes to Heraclitus' Fragment 94: "Time is a child playing a game of draughts; the kingship belongs to the child."

1 Nietzsche contradicts the political tradition exemplified by Jean-Jacques Rousseau (1712–78) in his book *The Social Contract* (1762). Rather than the product of an agreement between consenting individuals, Nietzsche sees the will to power at work.

is present, too fearsome, too sudden, too convincing, too "different" even to become merely hated. Their work is the instinctive creation of forms, the imposition of forms. They are the most involuntary and most unconscious artists in existence:—where they appear something new is soon present, a power structure which *lives*, something in which the parts and functions are demarcated and coordinated, in which there is, in general, no place for anything which does not first derive its "meaning" from its relationship to the totality. These men, these born organizers, have no idea what guilt, responsibility, and consideration are. In them that fearsome egotism of the artist is in charge, which stares out like bronze and knows how to justify itself for all time in the "work," just as a mother does in her child. *They* are not the ones in whom "bad conscience" grew—that point is obvious from the outset. But this hateful plant would not have grown *without them*. It would have failed if an immense amount of freedom had not been driven from the world under the pressure of their hammer blows, their artistic violence, or at least had not been driven from sight and, as it were made *latent*. This powerful *instinct for freedom*, once made latent—we already understand how—this instinct for freedom driven back, repressed, imprisoned inside, and finally still able to discharge and direct itself only against itself—that and that alone is what *bad conscience* is in its beginning.

18

We need to be careful not to entertain a low opinion of this entire phenomenon simply because it is from the start nasty and painful. In fact, it is basically the same active force which is at work on a grander scale in those artists of power and organizers and which builds states. Here it is inner, smaller, more mean-spirited, directing itself backwards, into "the labyrinth of the breast," to use Goethe's words,[1] and it creates bad conscience for itself and builds negative ideals, just that *instinct for freedom* (to use my own language, the will to power). Only the material on which the shaping and violating nature of this force directs itself here is simply man himself, his entire old animal self—and *not*, as in that greater and more striking phenomenon, on *another* man or on *other* men. This furtive violation of the self, this artistic cruelty, this pleasure in giving a shape to oneself as

---

1 Nietzsche quotes Goethe's lyric poem "To the Moon," line 35.

a tough, resisting, suffering material, to burn into it a will, a critique, a contradiction, a contempt, a denial, this weird and horribly pleasurable work of a soul willingly divided against itself, which makes itself suffer for the pleasure of creating suffering, all this *active* "bad conscience," as the essential womb of ideal and imaginative events, finally brought to light—we have already guessed—also an abundance of strange new beauty and affirmation and perhaps for the first time the idea of the beautiful in general.... For what would be "beautiful," if its opposite had not yet come to an awareness of itself, if ugliness had not already said to itself, "I am ugly"? At least, after this hint the paradox will be less puzzling, the extent to which in contradictory ideas, like *selflessness, self-denial, self-sacrifice,* an ideal can be indicated, something beautiful. And beyond that, one thing we do know—I have no doubt about it—namely, the nature of the *pleasure* which the selfless, self-denying, self-sacrificing person experiences from the beginning: this pleasure belongs to cruelty. So much for the moment on the origin of the "unegoistic" as something of *moral* worth and on the demarcation of the soil out of which this value has grown: only bad conscience, only the will to abuse the self, provides the condition for the *value* of the un-egoistic.

19

Bad conscience is a sickness—there's no doubt about that—but a sickness the way pregnancy is a sickness. Let's look for the conditions in which this illness has arrived at its most terrible and most sublime peak:—in this way we'll see what really brought about its entry into the world at the start. But that requires a lot of endurance—and we must first go back once more to an earlier point of view. The relationship in civil law between the debtor and his creditor, which I have reviewed extensively already, has been interpreted once again in an extremely remarkable and dubious historical manner into a relationship which we modern men are perhaps least capable of understanding, namely, into the relationship between *those people presently alive* and their *ancestors.* Within the original tribal cooperatives—we're talking about primeval times—the living generation always acknowledged a legal obligation to the previous generations, and especially to the earliest one which had founded the tribe (and this was in no way merely a sentimental obligation: the latter is something we could even reasonably claim was, in general, absent for the longest period of the human race). Here the reigning conviction is that the tribe *exists* at all only because of the sacrifices and achievements of its ancestors—and that people have to *pay them back* with sacrifices and achievements. In this people recognize a *debt* which keeps steadily growing because these ancestors in their continuing existence as powerful spirits do not stop giving the tribe new advantages and lending them their power. Do they do this gratuitously? But there is no "gratuitously" for those raw and "spiritually destitute" ages. What can people give back to them? Sacrifices (at first as nourishment understood very crudely), festivals, chapels, signs of honor, above all, obedience—for all customs, as work of one's ancestors, are also their statutes and commands. Do people ever give them enough? This suspicion remains and grows. From time to time it forcefully requires a huge wholesale redemption, something immense as a repayment to the "creditor" (the notorious sacrifice of the first born, for example, blood, human blood in any case). The *fear* of ancestors and their power, the awareness of one's debt to them, according to this kind of logic, necessarily increases directly in proportion to the increase in the power of the tribe itself, as the tribe finds itself constantly more victorious, more independent, more honored, and more feared. It's not the other way around! Every step towards the decline of the tribe, all conditions of misery, all indications of degeneration, of approaching dissolution, rather lead to a constant *lessening* of the fear of the spirit of its founder and give a constantly smaller image of his wisdom, providence, and powerful presence. If we think this crude form of logic through to its conclusion, then the ancestors of the *most powerful* tribes must, because of the fantasy of increasing fear, finally have grown into something immense and have been pushed back into the darkness of a divine mystery, something beyond the powers of imagination, so that finally the ancestor is necessarily transfigured into a *god*. Here perhaps lies even the origin of the gods, thus an origin out of *fear*! ... And the man to whom it seems obligatory to add "But also out of piety" could hardly claim to be right for the longest period of the human race, for his primaeval age. Of course, he would be all the more correct for the *middle* period, in which the noble tribes developed—those who in fact paid back to their founders, their ancestors (heroes, gods), with interest, all the characteristics which in the meantime had become manifest in themselves, the *noble* qualities. Later we will have another look at the process by which the gods were ennobled and exalted (which is naturally not at all the same thing as their becoming "holy"). But now, for the moment, let's follow the path of this whole development of the consciousness of guilt to its conclusion.

20

As history teaches us, the consciousness of being in debt to the gods did not in any way come to an end after the downfall of the organization of the "community" based on blood relationships. Just as humanity inherited the ideas of "good and bad" from the nobility of the tribe (together with its fundamental psychological tendency to set up orders of rank), in the same way people also inherited, as well as the divinities of the tribe and of the extended family, the pressure of as yet unpaid debts and the desire to be relieved of them. (The transition is made with those numerous slave and indentured populations which adapted themselves to the divine cults of their masters, whether through compulsion or through obsequiousness and *mimicry* [English in original]; from them this inheritance then overflowed in all directions). The feeling of being indebted to the gods did not stop growing for several thousands of years, always, in fact, in direct proportion to the extent to which the idea of god and the feeling for god grew on earth and were carried to the heights. (The entire history of ethnic fighting, victory, reconciliation, mergers, everything which comes before the final rank ordering of all the elements of a people in every great racial synthesis, is mirrored in the tangled genealogies of its gods, in the sagas of their fights, victories, and reconciliations. The progress towards universal empires is always also the progress towards universal divinities. In addition, despotism, with its overthrow of the independent nobility, always builds the way to some variety of monotheism). The arrival of the Christian god, as the greatest [*Maximal*] god which has yet been reached, thus brought about the maximum feeling of indebtedness on earth. Assuming that we have gradually set out in the *reverse* direction, we can infer with no small probability that, given the inexorable decline of faith in the Christian god, even now there may already be a considerable decline in the human consciousness of guilt. Indeed, we cannot dismiss the idea that the complete and final victory of atheism could release humanity from this entire feeling of being indebted to its origin, its *causa prima* [Latin: first cause]. Atheism and a kind of *second innocence* belong together.—

21

So much for a brief and rough preface concerning the connection between the ideas of "guilt" and "obligation" with religious assumptions. Up to this point I have deliberately set aside the actual moralizing of these ideas (the repression of them into the conscience, or more precisely, the complex interaction of the *bad* conscience with the idea of god). At the end of the previous section, I even talked as if there were no such thing as this moralizing and thus as if those ideas were now necessarily coming to an end after the collapse of their presuppositions, the faith in our "creditor," in God. But to a terrifying extent the facts indicate something different. The moralizing of the ideas of debt and duty, with their repression into the *bad* conscience, actually gave rise to the attempt to *reverse* the direction of the development I have just described, or at least to bring its motion to a halt. Now, in a fit of pessimism, the prospect of a final instalment *must* once and for all be denied; now, our gaze *must* bounce and ricochet back despairingly off an iron impossibility, now those ideas of "debt" and "duty" *must* turn back. But against *whom*? There can be no doubt: first of all against the "debtor," in whom from this point on bad conscience sets itself firmly, gnaws away, spreads out, and, like a polyp, grows wide and deep to such an extent that finally, with the impossibility of discharging the debt, people also come up with the notion that it is impossible to remove the penance, the idea that it cannot be paid off ("*eternal* punishment"):—finally however, those ideas of "debt" and "duty" turn back even against the "creditor." People should, in this matter, now think about the *causa prima* [Latin: first cause] of humanity, about the beginning of the human race, about their ancestor who from now on is loaded down with a curse ("Adam," "original sin," "no freedom of the will") or about nature from whose womb human beings arose and into which the principle of evil is now inserted ("the demonizing of nature") or about existence in general, which remains something *inherently without value* (nihilistic turning away from existence, longing for nothingness, or a desire for its "opposite," in an alternate state of being, Buddhism and things like that)—until all of a sudden we confront the paradoxical and horrifying expedient with which a martyred humanity found temporary relief, that stroke of genius of *Christianity*: God sacrificing himself for the guilt of human beings, God paying himself back with himself, God as the only one who can redeem man from what for human beings has become impossible to redeem—the creditor sacrificing himself for the debtor, out of *love* (can people believe that?), out of love for his debtor! ...

22

You will already have guessed *what* really went on with all this and *under* all this: that will to self-torment, that repressed cruelty of animal man pushed inward and forced back into himself, imprisoned in the "state" to make him tame, who invented bad conscience in order to lacerate himself, after the *more natural* discharge of this will to inflict pain had been blocked—this man of bad conscience seized upon religious assumptions to drive his self-torment to its most horrifying hardship and ferocity. Guilt towards *God*: this idea becomes his instrument of torture. In "God" he seizes on the ultimate contrast he is capable of discovering to his real and indissoluble animal instincts. He interprets these animal instincts themselves as a crime against God (as enmity, rebellion, revolt against the "master," the "father," the original ancestor and beginning of the world). He grows tense with the contradiction of "God" and "devil." He hurls from himself every "No" which he says to himself, to nature, naturalness, the factual reality [*Tatsächlichkeit*] of his being as a "Yes," as something existing, as living, as real, as God, as the blessedness of God, as God the Judge, as God the Hangman, as something beyond him, as eternity, as perpetual torment, as hell, as punishment and guilt beyond measure. In this spiritual cruelty there is a kind of insanity of the will which simply has no equal: a man's *will* finding him so guilty and reprehensible that there is no atonement, his *will* to imagine himself punished, but in such a way that the punishment could never be adequate for his crime, his *will* to infect and poison the most fundamental basis of things with the problem of punishment and guilt in order to cut himself off once and for all from any exit out of this labyrinth of *idées fixes* [French: obsessions], his *will* to erect an ideal—that of the "holy God"—in order to be tangibly certain of his own absolute worthlessness when confronted with it. O this insane, sad beast man! What ideas it has, what unnaturalness, what paroxysms of nonsense, what *bestiality of thought* breaks from it as soon as it is prevented, if only a little, from being *a beast in deed*! ... All this is excessively interesting, but there's also a black, gloomy, unnerving sadness about it, so that man must forcefully hold himself back from gazing too long into these abysses. Here we have *illness*—no doubt about that—the most terrifying illness that has raged in human beings up to now:—and anyone who can still hear (but nowadays people no longer have the ear for that!—) how in this night of torment and insanity the cry of *love* has resounded, the cry of the most yearning delight, of redemption through *love*, turns away, seized by an invincible horror ... In human beings there is so much that is terrible! ... The world has already been a lunatic asylum for too long!

23

These remarks should be sufficient, once and for all, concerning the origin of the "holy God."—The fact that conceiving gods does not necessarily, *in itself*, have to lead to this degraded imagination, that's something we could not excuse ourselves from recalling for a moment, the point that there are *more uplifting* ways to use the invention of the gods than for this human self-crucifixion and self-laceration, in which Europe in the last millennia has become an expert—fortunately that's something we can still infer with every glance we cast at the *Greek gods*, these reflections of nobler men, more rulers of themselves, in whom the *animal* in man felt himself deified and did *not* tear himself apart, did *not* rage against himself! These Greeks for the longest time used their gods for the very purpose of keeping that "bad conscience" at a distance, in order to be permitted to continue enjoying their psychic freedom. Hence, their understanding was the opposite of how Christianity used its God. In this matter the Greeks went *a very long way,* these splendid and lion-hearted Greeks, with their child-like minds. And no lesser authority than that of Homer's Zeus himself now and then lets them understand that they are making things too easy for themselves. "It's strange," he says at one point in relation to the case of Aegisthos, a *very* serious case—

It's strange how these mortal creatures complain about the gods!

Evil comes only from us, they claim, but they themselves Stupidly make themselves miserable, even contrary to fate.[1]
But at the same time we hear and see that even this Olympian

---

1 Zeus makes these remarks to the other Olympian gods at the start of Homer's *Odyssey* (i. 32–34). Aegisthos seduces Clytaemnestra and together they murder Agamemnon, her husband, as soon as he returns home from the Trojan War. The gods, according to Homer, had warned him in advance.

spectator and judge is far from being irritated and from thinking them evil because of this: "How *foolish* they are," he thinks in relation to the bad deeds of mortal men—and even the Greeks of the strongest and bravest times *conceded* that much about themselves—the "foolishness," "stupidity," a little "disturbance in the head" were the basis for many bad and fateful things— foolishness, *not* sin! Do you understand that? ... But even this disturbance in the head was a problem. "Indeed, how is this even possible? Where could this have really come from in heads like the ones *we* have, we men of noble descent, happy, successful, from the best society, noble, and virtuous?"—for hundreds of years the aristocratic Greek posed this question to himself in re- lation to every horror or outrage incomprehensible to him which had defiled one of his peers. "Some *god* must have deluded him," he finally said, shaking his head ... This solution is *typical* of the Greeks ... In this way, the gods then served to justify men to a certain extent, even in bad things. They served as the origins of evil—at that time the gods took upon themselves, not the execu- tion of punishment, but rather, what is *nobler*, the guilt ...

24

—I'll conclude with three question marks—that's clear enough. You may perhaps ask me, "Is an ideal actually being built up here or shattered?" ... But have you ever really asked yourself enough how high a price has been paid on earth for the construc- tion of *every* ideal? How much reality had to be constantly vilified and misunderstood for that to happen, how many lies had to be consecrated, how many consciences corrupted, how much "god" had to be sacrificed every time? In order to enable a shrine to be built, *a shrine must be destroyed*: that is the law—show me the case where it has not been fulfilled! We modern men, we are the inheritors of thousands of years of vivisection of the conscience and self-inflicted animal torture. That's what we have had the longest practice doing, that is perhaps our artistry; in any case, it's something we have refined, the corruption of our taste. For too long man has looked at his natural inclinations with an "evil eye," so that finally in him they have become twinned with "bad conscience." An attempt to reverse this might, *in itself*, be possi- ble—but who is strong enough for it, that is, to link as siblings bad conscience and the *unnatural* inclinations, all those aspi- rations for what lies beyond, those things which go against our senses, against our instincts, against nature, against animals—in short, the earlier ideals, all the ideals which are hostile to life, ideals of those who vilify the world? To whom can we turn to today with *such* hopes and demands? ... In this we would have precisely the *good* people against us, as well, of course, as the comfortable, the complacent, the vain, the enthusiastic, the tired.... But what is more deeply offensive, what cuts us off so fundamentally, as letting them take some note of the severity and loftiness with which we deal with ourselves? And, by contrast, how obliging, how friendly all the world is in relation to us, as soon as we act as all the world does and "let ourselves go" just like all the world! To attain the goal I'm talking about requires a *different* sort of spirit from those which are likely to exist at this particular time: spirits empowered by war and victory, for whom conquest, adventure, danger, and even pain have become a need. That would require getting acclimatized to keen, high air, winter wanderings, to ice and mountains in every sense. That would require even a kind of sublime maliciousness, an ultimate self-conscious wilfulness of knowledge, which comes with great health. Simply and seriously put, that would require just this *great health*! ... Is this even possible today? ... But at some time or other, in a more powerful time than this moldy, self-doubting present, he must nonetheless come to us, the *redeeming* man of great love and contempt, the creative spirit, constantly pushed again and again away from every sideline or from the beyond by his own driving power, whose isolation is misunderstood by people as if it were a flight *from* reality—whereas it is only his immersion, burial, and absorption *in* reality, so that, once he comes out of it into the light again, he brings home the *redemption* of this reality, its redemption from the curse which the previous ideal has laid upon it. This man of the future, who will release us from that earlier ideal just as much as from what *had to grow from it*, from the great loathing, from the will to nothingness, from nihilism—that stroke of noon and of the great decision which makes the will free once again, who gives back to the earth its purpose and to the human being his hope, this anti-Christian[1] and anti-nihilist, this conqueror of God and of nothingness—at some point he must come ...

---

1 The German word *Antichrist* can be translated as either "anti-Christ" or "anti-Christian." As it comes before "anti-nihilist," it is safe to assume that Nietzsche means "anti-Christian."

25

But what am I talking about here? Enough, enough! At this stage there's only one thing appropriate for me to do: keep quiet. Otherwise, I'll make the mistake of arrogating to myself something which only someone younger is free to do, someone "more of the future," someone more powerful than I am—something that only *Zarathustra* is free to do, *Zarathustra the Godless*....[1]

---

1 Zarathustra was the founder of the ancient Persian religion of Zoroastrianism. The significance of Zoroaster for Nietzsche's thought is the former's invention of dualism (good vs. evil). The overcoming of this difference is the purpose of Nietzsche's *Thus Spoke Zarathrustra* (1883–85).

THIRD ESSAY

WHAT DO ASCETIC IDEALS MEAN?

Carefree, mocking, violent—
that what Wisdom wants us to be.
She is a woman. She always loves only a man of war.
Thus Spoke Zarathustra (Part I)

1

What do ascetic ideals mean?—Among artists they mean nothing or too many different things; among philosophers and scholars they mean something like having a nose or an instinct for the most auspicious conditions of a higher spirituality; among women, at best, one *additional* seductive charm, a little *morbidezza* [Italian: sickliness] on beautiful flesh, the angelic quality of a nice-looking, plump animal; among physiologically impaired and peevish people (that is, among the *majority* of mortals) they are an attempt to imagine themselves as "too good" for this world, a holy form of orgiastic excess, their chief tool in the fight with their enduring pain and boredom; among the clergy they are the essential priestly belief, their best instrument of power, and also the "highest of all" permits for power; finally among the saints they are a pretext for hibernation, their *novissima gloriae cupido* [Latin: most recent desire for fame],[1] their repose in nothingness ("God"), their form of insanity. However, *the fact that* generally the ascetic ideal has meant so much to human beings is an expression of the basic fact of the human will, its *horror vacui* [Latin: horror of a vacuum or emptiness]. *It requires a goal*—and it prefers to will *nothingness* than *not* to will.—Do you understand me? ... Have you understood me? ... *"Not in the slightest, my dear sir!"* — so, let's start from the beginning.

---

1 Nietzsche quotes from Tacitus, *Histories*, iv.6.

2

What do ascetic ideals mean?—Or, to take a single example which I have been asked to give advice about often enough, what does it mean, for instance, when an artist like Richard Wagner[1] in his later years pays homage to chastity? In a certain sense, of course, he always did this, but in an ascetic sense he did it for the first time at the very end. What does this change in "sense" mean, this radical change in sense?—For that's what it was: with it Wagner leapt right over into his opposite. What does it mean when an artist leaps over into his opposite? ... If we are willing to pause for a while at this question, we immediately encounter here the memory of perhaps the best, strongest, most cheerful, and *bravest* period in Wagner's life, the time when he was inwardly and deeply preoccupied with the idea of Luther's marriage. Who knows the circumstances which really saw to it that today, instead of this wedding music, we have *Die Meistersinger*? And how much of the former work may perhaps still echo in the latter? But there is no doubt that this "Luther's Wedding" would also have involved the praise of chastity. Of course, it would have contained a praise of sensuality, as well—and that, it strikes me, would have been very much in order, very "Wagnerian," too. For between chastity and sensuality there is no necessary opposition. Every good marriage, every genuine affair of the heart transcends this opposition. In my view, Wagner would have done well if he had enabled his Germans to take this *pleasant* fact to heart once more, with the help of a lovely and brave comedy about Luther, for among the Germans there are and always have been a lot of people who slander sensuality, and Luther's merit is probably nowhere greater than precisely here: in

---

1 Richard Wagner (1813–83), innovative German composer known for the development of the *Gesamtkunstwerk* (total work of art) in his music dramas. After passing through a hero-worshipping stage in his relationship to Wagner—indeed, Nietzsche's first book, *The Birth of Tragedy* (1872), argued for a rebirth of German culture by adopting the example of Wagner's method in his music dramas—Nietzsche suffered extreme disillusionment, especially after Wagner turned to Roman Catholic mysticism in his later work. Wagner's *Die Meistersinger von Nürnberg* (*The Mastersingers of Nuremburg*) was first performed in 1868. Nietzsche speculates that Wagner's *Luther's Wedding*, which was never completed, would have celebrated both chastity *and* sensual experience and thus anticipated the transcendent sensuality of *Parsifal*, which was first performed in 1882.

having had the courage of his own *sensuality* (—at that time people called it, delicately enough, "evangelical freedom"). But even if it were the case that there really is that antithesis between chastity and sensuousness, fortunately there is no need for it to be a tragic antithesis. At least this should be the case for all successful and cheerful mortals, who are far from considering their unstable equilibrium between "animal and angel" an immediate argument against existence—the finest and brightest, like Goethe, like Hafiz, even saw in this one *more* attraction of life.[1] It's precisely such "contradictions" that make existence enticing.... On the other hand, it's easy enough to understand that once pigs who have had bad luck are persuaded to worship chastity—and there are such swine!—they see in chastity only their opposite, the opposite to unlucky pigs, and will worship that—and with such zealous tragic grunting! We can imagine it—that embarrassing and unnecessary antithesis, which Richard Wagner at the end of his life unquestioningly still wanted to set to music and produce on stage. *But what for?* That's a fair question. For why should he be concerned about pigs? Why should we?—

3

In this matter there is, of course, another question we cannot circumvent: why was Wagner really concerned about that manly (alas, so unmanly) "simpleton from the country," that poor devil and nature boy Parsifal,[2] whom he finally turned into a Catholic in such an embarrassing way. What? Was this Parsifal meant to be taken at all *seriously*? For we could be tempted to assume the reverse, even to desire it—that the Wagnerian Parsifal was intended to be cheerful, a concluding piece and satyr play,[3] as it were, with

---

1 Hafiz: Muhammad Schamaddhin (1330–89), Persian poet who inspired Goethe's cycle of poems *West-Eastern Divan* (1819, 1827), which functioned throughout the nineteenth century as an influential example of how the cultures of the Occident and the Orient could be synthesized.

2 Protagonist of Wagner's eponymous opera (1882), which is based loosely on Wolfram von Eschenbach's Arthurian romance *Parzival* (c. 1225).

3 In ancient Greece the performance of tragedies was traditionally followed by a satyr play, whose main feature was a chorus of satyrs—half-men, half-horses—dressed in phallic costumes who provided bawdy commentary and obscene humor.

which the tragic writer Wagner wanted to take his farewell, in a respectful manner worthy of him, from us, also from himself, and, above all, *from tragedy*, that is, with an excess of the highest and most high-spirited parody of the tragic itself, of the entire dreadful earthly seriousness and earthly wailing of his earlier works, of the *crudest form* in the anti-nature of the ascetic ideal, conquered at last. That would have been, as mentioned, particularly worthy of a great tragedian, who, like every artist, first attains the final peak of his greatness when he knows how to see himself and his art *beneath* him—when he knows how to *laugh* at himself. Is *Parsifal* Wagner's secret superior laughter at himself, the triumph of his achieving the ultimate and highest artistic freedom, the artist's movement into another world [*Künstler-Jenseitigkeit*]? As I've said, we might wish that. For what would *Parsifal* be *if intended seriously*? Do we need to see in it (as it was put to me) "the epitome of an insane hatred for knowledge, spirit, and sensuality"? A curse on the senses and the spirit in one breath of hatred? An apostasy and going back to sickly Christian and obscurantist ideals?[1] And finally even a denial of the self, a cancellation of the self on the part of an artist who up to that point had directed all the power of his will to attain the reverse, namely, the *highest spiritualization and sensuousness* in his art? And not only in his art, but also in his life. We should remember how Wagner in his day so enthusiastically followed in the footsteps of the philosopher Feuerbach.[2] Feuerbach's phrase about "healthy sensuality"—in Wagner's thirties and forties, as with many Germans (—they called themselves the "*young* Germans*"[3]), that phrase rang out like a word of redemption. Did Wagner finally *learn something different*? It appears, at least, that

---

1 Obscurantism pejoratively describes opponents of the Enlightenment, the diffusion of knowledge, and liberal values. In *Human, All-Too Human*, Nietzsche writes, "The essential element in the black art of obscurantism is not that it wants to darken individual understanding, but that it wants to blacken our picture of the world and darken our idea of existence" (Volume II, Part I, 7).

2 Ludwig Feuerbach (1804–72), German philosopher, anthropologist, and influential critic of Christianity. In his most famous book, *The Essence of Christianity* (1841), Feuerbach argues that God is merely an idealized projection of human identity.

3 Nietzsche is referring to Wagner's involvement with *Junges Deutschland* (Young Germany), a group of writers active between 1830 and 1850 who were influenced by French revolutionary ideas and rejected monarchy and religious obscurantism.

he finally wanted to *teach something different.* And not only on the stage with the trombones[1] of *Parsifal:*—in the cloudy writings of his last years—as constricted as they are baffling—there are a hundred places which betray a secret wish and will, a despondent, uncertain, unacknowledged will essentially to preach nothing but going back, conversion, denial, Christianity, medievalism, and to say to his followers "It's nothing! Seek salvation somewhere else!" In one place he even calls out to the "Blood of the Redeemer"....

4

In a case like Wagner's, which is in many ways an embarrassing one, although the example is typical, my opinion is that it's certainly best to separate an artist far enough from his work, so that one does not take him with the same seriousness as one does his work. In the final analysis, he is only the precondition for his work, its maternal womb, the soil or, in some cases, the dung and manure, on and out of which it grows—and thus, in most cases, something that we must forget about, if we want to enjoy the work itself. Insight into the *origin* of a work is a matter for physiologists and vivisectionists of the spirit, never the aesthetic men, the artists—never! In a deep, fundamental, even terrifying way the poet and composer of *Parsifal* could not escape living inside and descending into the conflicts of the medieval soul, a hostile distance from all spiritual loftiness, rigor, and discipline, a form of intellectual *perversity* (if you will forgive the expression), any more than a pregnant woman can escape the repellent and strange aspects of pregnancy, something which, as I have said, one must *forget* if one wants to enjoy the child. We should be on our guard against that confusion which arises from psychological *contiguity* (to use an English word), a confusion in which even an artist can only too easily get caught up, as if he himself *were* what he can present, imagine, and express. In fact, the case is this: *if* that were what he was, he simply would not present, imagine, or express it. A Homer would not have written a poem about Achilles or a Goethe a poem about Faust if Homer had been an Achilles or if Goethe had been a Faust.[2] A complete and entire

---

1 Here referring to a brass instrument invented by Wagner that is a hybrid of the French horn and the trombone.

2 Faust is the eponymous hero of Johann Wolfgang von Goethe's most famous work, published in two parts (1808, 1832). The idea here is that works of art are the product of projection and of efforts to compensate for and to overcome loss as well as personal inadequacies.

artist is forever separated from the "real," from what actually is. On the other hand, one can understand how he can sometimes grow weary of this eternal "unreality" and falseness of his innermost existence to the point of desperation—and that he then makes an attempt for once to reach over into what is forbidden precisely to him, into reality, in an attempt truly *to be*. What success does he have? We can guess ... That is the *typical wishfulness* of the artist: the same wishfulness which fell over Wagner once he'd grown old and for which he had to pay such a high, fatal price (—because of it he lost a valuable number of his friends). Finally, however, and quite apart from this mere wishfulness of his, who could not desire—for Wagner's own sake—that he had taken his leave of us and his art *in a different manner*, not with a *Parsifal*, but more victoriously, more self-confidently, more like Wagner—less deceptive, less ambiguous about all his intentions, less like Schopenhauer, less nihilistic?

5

—So, what do ascetic ideals mean? In the case of an artist, we know the answer immediately:—*absolutely nothing*! ... Or they mean so many things, that they amount to nothing at all! ... So let's eliminate the artists right away.[1] They do not stand independent of the world and *against* the world long enough for their evaluations and the changes in those evaluations to merit our interest *for their own sake*! They have in all ages been valets to a morality or philosophy or religion, quite apart from the fact that, often enough, they unfortunately have been the all-too-adaptable courtiers of groups of their followers and their patrons and flatterers with a fine nose for old or simply newly arriving powers. At the very least, they always need a means of protection, a support, an already established authority. The artists never stand for themselves—standing alone contravenes their deepest instincts. Hence, for example, "once the time had come" Richard Wagner took the philosopher Schopenhauer as his point man, as his protection. Who could have even imagined that he would have had the *courage* for an ascetic ideal without the support which Schopenhauer's philosophy offered him, without the authority of Schopenhauer, which was *becoming predominant* in Europe in the 1870s? (And that's not even considering whether

---

1 Nietzsche echoes Socrates' judgment in *The Republic* that, because they are mere imitators who exercise a subversive influence on the young, poets would need to be expelled from Plato's ideal state.

in the *new* Germany it would have been generally possible to be an artist without the milk of a human, imperially human kindness).[1]—And with this we come to the more serious question: What does it mean when a real *philosopher* pays homage to the ascetic ideal, a truly independent spirit like Schopenhauer,[2] a man and a knight with a bronze gaze, who is courageous to himself, who knows how to stand alone and does not first wait for a front man and hints from higher up?—Here let us consider right away the remarkable and for many sorts of people even fascinating position of Schopenhauer on *art*, for that was apparently the reason Richard Wagner *first* moved over to Schopenhauer (persuaded to do that, as we know, by a poet, by Herwegh).[3] That shift was so great that it opened up a complete theoretical contrast between his earlier and his later aesthetic beliefs—between, for example, the earlier views expressed in "Opera and Drama" and the later views in the writings which he published from 1870 on.[4] In particular, what is perhaps most surprising is that from this point on Wagner ruthlessly altered his judgment of the value and place of *music* itself. Why should it concern him that up to that point he had used music as a means, a medium, a "woman," something which simply required a purpose, a man, in order to flourish— that is, drama! Suddenly he realized that with Schopenhauer's theory and innovation he could do more *in majorem musicae gloriam* [Latin: for the greater glory of music][5]—that is, through the

---

1 Nietzsche alludes to the famous speech by Lady Macbeth in Shakespeare's tragedy (I.v.15–18): "Glamis thou art, and Cawdor, and shalt be / What thou art promis'd. Yet do I fear thy nature, / It is too full o' th' milk of human kindness / To catch the nearest way."

2 Schopenhauer emphasizes the role of art as a source of transcendence free of sexual desire and dependence on the physical body.

3 Georg Herwegh (1817–75), radical German poet who sought political refuge in Switzerland, where he met the similarly exiled Wagner. In addition to introducing Wagner to the works of Schopenhauer, Herwegh broadened the composer's horizon to include the writings of the reform-minded British poets Lord Byron (1788–1824) and P.B. Shelley (1792–1822), as well as the Persian poet Hafiz.

4 In the years after 1870, Wagner published the articles "Judaism in Music" (1869), "Religion and Art" (1880), and "What is a German?" (1878), in which German nationalism, reactionary politics, and antisemitism emerge as key components of his worldview.

5 Nietzsche refers to the privileged place that music occupies in Schopenhauer's aesthetics, which permits the listener *(continued)*

sovereignty of music, as Schopenhauer understood it: music set apart from all other arts, the inherently independent art, *not*, like the other arts, offering copies of phenomena, but rather the voice *of the* will itself speaking out directly from the "abyss" as its most authentic, most primordial, least derivative revelation. With this extraordinary increase in the value of music, as this seemed to grow out of Schopenhauer's philosophy, *the musician* himself also suddenly grew in value to an unheard of extent: from now on he would be an oracle, a priest, more than a priest, in fact, a kind of mouthpiece of the "essence" of things, a telephone from the world beyond—in future he didn't speak only of music, this ventriloquist of God—he talked metaphysics. Is it any wonder that finally one day he spoke about *ascetic ideals*? ...

6

Schopenhauer used Kant's formulation of the aesthetic problem[1]— although he certainly did not examine it with Kantian eyes. Kant thought he had honored art when among the predicates of the beautiful he gave priority to and set in the foreground those which constitute the honor of knowledge—impersonality and universal validity. Here is not the place to explore whether or not this is for the most part a false idea. The only thing I wish to stress is that Kant, like all philosophers, instead of taking aim at the aesthetic problem from the experiences of the artist (the creator), thought about art and the beautiful only from the point of view of the "looker on" and in the process, without anyone noticing it, brought the "spectator" himself into the concept "beautiful." If only these philosophers of beauty had also been at least sufficiently knowledgeable about this "spectator"!— that is, as a great *personal* fact and experience, as a wealth of very particular, strong experiences, desires, surprises, and delights in the realm of the beautiful! But I fear the opposite has always been the case. And so, from the very start, we get from them definitions like that famous one which Kant gives for the beautiful, in which the lack of a finer self-experience sits in the shape of a thick worm of fundamental error. "The beautiful," Kant said, "is what pleases in a *disinterested* way." In a

---

to escape the trammels of the physical world and attain liberation from the tyranny of the will.

1 In *The Critique of Judgment* (1790), Kant notes that the contemplation of works of art is necessarily "disinterested" and does not engage the viewer's feelings or desires.

disinterested way! Let's compare this definition with that other one formulated by a true "spectator" and artist—Stendhal, who once called the beautiful a *promesse de bonheur* [French: promise of happiness]. Here, at any rate, the very thing which Kant emphasizes in the aesthetic state is clearly *rejected* and deleted: *désintéressement* [French: disinterestedness]. Who is right, Kant or Stendhal?[1]— Naturally, if our aestheticians never get tired of weighing the issue in Kant's favor, claiming that under the magic spell of beauty people can look *even* at unclothed female statues "without interest," we are entitled to laugh a little at their expense:—in relation to this delicate matter, the experiences of *artists* are "more interesting," and Pygmalion was in any event *not* necessarily an "unaesthetic man."[2] Let's think all the better of the innocence of our aestheticians, which is reflected in such arguments. For example, let's count it to Kant's honor that he knew how to lecture on the characteristic properties of the sense of touch[3] with the naïveté of a country parson.—This point brings us back to Schopenhauer, who stood measurably closer to the arts than Kant but who nonetheless did not get away from the spell of the Kantian definition. How did that happen? The circumstance is sufficiently odd. He interpreted the word "disinterested" in the most personal manner from a single experience which must have been something routine with him. There are few things Schopenhauer talks about with as much confidence as he does about the effect of aesthetic contemplation. In connection with that, he states that it counteracts *sexual* "interest" in particular—and thus acts like lupulin or camphor. He never got tired of extolling *this* emancipation from the "will" as the great advantage and use of the aesthetic state. Indeed, we could be tempted to ask whether his basic conception of "Will and Idea," the notion that there could be a redemption from the "will" only through "representation," might have taken

---

1 Stendhal is the pen name of Marie-Henri Beyle (1783–1842), French novelist greatly admired by Nietzsche for his psychological realism. In Stendhal's *Rome, Naples, and Florence* (1854), art is described as "a promise of happiness." Nietzsche contrasts this definition of art, which has its designs on human feelings, with Kant's idea of art as utterly purposeless.

2 In Book X of the *Metamorphoses* by the Roman poet Ovid (43 BCE–17/18 CE), Pygmalion is a sculptor who carved a woman so lifelike and beautiful that he falls in love with her.

3 Nietzsche alludes to Kant's essay "On the Sense of Touch," in *Anthropology from a Pragmatic Perspective* (1798).

its origin from a universalizing of that sexual experience.[1] (With all questions concerning Schopenhauer's philosophy, incidentally, we should never fail to consider that it is the conception of a twenty-six-year-old young man, so that it involves not merely the specific details of Schopenhauer but also the particular details of that time of life). If, for example, we listen to one of the most expressive passages from the countless ones he wrote to honor the aesthetic state (*World and Will and Idea*, I, 231), we hear its tone, the suffering, the happiness, the gratitude uttered in words like these: "That is the painless condition which Epicurus[2] valued as the highest good and as the condition of the gods. For that moment, we are relieved of the contemptible drive of the will. We celebrate a Sabbath from the penal servitude to the will. The wheel of Ixion stands motionless."[3] ... What vehemence in the words! What a picture of torment and long weariness! What an almost pathological temporal contrast between "that moment" and the usual "wheel of Ixion," the "penal servitude to the will," the "contemptible drive of the will"!—But assuming that Schopenhauer were right a hundred times about himself, what would that provide by way of insight into the essence of the beautiful? Schopenhauer wrote about one effect of the beautiful—the way it calms the will—but is it a regularly occurring effect? Stendhal, as mentioned, a no less sensual person, but with a natural constitution much happier than Schopenhauer's, emphasizes another effect of the beautiful: "the beautiful *promises* happiness." To him the fact of the matter seemed to be precisely the *arousal of the will* ("of interest") by the beautiful. And could we not finally object about Schopenhauer himself that he was very wrong to think of himself as a Kantian in this matter, that he had completely failed to understand Kant's definition of the beautiful in a Kantian manner—that even he found the beautiful pleasing out of an "interest," even out of the strongest and most personal interest of all, that of a torture victim

---

1 Nietzsche is hinting at what Freud would more fully elucidate on the sublimation of sexual energy in the creation of art.

2 Epicurus (342–270 BCE), Greek materialist philosopher who is colloquially associated with the pursuit of pleasure (i.e., Epicureanism).

3 In Greek mythology, Ixion is a mortal man who tried to seduce Zeus' wife, Hera. He was punished in Hades by being bound on a perpetually spinning wheel of fire and tortured by the Furies. For Schopenhauer "the wheel of Ixion" functions as a symbol for the inescapable torments of human existence caused by servitude to the will.

who escapes from his torture? ... And to come back to our first question, "What does it *mean* when a philosopher renders homage to the ascetic ideal?"—we get here at least our first hint: he wants *to escape a torture.*

7

Let's be careful not to make gloomy faces right away at that word "torture." In this particular case there remain enough objections to take into account, enough to subtract—there even remains something to laugh about. For let's not underestimate the fact that Schopenhauer, who in fact treated sexuality as a personal enemy (including its instrument, woman, this *"instrumentum diaboli"* [Latin: tool of the devil]), *needed* enemies in order to maintain his good spirits, that he loved grim, caustic, black-green words, that he got angry for the sake of getting passionately angry, that he would have become ill, would have become a *pessimist* (—and he wasn't a pessimist, no matter how much he wanted to be one) without his enemies, without Hegel,[1] woman, sensuousness, and the whole will for existence, for continuing on. Had that not been the case, Schopenhauer would not have kept going—on that we can wager. He would have run off. But his enemies held him securely; his enemies seduced him back to existence again and again. Just like the ancient Cynics,[2] his anger was his refreshment, his relaxation, his payment, his remedy for disgust, his *happiness.* So much with respect to the most personal features in the case of Schopenhauer. On the other hand, with him there is still something typical—and here we only come up against our problem once more. As long as there have been philosophers on earth and wherever there have been philosophers (from India to England, to name two opposite poles of talent in philosophy) there unquestionably have existed a genuine philosophical irritability with and rancor against sensuousness— Schopenhauer is only the most eloquent eruption of these and,

---

1 Georg Wilhelm Friedrich Hegel (1770–1831), dominant philosophical presence in the nineteenth century and beyond whose central argument is that history embodies the unfolding of absolute *Geist* (spirit) according to a teleological, ultimately mechanical blueprint. Schopenhauer was an early adversary and tireless critic.

2 Greek philosophers inspired by Antisthenes (444–368 BCE), a student of Socrates, who lived free of possessions and other worldly attachments.

if one has an ear for it, also the most captivating and delightful. In addition, there exist a real philosophical bias and affection favoring the whole ascetic ideal. No one should fool himself about or against that. As mentioned, both belong to the philosophical type: if both are missing in a philosopher then he is always only a "so-called philosopher"—of that we may be certain. What does that *mean*? For we must first interpret these facts of the case: *in itself* stands there eternally stupid, like every "thing in itself." Every animal, including also *la bête philosophe* [French: the philosophical beast], instinctively strives for the optimal beneficial conditions in which it can let out all its power and attain the strongest feeling of its strength. Every animal in an equally instinctual way and with a refined sense of smell that "is loftier than all reason" abhors any kind of trouble maker and barrier which lies or which could lie in its way to these optimal conditions (—I'm *not* speaking about its path to "happiness," but about its way to power, to action, to its most powerful deeds, and, in most cases, really about its way to unhappiness). Thus, the philosopher abhors *marriage*, as well as what might persuade him into it—marriage is a barrier and a disaster along his route to the optimal. What great philosopher up to now has been married? Heraclitus, Plato, Descartes, Spinoza, Leibnitz,[1] Kant, Schopenhauer—none of these got married. What's more, we cannot even *imagine* them married. A married philosopher belongs *in a comedy*, that's my principle. And Socrates, that exception, the malicious Socrates, it appears, *ironice* [Latin: ironically] got married specifically to demonstrate *this* very principle.[2] Every philosopher would speak as once Buddha spoke when someone told him of the birth of a son, "Rahula has been born to me. A shackle has been forged for me." (Rahula here means "a little demon").[3] To every "free spirit" there must

---

1 Gottfried Wilhelm Leibniz (1646–1716), German philosopher and polymath who is considered, along with René Descartes (1596–1650) and Spinoza, one of the great seventeenth-century philosophers of rationalism.

2 Socrates (470/69–399 BCE), central figure in Western philosophy and the "protagonist" in the *Dialogues* of Plato (428/27–348/47 BCE). Socrates' marriage to the reputedly ill-tempered Xanthippe proves Nietzsche's argument that philosophers should never wed.

3 Nietzsche's quotation—from Hermann Oldenberg, *Buddha: His Life, His Teachings, His Community* (1881)—is reputed to have been the Buddha's reaction to the birth of Rahula (Veda Sanskrit for shackle, chain), his only son, in c. 534 BCE.

come a reflective hour, provided that previously he has had one without thought, of the sort that once came to this same Buddha—"Life in a house," he thought to himself, "is narrow and confined, a polluted place. Freedom consists of abandoning the house"; "because he thought this way, he left the house." The ascetic ideal indicates so many bridges to *independence* that a philosopher cannot, without an inner rejoicing and applause, listen to the history of all those decisive people who one day said "No" to all lack of freedom and went off to some *desert* or other, even assuming that such people were merely strong donkeys and entirely opposite to a powerful spirit. So what, then, does the ascetic ideal mean as far as a philosopher is concerned? My answer is—you will have guessed it long ago—the philosopher smiles when he sees in it an optimal set of conditions for the loftiest and boldest spirituality—in so doing, he does *not* deny "existence"; rather that's how he affirms *his* existence and *only* his existence and does this perhaps to such a degree that he is not far from the wicked desire *pereat mundus, fiat philosophia, fiat philosophus, fiam!* [Latin: let the world perish, let philosophy exist, let the philosopher exist, let me exist!] ...[1]

8

You see that these philosophers are not unprejudiced witnesses to and judges of the *value* of ascetic ideals! They think about *themselves*—what concern to them is "the saint"! In this matter they think about what is most immediately indispensable *to them*: freedom from compulsion, disturbance, fuss, from business, duties, worries: a bright light in the head, dance, the leap and flight of ideas; good air—thin, clear, free, dry—like the air at high altitudes, with which everything in animal being grows more spiritual and acquires wings; calm in all basement areas; all dogs nicely tied up in chains; no hostile barking and shaggy rancor; no gnawing worm of wounded ambition; modest and humble inner organs busy as windmills but at a distance; the heart in an alien place, beyond, in the future, posthumous—all in all, so far as the ascetic ideal is concerned, they think of the cheerful asceticism of some deified animal which has become independent, roaming

---

1 The Latin here is Nietzsche's reworking of the famous legal saying "*Fiat Justitia et pereat mundus*" (Let justice be done, though the world would perish), attributed to Ferdinand I (1503–64), the Holy Roman emperor, who adopted it as his motto.

above life rather than being at rest. We know what the three great catch phrases of the ascetic ideal are: poverty, humility, chastity. Now look closely at the lives of all great, prolific, inventive spirits—over and over again you'll rediscover all three there to a certain degree. *Not at all*—this is self-evident—as if it were something to do with their "virtues"—what does this kind of man have to do with virtues?—but as the truest and most natural conditions of their *best* existence, their *most beautiful* fecundity. At the same time, it is indeed entirely possible that their dominating spirituality at first had to set aside an unbridled and sensitive pride or the reins of a wanton sensuality or that they perhaps had difficulty enough maintaining their will for the "desert" against an inclination for luxury, for something very exquisite, as well as against a lavish liberality of heart and hand. But their spirituality did it, simply because it was the *dominating* instinct, which achieves its own demands in relation to all the other instincts—it still continues to do so. If it did not, then it would simply not dominate. Hence, this has nothing to do with "virtue." Besides, the *desert* I just mentioned, into which the strong spirits with an independent nature withdraw and isolate themselves—O how different it seems from the desert educated people dream about!—for in some circumstances these educated people are themselves this desert. And certainly, no actor of the spirit could simply endure it—for them it is not nearly romantic and Syrian enough, not nearly enough of a theatrical desert! It's true there's no lack of camels there, but that's the only similarity between them. Perhaps a voluntary obscurity, a detour away from one's self, a timidity about noise, admiration, newspapers, influence; a small official position, a daily routine, something which hides more than it brings to light, contact now and then with harmless, cheerful wildlife and birds whose sight is relaxing, a mountain for company, not a dead one but one with *eyes* (that means with lakes); in some circumstances even a room in a full, nondescript inn, where one is sure to be confused for someone else and can talk to anyone with impunity—that's what a "desert" is here. O, it's lonely enough, believe me! When Heraclitus withdrew into the courtyard and colonnades of the immense temple of Artemis,[1] that was a worthier "desert," I

---

1 Temple of Artemis in Ephesus (now Selçuk, Turkey), considered one of the Seven Wonders of the World until its destruction in 401 CE. Nietzsche is referring to an episode in the life of Heraclitus during a visit there as recounted in *Lives and Opinions of the Eminent*

admit. Why do we *lack* such temples? (—Perhaps we do *not* lack them. I've just remembered my most beautiful room for study, the Piazza San Marco,[1] assuming it's in the spring, and in the morning, too, between ten and twelve o'clock). But what Heraclitus was getting away from is still the same thing *we* go out of our way to escape nowadays: the noise and the democratic chatter of the Ephesians, their politics, their news about the "empire"[2] (you understand I mean the Persians), their market junk of "today"—for we philosophers need peace and quiet from one thing above all—from everything to do with "today."[3] We honor what is still, cold, noble, distant, past, in general everything at the sight of which the soul does not have to defend itself or tie itself up—something with which a person can speak without having to speak *aloud*. People should just listen to the sound which a spirit has when it is talking. Every spirit has its own sound, loves its own sound. The man over there, for example, must be a real agitator, I mean a hollow head, a hollow pot [*Hohlkopf*, *Hohltopf*]); no matter what goes into him, everything comes back out of him dull and thick, weighed down with the echo of a huge emptiness. That man over there rarely speaks in anything other than a hoarse voice. Has he perhaps *imagined* himself hoarse? That might be possible—ask the physiologists— but whoever thinks in *words* thinks as a speaker and not as a thinker (it reveals that fundamentally he does not think of things or think factually, but only in relation to things, that he really is thinking of *himself* and his listeners). A third man over there speaks with an insistent familiarity, he steps in too close to our bodies, he breathes over us—instinctively we shut our mouths, even though he is speaking to us through a book. The sound of his style tells us the reason for that—he has no time, he has little

---

Philosophers by Diogenes Laertes (third century CE). Heraclitus, while playing a game of jacks with children, responded to questions from onlookers as to why he was doing so: "Why, you rascals, are you astonished? Is it not better to do this than to take part in your civil life?" Translated by Robert Drew Hicks (Loeb Classical Library, 1925).

1 The Piazza San Marco is the main city square in Venice.
2 *Reich* in the original. Nietzsche alludes to the recent unification (in 1871) of Germany under Chancellor Otto von Bismarck (1815–98).
3 Nietzsche compares his own struggle against Christian "slave morality" with Heraclitus' conflict with the dominant Ephesian cult of Dionysus.

faith in himself, he'll have his say today or never again. But a spirit which is sure of itself, speaks quietly. He's looking for seclusion. He lets people wait for him. We recognize a philosopher by the following: he walks away from three glittering and garish things—fame, princes, and women. That doesn't mean that they might not come to him. He shrinks from light which is too bright. Hence, he shies away from his time and its "day." In that he's like a shadow: the lower the sun sinks, the bigger he becomes. So far as his "humility" is concerned, he endures a certain dependence and obscurity, as he endures the darkness. More than that, he fears being disturbed by lightning and recoils from the unprotected and totally isolated and abandoned tree on which all bad weather can discharge its mood, all moods discharge their bad weather. His "maternal" instinct, the secret love for what is growing in him, directs him to places where his need to think *of himself* is removed, in the same sense that the *maternal* instinct in women has up to now generally kept her in a dependent situation. Ultimately, they demand little enough, these philosophers. Their motto is "Whoever owns things is owned"—*not*, as I must say again and again, from virtue, from an admirable desire for modest living and simplicity, but because their highest master demands *that* of them, demands astutely and unrelentingly. He cares for only one thing and for that gathers up and holds everything—time, power, love, interest. This sort of man doesn't like to be disturbed by hostile things and by friendships; he easily forgets or scoffs. To him martyrdom seems something in bad taste—"to *suffer* for the truth"—he leaves that to the ambitious and the stage heroes of the spirit and anyone else who has time enough for it (—they themselves, the philosophers, have something to *do* for the truth). They use big words sparingly. It's said that they resist using even the word "truth": it sounds boastful.... Finally, as far as "chastity" concerns philosophers, this sort of spirit apparently keeps its fertility in something other than in children; perhaps they also keep the continuity of their names elsewhere, their small immortality (among philosophers in ancient India people spoke with even more presumption, "What's the point of offspring to the man whose soul is the world?"). There's no sense of chastity there out of some ascetic scruple and hatred of the senses, just as it has little to do with chastity when an athlete or jockey abstains from women. It's more a matter of what their dominating instinct wants, at least during its great pregnant periods. Every artist knows how damaging the effects of sexual intercourse are to states of great spiritual tension and preparation. The most powerful and most instinctual artists among them don't acquire this knowledge primarily by experience, by bad experience—no, it's simply that "maternal" instinct of theirs which here makes the decision ruthlessly to benefit the developing work among all the other stores and supplies of energy, of animal *vigor* [Latin: strength]. The greater power then *uses up* the lesser. Incidentally, apply this interpretation now to the above-mentioned case of Schopenhauer: the sight of the beautiful evidently worked in him as the stimulus for the *main power* in his nature (the power of reflection and the deep look), so that this then exploded and suddenly became master of his consciousness. In the process, we should in no way rule out the possibility that that characteristic sweetness and abundance typical of the aesthetic condition could originate precisely from the ingredient "sensuality" (just as from the same source is derived that "idealism" characteristic of sexually mature young girls)—so that thus, with the onset of the aesthetic condition, sensuality is not cancelled out, as Schopenhauer believed, but is transformed and does not enter the consciousness any more as sexual stimulation. (I will come back to this point of view at another time, in connection with the even more delicate problems of the *physiology of aesthetics*, so untouched up to this point, so unanalyzed).

9

A certain asceticism, as we have seen, a hard and cheerful renunciation with the best intentions, belongs to those conditions favorable to the highest spirituality and is also among its most natural consequences. So, it's no wonder from the outset that philosophers, in particular, never treat the ascetic ideal without some bias. A serious historical review demonstrates that the tie between the ascetic ideal and philosophy is even much closer and stronger. We could say it was in the *leading reins* of this ideal that philosophy in general learned to take its first steps and partial steps on earth—alas, still so awkwardly, alas, still with such a morose expression, alas, so ready to fall over and lie on its belly, this small, tentative, clumsy, loving infant with crooked legs! With philosophy things initially played themselves out as with all good things: for a long time, it had no courage for itself—it always looked around to see if anyone would come to its assistance, and even more it was afraid of all those who gazed at it. Just make a list of the individual drives and virtues of the philosopher—his impulse to doubt, his impulse to deny, his impulse to wait (the "ephectic" impulse[1]), his impulse to analyze, his impulse to research, to seek out, to take chances, his impulse to compare, to weigh evenly, his desire for neutrality and objectivity, his will to every "*sine ira et studio*" [Latin: without anger or ambition]—have we not already understood that for the longest time all of them went against the first demands of morality and conscience (to say nothing at all about *reason* in general, which even Luther liked to call Madam Sophistry, the Clever Whore[2]) and that if a philosopher *were* to have come to an awareness of himself, he would really have had to feel that he was almost the living manifestation of "*nitimur invetitum*" [Latin: we search for what is forbidden][3]— and thus *taken care not* to "feel himself," not to become conscious of himself? As I've said, the case is no different with all the good things of which we are nowadays so proud. Even measured by the standards of the ancient Greeks, our entire modern being, insofar as it is not weakness but power and consciousness of power, looks like sheer *hubris* [Greek: overweening pride][4] and godlessness; for the very opposite of those things we honor today have for the longest period had conscience on their side and God to guard over them. Our entire attitude to nature today, our violation of nature, with the help of machines and the unimaginable inventiveness of our technicians and engineers, is *hubris*; our attitude to God is *hubris*—I mean our attitude to some alleged spider spinning out purposes and morality behind the fabric of the huge fishing net of causality—we could say with Charles the Bold in his struggle with Louis XI, "*Je combats l'universelle araignée*" [French: I am fighting the universal spider];[5] our attitude to *ourselves* is *hubris*—for we experiment with ourselves in a manner

---

1 "Ephectic" refers to the practice of philosophical skepticism and is derived from the Greek *ephektikos* (to withhold or to hesitate).

2 Luther, final sermon in Wittenberg, 17 January 1546: "Reason is a whore, the greatest enemy that faith has; it never comes to the aid of spiritual things, but more frequently than not struggles against the Divine Word, treating with contempt all that emanates from God."

3 Nietzsche quotes from Ovid, *Amores* (16 BCE), III, iv.7.

4 *Hubris* is the fatal flaw in tragic heroes, leading to their demise.

5 Charles the Bold (1433–77), Duke of Burgundy (1467–77) during a conflict-ridden period in Western European history. His principal foe was Louis XI (1423–83), King of France, nicknamed the "universal spider" for the enormous web of conspiracies and intrigues that marked his reign.

we would not permit with any animal and happily and inquisitively slit the souls of living bodies open. What do we still care about the "salvation" of the soul? We cure ourselves later. Being sick teaches us things—we don't doubt that—it's even more instructive than being healthy. The *person who makes us ill* appears to us nowadays to be more important even than any medical people and "saviors." We violate ourselves now, no doubt about it, we nutcrackers of the soul, we questioning and questionable people, as if life were nothing else but cracking nuts. And in so doing, we must necessarily become every day constantly more questionable, *more worthy* of being questioned, and in the process perhaps also worthier—to live? All good things were once bad things; every original sin has become an original virtue. For example, marriage for a long time seemed to be a sin against the rights of the community. Once people paid a fine for being so presumptuous as to arrogate a woman to themselves (that involves, for instance, the *jus primae noctis* [Latin: the right of the first night],[1] even today in Cambodia the privilege of the priest, this guardian of "good ancient customs"). The gentle, favorable, yielding, sympathetic feelings—which over time grew so valuable that they are almost "value in itself"—for the longest period were countered by self-contempt against them. People were ashamed of being mild, just as today they are ashamed of being hard (compare *Beyond Good and Evil*, Section 260). Subjugation under the *law*—O with what resistance of conscience the noble races throughout the earth had to renounce the *vendetta* [Italian: blood feud] and to concede the power of the law over themselves! For a long time, the "law" was a *vetitum* [Latin: something prohibited], a sacrilege, an innovation; it appeared with force, *as* force, something to which people submitted only with a feeling of shame for their conduct. Every one of the smallest steps on earth in earlier days was fought for with spiritual and physical torture. This whole historical point, "that not only moving forward—no!—but walking, moving, and changing necessarily required their countless martyrs," nowadays sounds so strange to us. In *The Dawn*, Section 18, I brought out this point. "Nothing has come at a higher price," it says there, "than the small amount of human reason and feeling of freedom, which we are now so proud of. But because of this pride it is now almost impossible for us to sense how that huge stretch of time of the 'morality of

---

1 In feudal times, the right of the lord of the estate to sleep with the brides of his serfs on their wedding nights.

custom,' which comes before 'world history,' is the really decisive and important history which established the character of humanity, when everywhere people recognized suffering as virtue, cruelty as virtue, pretence as virtue, revenge as virtue, the denial of reason as virtue and, by contrast, well-being as danger, the desire for knowledge as danger, peace as danger, pity as danger, being pitied as disgrace, work as disgrace, insanity as divinity, *change* as inherently immoral and pregnant with ruin!"

10

The same book, in Section 42, explains the system of values, the *pressure* of a system of values, under which the most ancient race of contemplative men had to live—a race that was despised exactly to the extent that it was not feared! Contemplation first appeared on earth in a disguised shape, with an ambiguous appearance, with an evil heart, and often with a worried head. There's no doubt about that. For a long time, the inactive, brooding, unwarlike elements in the instincts of contemplative people fostered a deep mistrust around them, against which the only way to cope was to arouse an emphatic fear of them. The ancient Brahmins, for example, understood that! The oldest philosophers knew how to earn meaning for their existence and their appearance, some security and background, because of which people learned to fear them. To look at the matter more closely, this happened because of an even more fundamental need, that is, the need to win fear and respect for themselves. For they discovered that inside them all judgments of value had turned *against* them; they had to beat down all kinds of suspicions about and resistance to "the philosopher inside them." As men of dreadful times, they achieved this with dreadful means: cruelty against themselves, inventive self-denial—that was the major instrument of these power-hungry hermits and new thinkers, who found it necessary first to overthrow the gods and traditions inside themselves, in order to be able *to believe* in their innovation. I recall the famous story of King Vishvamitra,[1] who, through a thousand years of self-torments, acquired such a feeling of power and faith in himself that he committed himself to building a *new heaven*, that weird symbol of the oldest and most recent history of philosophers on earth. Everyone who at some

---

1 Vishvamitra was a king of ancient India legendary for undertaking a spiritual journey of severe austerity.

time or another has built a "new heaven," found the power to do that first in *his own hell*.... Let's condense all these facts into short formulas: the philosophical spirit always had to begin by disguising itself, wrapping itself in a cocoon of the *previously established* forms of the contemplative man, as priest, magician, prophet, generally as a religious man, in order to make any kind of life *at all possible*. *The ascetic ideal* for a long time served the philosopher as a form in which he could appear, as a condition for his existence—he had to *play the role*, in order to be able to be a philosopher. And he had to *believe in* what he was doing, in order to play that role. The characteristically detached stance of philosophers, something which denies the world, is hostile to life, has no faith in the senses, and is free of sensuality, which was maintained right up to the most recent times and thus became valued almost as *the essence of the philosophical posture*—that is, above all, a consequence of the critical conditions under which, in general, philosophy arose and survived. In fact, for the longest time on earth philosophy would *not have been at all possible* without an ascetic cover and costume, without an ascetic misunderstanding of the self. To put the matter explicitly and vividly: up to the most recent times the *ascetic priest* has provided the repellent and dark caterpillar form which was the only one in which philosophy could live and creep around.... Has that really *changed*? Is the colorful and dangerous winged creature, that "spirit" which this caterpillar hid within itself, at last really been released and allowed out into the light, thanks to a sunnier, warmer, brighter world? Nowadays do we have sufficient pride, daring, bravery, self-certainty, spiritual will, desire to assume responsibility, and *freedom of the will* so that, from now on, "the philosopher" is truly *possible* on earth? ...

11

Only now that we have taken a look at the *ascetic priest* can we seriously get at our problem: What does the ascetic ideal mean—only now does it become "serious." From this point on we confront the actual *representative of seriousness*. "What does all seriousness mean?"—this even more fundamental question perhaps lies already on our lips, a question for physiologists, naturally, but nonetheless one which we will still evade for the moment. In that ideal, the ascetic priest preserves, not merely his faith, but also his will, his power, his interest. His right to existence stands and falls with that ideal. No wonder that here we run into a fearful opponent, given, of course, that we were people antagonistic to that ideal?—an opponent of the sort who fights for his existence against those who deny the ideal ... On the other hand, it is from the outset improbable that such an interesting stance to our problem will be particularly beneficial to it. The ascetic priest will hardly in himself prove the most successful defender of his ideal, for the same reason that a woman habitually fails when it's a matter of defending "woman as such"—to say nothing of his being able to provide the most objective assessment of and judgment about the controversy we are dealing with here. Rather than having to fear that he will refute us too well— this much is clear enough—it's more likely we'll still have to help him defend himself against us.... The idea being contested at this point is the *value* of our lives in the eyes of ascetic priests: this same life (along with what belongs to it, "nature," "the world," the whole sphere of becoming and transience) they set up in relation to an existence of a totally different kind, a relationship characterized by opposition and mutual exclusion, *except* where life somehow turns against itself, *denies itself.* In this case, the case of an ascetic life, living counts as a bridge over to that other existence. The ascetic treats life as an incorrect road, where we must finally go backwards, right to the place where it begins, or as a misconception which man refutes by his actions—or *should* refute. For he *demands* that people go with him. Where he can, he enforces *his* evaluation of existence. What's the meaning of that? Such a monstrous way of assessing value does not stand inscribed in human history as something exceptional and curious. It is one of the most widespread and enduring extant facts. If read from a distant star, the block capital script of our earthly existence might perhaps lead one to conclude that the earth is the inherently *ascetic star*, a corner for discontented, arrogant, and repellent creatures, incapable of ridding themselves of a deep dissatisfaction with themselves, with the earth, with all living, creatures who inflict as much harm on themselves as possible for the pleasure of inflicting harm—probably their single pleasure. We should consider how regularly, how commonly, how in almost all ages the ascetic priest makes an appearance. He does not belong to one single race. He flourishes everywhere. He grows from all levels of society. And it's not the case that he breeds and replants his way of assessing value somehow through biological inheritance: the opposite the case—generally speaking, a deep instinct forbids him from reproducing. There must be a high-order necessity which makes this species *hostile to life* always grow again and flourish—it must be in the *interest of life itself* not to have such a type of self-contradiction die out. For an ascetic life is a self-contradiction. Here a *ressentiment* without equal is in control, something with an insatiable instinct and will to power, which wants to become master, not over something in life but over life itself, over its deepest, strongest, most basic conditions; here an attempt is being made to use one's power to block up the sources of that power; here one directs one's green and malicious gaze against one's inherent physiological health, particularly against its means of expression—beauty, joy—while one experiences and *seeks* for a feeling of pleasure in mistrust, atrophy, pain, accident, ugliness, voluntary loss, self-denial, self-flagellation, self-sacrifice. All this is paradoxical to the highest degree. Here we stand in front of a dichotomy which essentially *wants* a dichotomy, which *enjoys* itself in this suffering and always gets even more self-aware and more triumphant in proportion to the *decrease* in its own prerequisite, the physiological capacity for life. "Triumph precisely in the ultimate agony"—under this supreme sign the ascetic ideal has fought from time immemorial. Inside this riddle of seduction, in this picture of delight and torment, it sees its highest light, its salvation, its final victory. *Crux, nux, lux* [Latin: cross, nut, light]—for the ascetic ideal these are all one thing.

12

Given that such a living desire for contradiction and hostility to nature is used to *practice philosophy*, on what will it discharge its most inner arbitrary power? It will do that on something it perceives, with the greatest certainty, as true, as real. It will seek out *error* precisely where the essential instinct for life has established its most unconditional truth. For example, it will demote physical life to an illusion, as the ascetics of the Vedanta philosophy did.[1] Similarly it will treat pain, the multiplicity of things, the whole ideational opposition between "subject" and "object"[2] as error,

---

1 The *Vedanta* school of Indian philosophy is derived from the *Principal Upanishads* (800–600 BCE) and is distinguished from the *Veda* by identifying a complete devotion to Brahma as the only possible escape from an endless cycle of reincarnations.

2 The knowing subject is the knower, while the object of knowledge is what is known.

nothing but error! To deny faith in one's own self, to deny one's own "reality"—what a triumph!—and not just over the senses, over appearances, but a much loftier kind of triumph, an over-powering of and act of cruelty against *reason*: a process in which the highest peak of delight occurs when ascetic self-contempt and self-mockery of reason proclaims: "There *is* a kingdom of truth and being, but reason is expressly *excluded* from it" ... (By the way, even in the Kantian idea of the "intelligible character of things" there still remains something of this lecherous ascetic dichotomy, which loves to turn reason against reason: for the "intelligible character" with Kant means a sort of composition of things about which the intellect understands just enough to know that for the intellect it is—*wholly and completely unintelligible*).—But precisely because we are people who seek knowledge, we should finally not be ungrateful for such determined reversals of customary perspectives and evaluations with which the spirit has for so long raged against itself with such apparent wickedness and futility. To use this for once to see differently, the *will* to see things differently, is no small discipline and preparation of the intellect for its coming "objectivity"—the latter meant not in the sense of "disinterested contemplation" (which is inconceivable nonsense), but as the capability of *having power* over one's pos-itive and negative arguments and of raising them and disposing of them so that one knows how to make the very *variety* of per-spectives and interpretations of emotions useful for knowledge. From now on, my philosophical gentlemen, let us protect our-selves better from the dangerous old conceptual fantasy which posits a "pure, will-less, painless, timeless subject of cognition"; let's guard ourselves against the tentacles of such contradictory ideas as "pure reason," "absolute spirituality," "knowledge in it-self"—those things which demand that we think of an eye which simply cannot be imagined, an eye which is to have no direction at all, in which the active and interpretative forces are supposed to stop or be absent—the very things through which seeing first becomes seeing something. Hence, these things always demand from the eye something conceptually absurd and incomprehen-sible. The *only* seeing we have is seeing from a perspective; the *only* knowledge we have is knowledge from a perspective; and *the more* emotions we allow to be expressed in words concerning something, *the more* eyes, different eyes, we know how to train on the same thing, the more complete our "idea" of this thing, our "objectivity," will be. But to eliminate the will in general, to suspend all our emotions without exception—even if we were capable of that—what would that be? Wouldn't we call that castrating the intellect?

13

But let's go back to our problem. The sort of self-contradiction which seems to be present in ascetic people, "life *opposing* life," is—this much is clear—physio-logically (and not only physio-logically) considered—simply absurd. It can only be *apparent*. It must be some kind of temporary expression, an interpretation, formula, make up, a psychological misunderstanding of something whose real nature could not be understood for a long time, could not for a long time be described *in itself*—a mere word, caught in an old *gap* in human understanding. So let me counter that briefly with the facts of the matter: *the ascetic ideal arises out of the instinct for protection and salvation in a degenerating life*, which seeks to keep itself going by any means and struggles for its existence. It indicates a partial physiological inhibition and exhaustion, against which those deepest instincts for living which still remain intact continuously fight on with new methods and innovations. The ascetic ideal is one such method. The facts are thus precisely the opposite of what those who honor this ideal claim— life is struggling in that ideal and by means of that ideal with death and *against* death: the ascetic ideal is a maneuver for the *preservation* of life. As history teaches us, to the extent that this ideal could prevail over men and become powerful, particularly wherever civilization and the taming of humans have been successfully implemented, it expresses an important fact: the *pathological nature* of the earlier form of human beings, at least of those human beings who had been tamed, the physiological struggle of men against death (more precisely, against weariness with life, against exhaustion, against desire for the "end"). The ascetic priest is the incarnation of the desire for another state of being, an existence somewhere else—indeed, the highest stage of this desire, its characteristic zeal and passion. But the very *power* of this desire is the chain which binds him here. That's simply what turns him into a tool which has to work to create more favorable conditions for living here and for living as a human being—with this very *power* he keeps the whole herd of failures, discontents, delinquents, unfortunates, all sorts of people who inherently suffer, focused on existence, because instinctively he goes ahead of them as their herdsman. You understand already what I mean: this ascetic priest, this apparent enemy of living, this *man who denies*—he belongs precisely with all the great *conserving* and *affirming* forces of life ... To what can we ascribe this pathology? For the human being is more ill, less certain, more changeable, more insecure than any other animal—there's no doubt about that. He is *the* sick animal. Where does that come from? To be sure, he has also dared more, innovated more, defied more, and demanded more from fate than all the other animals combined. He is the great experimenter with himself, unhappy, dissatisfied, who struggles for ultimate mastery with animals, nature, and gods—still unconquered, always a man of the future, who no longer gets any rest from the force of his own powers, so that his future relentlessly burrows like a thorn into the flesh of his entire present:—how should such a brave and rich animal not also be the animal in most danger, the one which, of all sick animals, suffers the most lengthy and most profound illness? Human beings, often enough, get fed up: there are entire epidemics of this process of getting fed up (—for example, around 1348, at the time of the Dance of Death[1]): but even this very disgust, this exhaustion, this dissatisfaction with himself—all this comes out of him so powerfully that it immediately becomes a new chain. The No which he speaks to life brings to light, as if through a magic spell, an abundance of more tender Yeses; in fact, when he *injures* himself, this master of destruction, of self-destruction—it is the wound itself which later forces him to *live on*....

14

The more normal this pathology is among human beings—and we cannot deny its normality—the higher we should esteem the rare cases of spiritual and physical power, humanity's *strokes of luck*, and the more strongly successful people should protect themselves from the most poisonous air, the atmosphere of illness. Do people do that? ... Sick people are the greatest danger for healthy people. For strong people disaster does *not* come from the strongest, but from the weakest. Are we aware of that? ... If we consider the big picture, we should not wish for any diminution of the fear we have of human beings, for this fear compels

---

1 Dance of Death or *Danse Macabre*: The Black Death, a pandemic
  that wiped out a significant percentage of the European population
  during the fourteenth century, inspired a representational genre
  that combined amusement with a reminder of the ubiquity of death
  from which no one was safe.

the strong people to be strong and, in some circumstances, terri-ble—that fear *sustains* the successful types of people. What we should fear, what has a disastrous effect unlike any other, would not be a great fear of humanity but a great *loathing* for humanity; similarly, a great *pity* for humanity. If both of these were one day to mate, then something most weird would at once inevitably ap-pear in the world, the "ultimate will" of man, his will to nothing-ness, to nihilism. And, as a matter of fact, a great deal of preparation has gone on for this union. Whoever possesses, not only a nose to smell with, but also eyes and ears, senses almost everywhere, no matter where he steps nowadays, an atmosphere something like that of an insane asylum or hospital—I'm speak-ing, as usual, of people's cultural surroundings, of every kind of "Europe" there is right here on this earth. The *invalids* are the great danger to humanity: not the *evil* men, *not* the "predatory animals." Those people who are, from the outset, failures, op-pressed, broken—they are the ones, the *weakest*, who most un-dermine life among human beings, who in the most perilous way poison and question our trust in life, in humanity, in ourselves. Where can we escape it, that downcast glance with which people carry a deep sorrow, that reversed gaze of the man originally born to fail which betrays how such a man speaks to himself—that gaze which is a sigh. "I wish I could be someone else!"—that's what this glance sighs. "But there is no hope here. I am who I am. How could I detach myself from myself? And yet—*I've had enough of myself!*" ... On such a ground of contempt for one-self, a truly swampy ground, grows every weed, every poisonous growth, and all of them so small, so hidden, so dishonest, so sweet. Here the worms of angry and resentful feelings swarm; here the air stinks of secrets and duplicity; here are constantly spun the nets of the most malicious conspiracies—the plotting of suffering people against the successful and victorious; here the appearance of the victor is *despised*. And what dishonesty not to acknowledge this hatred as hatred! What an extravagance of large words and postures, what an art of "decent" slander! These failures: what noble eloquence streams from their lips! How much sugary, slimy, humble resignation swims in their eyes! What do they really want? At least *to make a show of* justice, love, wisdom, superiority— that's the ambition of these "lowest" peo-ple, these invalids! And how clever such an ambition makes peo-ple! For let's admire the skillful counterfeiting with which people here imitate the trademarks of virtue, even its resounding tinkle, the golden sound of virtue. They have now taken a lease on virtue entirely for themselves, these weak and hopeless invalids—there's no doubt about that: "We alone are the good men, the just men"—that's how they speak: "We alone are the *homines bonae voluntatis* [Latin: men of good will]." They wander around among us like personifications of reproach, like warnings to us—as if health, success, strength, pride, and a feeling of power were already inherently depraved things, for which people must atone someday, atone bitterly. O how ready they themselves basically are to *make* people atone, how they thirst to be *hangmen*! Among them there are plenty of people disguised as judges seeking revenge. They always have the word "Justice" in their mouths, like poisonous saliva, with their mouths always pursed, always ready to spit at anything which does not look discontented and goes on its way in good spirits. Among them there is no lack of that most disgusting species of vain people, the lying monsters who aim to present themselves as "beautiful souls" and who, for example, carry off to market their ruined sensuality, wrapped up in verse and other swaddling clothes, as "purity of heart," the species of self-gratifying moral masturbators.[1] The desire of sick people to present *some* form or other of superiority, their instinct for secret paths leading to a tyranny over the healthy—where can we not find it, this very will to power of the weakest people! The sick woman, in particular: no one outdoes her in refined ways to rule others, to exert pressure, to tyrannize. For that purpose, the sick woman spares nothing living or dead. She digs up again the most deeply buried things (the Bogos[2] say "The woman is a hyena"). Take a look into the background of every family, every corporation, every community: everywhere you see the struggle of the sick against the healthy—a quiet struggle, for the most part, with a little poison powder, with needling, with deceitful expressions of long suffering, but now and then also with that sick man's Pharisee tactic of *loud* gestures, whose favorite role is "noble indignation." It likes to make itself heard all the way into the consecrated rooms of science, that hoarse, booming indignation of the pathologically ill hound, the biting insincerity and rage of

---

1 Nietzsche ironically refers to a section of Goethe's novel *Wilhelm Meister's Apprenticeship* (1795–96), "Confessions of a Beautiful Soul."

2 The Bogos or Bilen people occupy territory in the Horn of Africa. "The Hyena Woman" is an Ethiopian folktale that mythologizes the supposed predatory nature of women.

such "noble" Pharisees[1] (—once again I remind readers who have ears of Eugene Dühring, that apostle of revenge from Berlin, who in today's Germany makes the most indecent and most revolting use of moralistic gibberish [*Bumbum*]—Dühring, the pre-eminent moral braggart we have nowadays, even among those like him, the anti-Semites). They are all men of *ressentiment*, these physiologically impaired and worm-eaten men, a totally quivering earthly kingdom of subterranean revenge, inexhaustible, insatiable in its outbursts against the fortunate, and equally in its masquerades of revenge, its pretexts for revenge. When would they truly attain their ultimate, most refined, most sublime triumph of revenge? Undoubtedly, if they could succeed *in pushing* their own wretchedness, all misery in general, *into the consciences* of the fortunate, so that the latter one day might begin to be ashamed of their good fortune and perhaps would say to themselves, "It's shameful to be fortunate. *There's too much misery!*" ... But there could be no greater and more fateful misunderstanding than if, through this process, the fortunate, the successful, the powerful in body and spirit should start to doubt their *right to happiness*. Away with this "twisted world"! Away with this disgraceful softening of feelings! That the invalids do *not* make the healthy sick—and that would be such a softening—that should surely be ruling point of view on earth:—but that would require above everything that the healthy remain *separated* from the sick, protected even from the gaze of sick people, so that they don't confuse themselves with the ill. Or would it perhaps be their assignment to attend on the sick or be their doctors? ... But they could not misjudge or negate *their* work more seriously—something higher *must* not demean itself by becoming the tool of something lower. The pathos of distance *must* keep the work of the two groups forever separate! Their right to exist, the privilege of a bell with a perfect ring in comparison to one that is cracked and off key, is indeed a thousand times greater. They alone are the *guarantors* of the future; they alone stand *as pledge* for humanity's future. Whatever *they* can do, whatever *they* should do—the sick can never do and should not do. But so *that* they are able to do what only *they* should do, how can they have the freedom to make themselves the doctor,

---

1 Pharisees, originally a branch of Judaism, critiqued by Jesus for their hypocrisy. In its modern usage "Pharisee" describes a self-righteous person.

the consoler, the "person who cures" for the invalids? ... And therefore let's have fresh air! fresh air! In any case, let's keep away from the neighborhood of all cultural insane asylums and hospitals! And for that let's have good companionship, *our* companionship! Or loneliness, if that's necessary! But by all means let's stay away from the foul stink of inner rotting and of the secret muck from sick worms! In that way, my friends, we can defend ourselves, at least for a while, against the two nastiest scourges which may be lying in wait precisely for us—against a *great disgust with humanity* and against a *great pity for humanity*!

15

If you've grasped the full profundity of this—and precisely here I require that you *grasp deeply*, understand profoundly—of the extent to which it simply *cannot* be the task of healthy people to attend to the sick, to make invalids well, then you've understood one more necessary matter—the necessity for doctors and nurses *who are themselves ill*. And now we have the meaning of the ascetic priest—we're holding it in both hands. We need to look on the ascetic priest as the preordained healer, shepherd, and advocate of the sick herd; in that way we can, for the first time, understand his immense historical mission. The *ruling power* over suffering people is his kingdom. His instinct instructs him to do that; in that he has his very own art, his mastery, his sort of success. He must be sick himself; he must be fundamentally related to the sick and those who go astray, in order to understand them—in order to be understood among them. But he must also be strong, master over himself even more than over others, that is, undamaged in his will to power, so that he inspires the confidence and fear of the invalids, so that he can be their support, resistance, protection, compulsion, discipline, tyrant, god. He has to defend his herd, but against whom? Against the healthy people undoubtedly, also against their envy of the healthy. He has to be the natural opponent *and critic* of all rough, stormy, unchecked, hard, violent, predatory health and power. The priest is the first form of the more delicate animal which despises more easily than it hates. He will not be spared having to conduct war with predatory animals, a war of cunning (of the "spirit") rather than of force, as is obvious—for that purpose, in certain circumstances it will be necessary for him to develop himself almost into a new type of beast of prey, or at least *to represent* himself as such a beast—with a new animal ferocity in which the polar bear, the sleek, cold, and patient tiger, and, not least, the fox seem to be combined in a unity which attracts just as much as it inspires fear. If need compels him to, he will walk even in the midst of the other sort of predatory animals with the seriousness of a bear, venerable, clever, cold, and with a duplicitous superiority, as the herald and oracle of more mysterious forces, determined to sow this ground, where he can, with suffering, conflict, self-contradiction, and only too sure of his art, to become the master over *suffering people* at all times. There's no doubt he brings with him ointments and balm. But in order to be a doctor, he first has to inflict wounds. Then, while he eases the pain caused by the wound, *at the same time he poisons the wound*—for that is, above all, what he knows how to do, this magician and animal trainer, around whom everything healthy necessarily becomes ill and everything sick necessarily becomes tame. In fact, he defends his sick herd well enough, this strange shepherd—he protects them also against themselves, against the smoldering wickedness, scheming, and maliciousness in the herd itself, against all those addictions and illnesses characteristic of their associating with each other. He fights shrewdly, hard, and secretly against the anarchy and self-dissolution which start up all the time within the herd, in which that most dangerous explosive stuff and blasting material, *ressentiment*, is constantly piling and piling up. To detonate this explosive stuff in such a way that it does not blow up the herd and its shepherd, that is his essential work of art and also his most important use. If we want to sum up the value of the priestly existence in the shortest slogan, we could at once put it like this: the priest is the *person who alters the direction* of *ressentiment*. For every suffering person instinctively seeks a cause for his suffering, or, more precisely, an agent, or, even more precisely, a *guilty* agent sensitive to suffering—in short, he seeks some living person on whom he can, on some pretext or other, unload his feelings, either in fact or *in effigie* [Latin: in effigy]: for the discharge of feelings is the most important way a suffering man seeks relief—that is, some anaesthetic—it's his involuntarily desired narcotic against any kind of torment. In my view, only here can we find the true physiological cause of *ressentiment*, revenge, and things related to them, in a longing for some anaesthetic against pain through one's emotions. People usually look for this cause, most incorrectly, in my opinion, in the defensive striking back, a merely reactive protective measure, a "reflex movement" in the event of some sudden damage and threat, of the sort a decapitated frog still makes in order to get rid of corrosive acid. But the difference is fundamental: in one case, people want to prevent suffering further damage; in the other case, people want to *deaden* a tormenting, secret pain which is becoming unendurable by means of a more violent emotion of some kind and, for the moment at least, to drive it from their consciousness—for that they need some emotion, as unruly an emotion as possible, and, in order to stimulate that, they need the best pretext available. "Someone or other must be guilty of the fact that I am ill"—this sort of conclusion is characteristic of all sick people, all the more so if the real cause of their sense that they are sick, the physiological cause, remains hidden (—it can lie, for example, in an illness of the *nervus sympathicus* [Latin: intestinal nervous system], or in an excessive secretion of gall, or in a lack of potassium sulfate and phosphate in the blood, or in some pressure in the lower abdomen, which blocks the circulation, or in a degeneration of the ovaries, and so on). Suffering people all have a horrible willingness and capacity for inventing pretexts for painful emotional feelings. They enjoy even their suspicions, their brooding over bad actions and apparent damage. They ransack the entrails of their past and present, looking for dark, dubious stories, in which they are free to feast on an agonizing suspicion and to get intoxicated on the poison of their own anger—they rip open the oldest wounds, they bleed themselves to death from long-healed scars, they turn friends, wives, children, and anyone else who is closest to them into criminals. "I am suffering. Someone or other must be to blame for that"—that's how every sick sheep thinks. But his shepherd, the ascetic priest, says to him: "That's right, my sheep! Someone must be to blame for that. But you yourself are this very person. You yourself are the only one to blame—*you alone are to blame for yourself!*" ... That is bold enough, and false enough. But one thing at least is attained by that, as I have said, the direction of *ressentiment* has been—*changed.*

16

By now you will have guessed what, according to my ideas, the healing artistic instinct for life at least has *attempted* with the ascetic priest and why he had to use a temporary tyranny of such paradoxical and illogical ideas, like "guilt," "sins," "sinfulness," "degeneration," and "damnation": to make sick people to a certain extent *harmless*, to enable the incurable to destroy themselves by their own actions, to redirect the *ressentiment* of the mildly ill sternly back onto themselves ("there's one thing necessary"—),[1] and in this manner to *utilize* the bad instincts of all suffering people to serve the purpose of self-discipline, self-monitoring, self-conquest. As is obvious, this kind of "medication," a merely emotional medication, has nothing at all to do with a real *cure* for an illness, in a physiological sense. We are never entitled to assert that the instinct for life has any sort of chance or intention to heal itself in this way. A kind of pressure to come together and organize the invalids on one side (—the word "church" is the popular name for this), some form of temporary guarantee for healthier successful people, the ones more completely fulfilled, on another side, and in the process the creation of *rift* between the healthy and sick—for a long time that's all there was. And that was a lot! It was a great deal! (In this essay, as you see, I proceed on an assumption which, so far as the readers I require are concerned, I do not have to prove first—that the "sinfulness" of human beings is not a matter of fact, but much rather only the interpretation of a factual condition, that is, of a bad psychological mood—with the latter seen from a moral-religious perspective, something which is no longer binding on us.—The fact that someone *feels* himself "guilty" or "sinful" does not in itself yet demonstrate clearly that he is justified in feeling like that, just as the mere fact that someone feels healthy does not mean that he is healthy. People should remember the famous witch trials[2]: at that time the most perspicacious and philanthropic judges had no doubt that they were dealing with guilt; the "witches" *themselves had no doubts about that point*—nonetheless, there was no guilt.—To express that assumption in broader terms: I consider that "spiritual pain" itself is not, in general, a fact, but only an interpretation [(a causal interpretation)] of facts which up to that point have not been precisely formulated, and thus something that is still completely up in the air and not scientifically binding—essentially a fat word set in place of a very spindly question mark. To put the matter crudely, when someone cannot cope with a "spiritual pain," that has *nothing* to do with his "soul"; it's more likely something to do with his belly [(speaking crudely, as

---

1 Luke 10:42: "But one thing is needful: and Mary hath chosen that good part, which shall not be taken away from her."

2 The three centuries between 1450 and 1750 constituted the main period of the persecution and execution of persons suspected of practicing witchcraft. An estimated 35,000 to 100,000 people, chiefly women and teenaged girls, were victims.

I said: but in saying that I'm not expressing the slightest wish to be crudely heard or crudely understood . . .)]. A strong and successful man digests his experiences [(his actions, including his misdeeds)] as he digests his meals, even when he has to swallow down some hard mouthfuls. If he is "unable to finish with" an experience, this kind of indigestion is just as much a physiological matter as that other one—and in many cases, in fact, only one of the consequences of that other one.—With such an view, a person can, just between ourselves, still be the strongest opponent of all materialism....)])[1]

17

But is he really a *doctor*, this ascetic priest?—We already understand the extent to which one can hardly be permitted to call him a doctor, no matter how much he likes feeling that he is a "savior" and allowing himself to be honored as a "savior." But he fights only against suffering itself, the unhappiness of the suffering person, *not* against its cause, *not* against the essential sickness—this must constitute our most fundamental objection to priestly medication. But if for once we look at things from the perspective which only the priest understands and adopts, then it will not be easy for us to limit our amazement at all the things he has noticed, looked for, and found by seeing things in that manner. The *alleviation* of suffering, every kind of "consolation"—that manifests itself as his particular genius: he has understood his task as consoler with so much innovation and has selected the means for that so spontaneously and so fearlessly! We could call Christianity, in particular, a huge treasure house of the most elegant forms of consolation—there are so many pleasant, soothing, narcotizing things piled up in it, and for this purpose it takes so many of the most dangerous and most audacious chances. It shows such sophistication, such southern refinement, especially when it guesses what kind of emotional stimulant can overcome, at least for a while, the deep depression, leaden exhaustion, and black sorrow of the physiologically impaired. For, generally speaking, with all great religions, the main issue concerns the fight against a certain endemic exhaustion and heaviness. We can from the outset assume as probable that from time to time, in particular places on the earth, a feeling of *physiological inhibition* must necessarily become master over wide

---

1 Nietzsche added the square brackets with parentheses.

masses of people, but, because of a lack of knowledge about physiology, it does not enter people's consciousness as something physiological, so they look for and attempt to find its "cause" and remedy only in psychology and morality (—this, in fact, is my most general formula for whatever is commonly called a "*religion*"). Such a feeling of inhibition can have a varied ancestry; for instance, it can be the result of cross-breeding between different races (or between classes—for classes also always express differences in origin and race: European "*Weltschmerz*" [pain at the state of the world][1] and nineteenth-century "pessimism" are essentially the consequence of an irrational, sudden mixing of the classes), or it can be caused by incorrect emigration—a race caught in a climate for which its powers of adaptation are not sufficient (the case of the Indians in India); or by the influence of the age and exhaustion of the race (Parisian pessimism from 1850 on); or by an incorrect diet (the alcoholism of the Middle Ages, the inanity of *vegetarians* [English in the original], who, of course, have on their side the authority of Shakespeare's foolish knight Sir Andrew Aguecheek); or by degeneration in the blood, malaria, syphilis and things like that (German depression after the Thirty Years' War, which spread bad diseases in an epidemic through half of Germany and thus prepared the ground for German servility, German timidity).[2] In such a case, a *war against the feeling of a lack of enthusiasm* will always be attempted in the grand style. Let's briefly go over its most important practices and forms. (Here I leave quite out of account, as seems reasonable, the actual war *of the philosophers* against this lack of enthusiasm, which always has a habit of appearing at the same time—that war is interesting enough, but too absurd, with too little practical significance, too full of cobwebs and loafing around—as, for example, when pain is to be shown an error, on the naive assumption that the pain *must* disappear as soon as it is recognized as a error—but, lo and behold, it

---

1 *Weltschmerz* was coined by the German Romantic author Jean Paul (Johann Paul Friedrich Richter) (1763–1825) in *Selina, or On the Immortality of the Soul* (1804).

2 The reference here, as proposed by Maudemarie Clark and Alan J. Swensen, is an allusion to Shakespeare's *Twelfth Night*, where Sir Andrew Aguecheek (called Junker Christoph in the Schlegel-Tieck German translation) comments on his eating habits. See Maudemarie Clark and Alan Swensen's translation of *The Genealogy of Morality* (Hackett, 1998), p. 156. Nietzsche refers to Junker Christoph's meat-eating habits again in this section.

sees to it that it does not disappear ...). *First*, people fight that domineering listlessness with means which, in general, set our feeling for life at their lowest point. Where possible, there is generally no more willing, no more desire; they stay away from everything which creates an emotional response, which makes "blood" (no salt in the diet, the hygiene of the fakir); they don't love; they don't hate—equanimity—they don't take revenge, they don't get wealthy, they don't work; they beg; where possible, no women, or as few women as possible; with respect to spiritual matters, Pascal's principle *"Il faut s'abêtir"* [French: One must make oneself stupid].[1] The result, expressed in moral-psychological terms, is "selflessness," "sanctification"; expressed in physiological terms: hypnotizing—the attempt to attain for human beings something approaching what *winter hibernation* is for some kinds of animals and what *summer sleep* is for many plants in hot climates, the minimum consumption and processing of material stuff which can still sustain life, but which does not actually enter consciousness. For this purpose, an astonishing amount of human energy has been expended. Has it all gone for nothing? ... We should not entertain the slightest doubts that such *sportsmen* [English in original] of "holiness," whom almost all populations have in abundance at all times, in fact found a real release from what they were fighting against with such a rigorous *training* [English in original]—with the help of their systemic methods for hypnosis, in countless cases they really were *released* from that deep physiological depression. That's the reason their methodology belongs with the most universal ethnological facts. For the same reason, we have no authority for considering such an intentional starving of one's desires and of one's physical well-being as, in itself, symptoms of insanity (the way a clumsy kind of roast-beef-eating "free spirit" and Sir Andrew Aguecheek/Juncker Christoph like to do). It's much more the case that it opens or can open the *way* to all sorts of spiritual disruptions, to "inner light," for example, as with Hesychasts on Mount Athos, to hallucinating sounds and shapes, to sensual outpourings and ecstasies of sensuality (the history of St. Theresa).[2]

---

1 Blaise Pascal (1623–62), French philosopher notable for examining the limits of human knowledge.

2 Hesychasts: a religious tradition in the Eastern Orthodox Church based on Mount Athos in Greece which emphasizes the abandonment of sensual experience. St. Theresa of Ávila (1515–82), Carmelite nun who founded a branch of her order that practiced flagellation and discalceation (going barefoot) in order to fight

It's self-evident that the interpretation which has been given for conditions of this sort by those afflicted with them has always been as effusively false as possible. Still, people should not fail to catch the tone of totally convincing gratitude ringing out in the very *will* to such a form of interpretation. They always value the highest state, *redemption* itself, that finally attained collective hypnosis and quietness, as the inherent mystery, which cannot be adequately expressed even by the highest symbols, as a stop at and return home to the basis of things, as an emancipation from all delusions, as "knowledge," as "truth," as "being," as the removal of all goals, all wishes, all acts, and thus as a place beyond good and evil. "Good and evil," says the Buddhist, "are both fetters: the perfect one became master over both"; "what's done and what's not done," says the man who believes in the Vedanta, "give him no pain; as a wise man he shakes good and evil off himself; his kingdom suffers no more from any deed; good and evil—he has transcended both"—an entirely Indian conception, whether Brahmin or Buddhist. (Neither in the Indian nor in the Christian way of thinking is this "redemption" considered *attainable* through virtue, through moral improvement—no matter how high a value they place on virtue as a form of hypnotism. People should note this point—it corresponds, incidentally, to the plain facts. That on this point they kept to the *truth* might perhaps be considered the best piece of realism in the three largest religions, which, apart from this, are religions so fundamentally concerned with moralizing. "The man who knows has no duties" ... "Redemption does not come about through an *increase* in virtue, for it consists of unity with Brahma, who is incapable of any increase in perfection; even less does it come through *setting aside* one's faults, for the Brahma, unity with whom creates redemption, is eternally pure"—these passages from the commentary of Shankara are cited by the first genuine *authority* on Indian philosophy in Europe, my friend Paul Deussen).[1] So we want to honor "redemption" in the great religions; however, it will be a little difficult for us to remain serious

---

spiritual laxity during the Counter-Reformation. Moreover, fearful that her experiences of religious ecstasy may have been diabolical in origin, she inflicted horrible tortures on herself.

1 Adi Shankara (c. 788–820 CE), Indian philosopher who played a formative role in the historical development of Hinduism. Paul Deussen (1845–1919), boyhood friend of Nietzsche, editor of Schopenhauer, and translator of the Indian religious texts quoted by Nietzsche in *The Genealogy*.

about the way these people, who've grown too weary of life even to dream, value *deep sleep*—that is, deep sleep as already an access to the Brahma, as an achieved *unio mystica* [Latin: mystical union or marriage] with God. On this subject, the oldest and most venerable "Scripture" states: "When he is soundly and completely asleep and is in a state of perfect calm, so that he is not seeing any more dream images, at that moment, O dear one, united with Being, he has gone into himself—now that he has been embraced by a form of his knowing self, he has no consciousness any more of what is outer or inner. Over this bridge comes neither night nor day, nor old age, nor death, nor suffering, nor good works, nor evil works." Similarly, believers in this most profound of the three great religions say, "In deep sleep the soul lifts itself up out of this body, goes into the highest light, and moves out in its own form: there it is the highest spirit itself which wanders around, while it jokes and plays and enjoys itself, whether with women or with carriages or with friends; there it no longer thinks back to its bodily append-ages, to which the *prana* (the breath of life) is harnessed like a draught animal to a cart." Nevertheless, as in the case of "redemp-tion," we also need to keep in mind here that no matter how great the splendor of oriental exaggeration, what this states is basically the same evaluation which was made by that clear, cool, Greek-cool, but suffering Epicurus:[1] the hypnotic feeling of nothingness, the silence of the deepest sleep, in short, the *loss of suffering*—something which suffering and fundamentally disgruntled people are already entitled to consider their highest good, their value of values, and which they *must* appraise as positive and experience as *the* positive in itself. (With the same logic of feeling, in all pessi-mistic religions nothingness is called *God*).

18

Against this condition of depression, a different and certainly easier training is tried far more often than such a hypnotic collective deadening of the sensibilities, of the ability to ex-perience pain, for the method requires rare powers, above all, courage, contempt for opinion, and "intellectual Stoicism."[2]

---

1 Nietzsche correctly notes that the apogee of Epicurean wisdom was the attainment of utter calmness and peace of mind amid the flux of experience.

2 Stoicism was school of ancient Greek philosophy which taught that happiness is achieved by accepting reality as it is.

This different *training* [English in original] is *mechanical activity*. There's no doubt whatsoever that this can alleviate a suffering existence to a degree which is not insignificant. Today we call this fact, somewhat dishonestly, "the blessings of work." The relief comes about because the interest of the suffering person is basically diverted from his suffering—because some action and then another action are always entering his consciousness, thus leaving little space there for suffering. For it's *narrow*, this room of human consciousness! Mechanical activity and what's associated with it—like absolute regularity, meticulous and mindless obedience, a style of life set once and for all, filling in time, a certain allowance for, indeed, training in, "impersonality," in forgetting oneself, in *"incuria sui"* [Latin: indifference to oneself]—how fundamentally, how delicately the ascetic priest knew how to use them in the struggle with suffering! Especially when it involved the suffering people of the lower classes, working slaves, or prisoners (or women, most of whom are, in fact, simultaneously both working slaves and prisoners) what was needed was little more than the minor art of changing names and re-christening, so as to make those people in future see a favor, some relative good fortune, in things they hated—the slave's discontent with his lot, in any case, was *not* invented by the priests. An even more valuable tool in the battle against depression is prescribing a *small pleasure* which is readily accessible and can be made habitual. People frequently use this medication in combination with the one just mentioned. The most common form in which pleasure is prescribed in this way as a cure is the pleasure in *creating* pleasure (as in showing kindness, giving presents, providing relief, helping, encouraging, trusting, praising, honoring). The ascetic priest orders "love of one's neighbor"; in so doing, he is basically prescribing an arousal of the strongest, most life-affirming drive, even if only in the most cautious doses—the *will to power*. The happiness which comes from "the smallest feeling of superiority," which all doing good, being useful, helping, and honoring bring with them, is the most plentiful way of providing consolation, which the physiologically impaired habitually use, provided that they have been well advised. In a different situation, they harm each other, doing so, of course, in obedience to the same basic instinct. If we look for the beginnings of Christianity in the Roman world, we find organizations growing up for mutual support, combinations of the poor and sick, for burial, on the lowest levels of society at the time, in which that major way of combating depression, the minor joys which habitually develop out of mutual demonstrations of kindness, were consciously employed—perhaps at the time this was something new, a real discovery? "The will to mutual assistance," to the formation of the herd, to "a community," to a *cénacle* [French: community] summoned in this manner, must call up again, if only in the smallest way, that aroused will to power and come to a new and much greater outburst. In the fight against depression, the *development of the herd* is an essential step and a victory. By growing, the community also reinforces in the individual a new interest, which often enough raises him up over the most personal features of his bad disposition, his dislike of *himself* (Geulincx's *despectio sui* [Latin: contempt for oneself]).[1] All sick pathological people, in their desire to shake off a stifling lack of enthusiasm and a feeling of weakness, instinctively strive for the organization of a herd. The ascetic priest senses this instinct and promotes it. Where there is a herd, it's the instinct of weakness which has willed the herd and the cleverness of the priest which has organized it. For we should not overlook the following point: through natural necessity strong people strive to separate *from* each other, just as much as weak people strive to be *with* each other. When the former unite, that happens only at the prospect of an aggressive combined action and a collective satisfaction of their will to power, with considerable resistance from the individual conscience. By contrast, the latter organize themselves collectively, taking *pleasure* precisely in this collective—their instinct is satisfied by this in the same way that the instinct of those born "Masters" (i.e., the solitary man of the predatory species of human being) is basically irritated and upset by organization. Under every oligarchy—all history teaches us— is always concealed the craving for *tyranny*. Every oligarchy is constantly trembling with the tension which every individual in it necessarily has in order to remain master of this craving. (That was the case, for example, with the *Greeks*. Plato provides evidence of this in a hundred passages—Plato, who understood his peers—and himself ...).

---

1 Arnold Geulincx (1624–69), Flemish rationalist philosopher who taught that God would occasionally intervene in the physical world. One's proper attitude toward such events was "contempt for oneself."

19

The ascetic priest's methods, which we learned about earlier—
the collective deadening of the feeling for life, mechanical activity, minor joys, above all, the joy in "loving one's neighbor," the
organization of the herd, the awakening of the feeling of power
in the community, as a result of which the dissatisfaction of the
individual with himself is drowned out by his pleasure in the
flourishing of the community—these things are, measured by
modern standards, his *innocent* methods in the war against unhappiness. But now let's turn our attention to more interesting
methods, to his "guilty" ones. With all of them there is one thing
involved: some kind of *excess of feeling*—employed as the most
effective anaesthetic against stifling, crippling, and long-lasting
pain. For that reason, the priest's powers of innovation have been
tireless in addressing this one question in particular: *"Through
what means* do people reach emotional excess?" ... That sounds
harsh. It's clear enough that it would sound more appealing and
perhaps please our ears better if I said something like "The ascetic priest has always used the *enthusiasm* which lies in all strong
emotions." But why keep caressing the mollycoddled ears of our
modern delicate sensibilities? Why should we, *for our part*, retreat
even one step back from the *Tartufferie* [French: hypocrisy] of
their vocabulary? Doing something like that would already make
us psychologists active hypocrites—apart from the fact that for
us it would be disgusting. For if a psychologist today has *good
taste* anywhere (others might say his honesty), it's because he de-
tests that disgraceful *moralizing* way of talking, which effectively
covers in slime all modern judgments about human beings and
things. For we must not deceive ourselves in this business. The
most characteristic feature which forms modern souls and modern books is not lying but the ingrained *innocence* in their moralistic lying. To have to discover this "innocence" again all over
the place—that is perhaps the most repellent part of our work, of
all the inherently dangerous work which nowadays a psychologist has to undertake. It is a part of *our* great danger—it is a path
that perhaps takes *us* in particular to a great revulsion. I have no
doubt about what single purpose will be served, or can be served,
in a coming world by modern books (provided they last, which,
of course, we need not fear, and provided there will one day be
a later world with a stronger, harder, and *healthier* taste), or what
general purpose *all things* modern will have: they will serve as
emetics—and they'll do that thanks to their moralistic sweetness

and falsity, their innermost feminism, which likes to call itself "idealism" and which, at all events, has faith in Idealism.[1] Today our educated people, our "good people," don't tell lies—that's true. But that's *no reason* to respect them! The real lie, the genuine, resolute, "honest" lie (people should listen to Plato on its value[2]) for them would be something far too demanding, too strong. It would require what people are not allowed to demand of them, that they opened up their eyes and looked at themselves, so that they would know how to differentiate between "true" and "false" with respect to themselves. But they are fit only for *ignoble lies*. Everyone today who feels that he is a "good man" is completely incapable of taking a stand on any issue at all, other than with *dishonest falseness*—an abysmal falsity, which is, however, innocent falsity, true-hearted falsity, blue-eyed falsity, virtuous falsity. These "good people"—collectively they are now utterly and completely moralized and, so far as their honesty is concerned, they've been disgraced and ruined for all eternity. Who among them could endure even one *truth* "about human beings"! ... Or, to ask the question more precisely, who among them could bear a *true* biography! Here are a couple of indications: Lord Byron recorded some very personal things about himself, but Thomas Moore was "too good" for them. He burned his friend's papers. The executor of Schopenhauer's will, Dr. Gwinner, is alleged to have done the same thing, for Schopenhauer had also recorded some things about himself and also, perhaps, against himself (*"eis heauton"* [Greek: against himself]). The capable American Thayer, the biographer of Beethoven, abruptly stopped his work: at some point or other in this venerable and naive life he could no longer continue ...[3] Moral: What intelligent man nowadays

---

1 Throughout *The Genealogy* Nietzsche conflates all tendencies which he identifies with the search for an escape from reality, such as feminism, socialism, and idealism.

2 In Book III of Plato's *Republic*, Socrates describes the benefits of the "noble" or "good lie" (*gennaion pseudos*)—a myth or falsehood told the people by the ruling elites—in maintaining the well-being of society.

3 George Gordon, Lord Byron, British Romantic poet who was chiefly a satirist and a rebel against conventional mores. Thomas Moore (1779–1852), Irish poet notorious for burning Byron's unpublished memoirs at the latter's death. Wilhelm von Gwinner (1825–1917), German lawyer and civil servant who served as Schopenhauer's executor and biographer. Alexander Wheelock

would still write an honest word about himself?—He would already have to be a member of the Order of Holy Daredevils. We have been promised an autobiography of Richard Wagner. Who has any doubts that it will be a *prudent* autobiography? Let's remember the comical horror which the Catholic priest Janssen aroused in Germany with his incomprehensibly bland and harmless picture of the German Reformation movement.[1] How would people react if one day someone explained this movement *differently*, if, for once, a true psychologist with *spiritual strength* and not a shrewd indulgence toward strength pictured a true Luther for us, no longer with the moralistic simplicity of a country parson, no longer with the sweet and considerate modesty of a protestant historian, but with something like the fearlessness of a *Taine?*[2] . . . (Parenthetically, the Germans have finally produced a sufficiently beautiful classical type of such shrewd indulgence—they can classify him as one of their own and be proud of him, namely, their Leopold Ranke, this born classical *advocatus* [Latin: advocate] of every *causa fortior* [Latin: stronger cause], the shrewdest of all the shrewd "realists").[3]

20

But you will already have grasped what I'm getting at. All in all, that's surely reason enough, is it not, why we psychologists nowadays cannot rid ourselves of a certain distrust *in ourselves?* ... We also are probably "too good" for the work we do. We are probably sacrificial victims and prey, as well, made sick by this contemporary taste for moralizing, no matter how much we also feel

---

Thayer (1817–97), originally a New England schoolteacher; his German-language biography of Ludwig van Beethoven (1770–1827), considered a heroic feat, remains the standard reference on the German composer.

1 Johannes Janssen (1829–91), Catholic priest and German historian whose *Geschichte des deutschen Volkes seit dem Ausgang des Mittelalters* (*History of the German People since the End of the Middle Ages*) (1878–94) was controversial for its unsparing treatment of the shortcomings of the leaders of the Protestant Reformation.

2 Hippolyte Adolphe Taine (1828–93), French literary critic who promoted the school of Naturalism in France.

3 Leopold von Ranke (1795–1886), German historian who established modern historiographical standards for archival research and factual reconstruction of historical events.

we're its critics—it probably infects even *us* as well. What was that diplomat[1] warning about when he addressed his colleagues? "Gentlemen, let us mistrust our first impulses above all!" he declared; "*they are almost always good*" That's also how every psychologist today should speak to his peers. And so, we come back to our problem, which, in fact, requires a certain rigor from us, especially some distrust of our "first impulses." *The ascetic ideal in the service of intentional emotional excess*—whoever remembers the previous essay will, with the compressed content of these ten words, already have a preliminary sense of the essential content of what I now have to demonstrate. To remove the human soul for once from its entire frame, to immerse it in terror, frost, glowing embers, and joys of that kind, so that it rids itself, as if with a bolt of lightning, of all pettiness and small-mindedness of lack of interest, apathy, and irritation. What paths lead to *this* goal? And which of them is the most reliable? ... All the greatest emotions basically have this capacity, provided they discharge themselves suddenly—anger, fear, lust, revenge, hope, triumph, despair, cruelty. And the ascetic priest has, in fact, without a second thought, taken the *entire* pack of wild hounds in the human being into his service and let loose one of them at one time, another at another time, always for the same purpose, to wake human beings up out of their long sadness, to chase away, at least for a while, their stifling pain, their tentative misery, and always covered up in a religious interpretation and "justification." Every emotional excess of this sort demands *payment* later; that's self-evident—it makes sick people sicker. And thus, this way of providing a remedy for pain, measured by modern standards, is a "guilty" method. However, to be fair, we must insist all the more that it was used *in good conscience*, that the ascetic priest prescribed it with the deepest faith in its utility, indeed, its indispensability—often enough almost falling apart himself in front of the misery he created; and, similarly, that the vehement physiological revenges of such excesses, perhaps even psychic disturbances, basically do not really contradict the whole meaning of this kind of medication, which, as I've pointed out above, was *not* designed to heal sick people, but to fight their enervating depression, to alleviate and anaesthetize it. *With this method* that goal was attained. The main instrumental fingering which

---

1 Here Nietzsche alludes to Charles-Maurice de Tallyrand (1754–1838), who served in multiple diplomatic posts in post-revolutionary French governments.

the ascetic priest allowed himself in order to bring every kind of disorienting ecstatic music ringing out in the human soul was achieved, as everyone knows, by the fact that he made use of the *feeling of guilt*. The previous essay indicated, in brief, the origin of this feeling—as a part of animal psychology, nothing more. The feeling of guilt we encountered there in its raw state, as it were. In the hands of the priest, this true artist in guilt feelings, it first acquired a form—and what a form! "Sin"—for that's how the priest's new interpretation of the animal "bad conscience" ran (cruelty turned backwards)—has been the greatest event in the history of the sick soul so far. In it we have the most dangerous and the most fateful artistic work of religious interpretation. The human being, suffering from himself somehow—at any rate, psychologically—something like an animal barred up in a cage, confused about why this has happened and what purpose it serves, longing for reasons—reasons provide relief—longing also for treatments and narcotics, finally discussed the matter with one who also knew about hidden things—and lo and behold! He gets a hint. He gets the *first* hint about the "cause" of his suffering from his magician, the ascetic priest. He is to seek this cause in *himself*, in his *guilt*, in a piece of the past. He is to understand his own suffering as a *condition of punishment* ... He heard, he understood—this unfortunate man: now things stand with him as with a hen around which a line has been drawn. He is not to come outside this circle of lines again. The "sick man" is turned into the "sinner" ... And now for a couple of millennia people have not rid themselves of the look of this new sick man, the "sinner."—Will people ever be rid of him?—No matter where we look, we see everywhere the hypnotic glance of the sinner, who always moves in one direction (in the direction of "guilt" as the *single* cause of suffering), everywhere the bad conscience, this "horrifying animal," to use Luther's words, everywhere the past regurgitated, the fact distorted, the "green eye" cast on all action, everywhere the *desire* to misunderstand suffering turned into the meaning of life, with suffering reinterpreted into feelings of guilt, fear, and punishment, everywhere the whip, the hair shirt, the starving body, remorse, everywhere the sinner's breaking himself on the terrible torture wheel of a restless conscience, greedy for its own sickness; everywhere silent torment, extreme fear, the agony of the tortured heart, the spasms of an unknown joy, the cry for "redemption." As a matter of fact, with this system of procedures the old depression, heaviness, and exhaustion were basically *overthrown*. Life became *very* interesting once again: lively, always lively, sleepless, glowing, charred, exhausted, and yet not tired—that's how man looked, the "sinner," who was initiated into *these* mysteries. This grand old magician in the war against the lack of excitement, the ascetic priest—he had apparently won. *His* kingdom had come. Now people no longer moaned *against* pain; they *longed* for pain: "*More* pain! *More* pain!"—that had been the demanding cry of his disciples and initiates for centuries. Every excess of feeling which brought grief, everything that broke apart, knocked over, smashed to bits, carried away, enraptured, the secrets of the torture chambers, the very invention of hell—from now on everything was discovered, surmised, put into practice. Everything now was available for the magician's use. Everything in future served for the victory of his ideal, the ascetic ideal.... "My kingdom is not of *this* world"[1]—he said afterwards (as he said before). Does he really have the right still to speak this way? ... Goethe asserted that there were only thirty-six tragic situations.[2] From that we can surmise, if we did not know it anyway, that Goethe was no ascetic priest. He—knows more ...

21

So far as *this* whole sort of priestly medication is concerned, the "guilty" sort, any word of criticism is too much. That an excess of feeling of the sort the ascetic priest habitually prescribes for his sick people in this case (under the holiest of names, as is obvious, while convinced of the sanctity of his purpose) has truly been *of use* to some invalid: who would really want to defend the truth of this kind of claim? At least we should come to an understanding of that phrase "been of use." If with those words people wish to assert that such a system of treatment has *improved* human beings, then I won't contradict them. I would only add what "improved" indicates to me—it's as much as saying "tamed," "weakened," "disheartened," "refined," "mollycoddled" (hence, almost equivalent to *damaged* ...). But when we are mainly concerned with sick, upset, and depressed people, such

---

1 John 18:36.
2 Goethe derived this schema from the Venetian playwright Carlo Gozzi (1720–1806). See Johann Peter Eckermann, *Gespräche mit Goethe in den letzten Jahren seines Lebens* (Verlag C.H. Beck, 1984), entry for 14 February 1830, p. 618. Nietzsche alludes to Goethe's numerous love affairs and fondness for good wine.

a system, even supposing that it makes them "better," always makes them *sicker*. You only have to ask doctors who treat the mentally ill [*Irrenärzte*] what a methodical application of the torments of repentance, remorse, and convulsions of redemption always brings with it. We should also consult history: wherever the ascetic priest has put in place this way of dealing with the sick, illness has always spread far and wide at terrifying speed. What has its "success" always involved? The person who was already ill gets in addition a shattered nervous system, and that occurs on the largest and smallest scale, among individuals and among masses of people. As a consequence of a *training* [English in original] in repentance and redemption, we witness huge epidemics of epilepsy, the greatest known to history, as in the St. Vitus's and St. John's dances in the Middle Ages.[1] We find its repercussions in other forms of fearful paralysis and enduring depression, with which, under certain circumstances, the temperament of an entire people or city (Geneva, Basel) is changed into its opposite once and for all—with these belong also the witch crazes, something related to sleep walking (eight major epidemics of this broke out between 1564 and 1605 alone)[2];—among its consequences we also find that death-seeking mass hysteria whose horrific cry "*evviva la morte*" [Italian: long live death] was heard far across the whole of Europe, interrupted by idiosyncratic outbursts— sometimes of lust, sometimes of destructive frenzies, just as the same alternation of emotions, with the same intermissions and reversals, can also still be observed nowadays all over the place, in every case where the ascetic doctrine of sin once again enjoys a great success (religious neurosis[3] *appears* as a form of an "evil nature"—that's indisputable. What is it? *Quaeritur* [Latin: that's what we need to ask]). Generally speaking, the ascetic ideal and

---

1 During the sixteenth century in Europe there were frequent outbreaks of dancing mania—initially considered a curse sent by a saint—that could last for hours, days, weeks, and even months. Its causes have been variously ascribed to pathology—epidemics of disease, mass psychosis, mass ergot poisoning of grain, or the stresses associated with poverty—or religious cults that staged group dances as rituals that mimicked such events in ancient Greece and Rome.

2 The bloody mass persecution of witches has been seen as a complex response to the effects of religious strife, war, and famine caused by the Little Ice Age.

3 Neurosis: an umbrella term for psychological disturbance in the pre-Freudian era.

its cult of moral sublimity, this supremely clever, most dubious, and most dangerous systematization of all the ways to promote an excess of emotion under the protection of holy purposes, has etched itself into the entire history of human beings in a dreadful and unforgettable manner, and, alas, *not only* into their history ... Apart from this ideal, there's scarcely anything else I would know to point to which has had such a destructive effect on the *health* and racial power, particularly of Europeans. Without any exaggeration, we can call it *the true disaster* in the history of the health of European people. At most, the specifically German influence might be comparable to its effect: I refer to the alcohol poisoning of Europe, which up to now has marched strictly in step with the political and racial superiority of the Germans (— wherever they have infused their blood, they have also infused their vices).—The third in line would be syphilis—*magno sed proxima intervallo* [Latin: next in line, but after a large gap].[1]

22

Wherever he achieved mastery, the ascetic priest has ruined spiritual health. As a result, he has also ruined *taste in artibus et litteris* [Latin: in arts and letters]—he is still ruining that. "As a result"?—I hope you will simply concede me this "as a result." At least, I have no desire to demonstrate it first. A single indication: it concerns the fundamental text of Christian literature, its essential model, its "book in itself." Still in the middle of the Greco-Roman magnificence, which was also a magnificent time for books, faced with an ancient world of writing which had not yet declined and fallen apart, an age in which people could still read some books for which one would now exchange half of all literature, the simplicity and vanity of Christian agitators—we call them the church fathers—already dared to proclaim, *"We also have our classical literature. We don't need Greek literature."*— And with that, they pointed with pride to books of legends, letters of the apostles, and little apologetic treatises, in somewhat the same way as nowadays the English "Salvation Army"[2] with its related literature fights its war against Shakespeare and other

---

1 Ironically, Nietzsche's mental collapse, illness, and death were long speculated to have been caused by syphilis.

2 Evangelical Christian charitable organization with uniforms and military ranks, established by the Methodist preacher William Booth (1829–1912).

"pagans." I don't like the "New Testament"[1]—you will already have guessed as much. It almost disturbs me that I stand alone in my taste with respect to this most highly regarded and most overvalued written work (the taste of two thousand years is *against* me). But how can I help it! "Here I stand. I can do no other"[2]—I have the courage of my own bad taste. The *Old Testament*—now, that's something totally different: all honor to the Old Testament! In that I find great men, a heroic landscape, and something of the very rarest of all elements on earth, the incomparable naïveté of the *strong heart*; even more—I find a people. In the New Testament, by contrast, I find nothing but small sectarian households, nothing but spiritual rococo, nothing but ornament, twisty little corners, oddities, nothing but conventional air, not to mention an occasional breeze of bucolic sweet sentimentality, which belongs to the age (*and* the Roman province), something not so much Jewish as Hellenistic. Humility and pomposity standing shoulder to shoulder; a chatting about feelings which are almost stupefying; vehement feelings but no passion, with awkward gestures. Here, it seems, there's a lack of all good upbringing. How can people make such a fuss about their small vices, the way these devout little men do? No cock—and certainly not God—would crow about such things. Finally, they even want to possess "the crown of eternal life,"[3] all these small people from the provinces. But what for? What for? It is impossible to push presumption any further. An "immortal" Peter: who could endure *him*? They have an ambition that makes one laugh: one of them spells out his most personal things, his stupidities, melancholy, and indolent worries, as if the essence of all things had a duty to worry about such matters. Another one never gets tired of wrapping up God himself in the smallest misery he finds himself stuck in. And the most appalling taste of this constant familiarity with God! This Jewish, and

---

1 The Old Testament contains the sacred scriptures of the Jewish faith, while Christianity interprets the New Testament as the fulfillment of the prophecies of the Old, chiefly in the identification of Jesus as the Messiah.

2 "Hier stehe ich. Ich kann nicht anders": allegedly Martin Luther's reply when asked, at the Diet of Worms (1521), to take back his criticisms of the Roman Catholic Church. His response launched the Protestant Reformation.

3 Revelations 2:10: "[B]e thou faithful unto death, and I will give thee a crown of life."

not merely Jewish, excessive importuning God with mouth and paw! ... There are small despised "pagan people" in east Asia from whom these first Christians could have learned something important, some *tact* in their reverence. As Christian missionaries reveal, such people are not generally allowed to utter the name of their god. This seems to me sufficiently delicate. It was certainly too delicate not only for the "first" Christians. To sense the contrast, we should remember something about Luther, the "most eloquent" and most presumptuous peasant Germany ever had, and the tone Luther adopted as the one he most preferred in his conversations with God. Luther's resistance to the interceding saints of the church (especially to "the devil's sow, the Pope") was undoubtedly, in the last analysis, the resistance of a lout irritated by the *good etiquette* of the church, that etiquette of reverence of the priestly taste, which lets only the more consecrated and the more discreet into the holy of holies and shuts the door against the louts, who in this particular place are never to speak. But Luther, the peasant, simply wanted something different—this situation was not *German* enough for him. Above all, he wanted to speak directly, to speak for himself, to speak "openly" with his God. Well, he did it.—You can conjecture easily enough that there has never been a place anywhere in which the ascetic ideal has been a school of good taste, even less of good manners—in the best cases, it was a school for priestly manners. That comes about because it carries something in its own body which is the deadly enemy of all good manners—it lacks moderation, it resists moderation, it is itself a *"non plus ultra"* [Latin: what cannot be surpassed].

23

The ascetic ideal has not only ruined health and taste; it has also ruined a third, fourth, fifth, and sixth something as well—I'll be careful not to mention *everything* (when would I come to the end!). I'm not going to reveal what this ideal has *brought about*. I would much rather confine myself to what it *means*, what it allows us to surmise, what lies hidden behind, under, and in it, what it provisionally and indistinctly expresses, overloaded with question marks and misunderstandings. And only with *this* purpose in mind, I cannot spare my readers a glimpse into the monstrosity of its effects, as well as its disastrous consequences, in order, that is, to prepare them for the ultimate and most terrifying aspects which the question of the meaning of this ideal has for me. Just what does the *power* of this ideal mean, the *monstrous* nature of this power? Why was it given room to grow to this extent? Why was there not a more effective resistance? The ascetic ideal is the expression of a will. *Where* is the opposing will, in which an *opposing ideal* finds its expression? The ascetic ideal has a *goal*—a goal which is universal enough that all other interests in human existence, measured against it, seem small and narrow. It interprets times, people, and humanity unsparingly with this goal in mind. It permits no other interpretation. No other goal counts. It rejects, denies, affirms, and confirms only through *its own* interpretative meaning (—and has there ever been a system of interpretation more thoroughly thought through?); it does not submit to any power; by contrast, it believes in its privileged position in relation to all power, in its absolutely *higher ranking* with respect to every power—it believes that there is no power on earth which does not have to derive its meaning first from it, a right to exist, a value, as a tool in *its own* work, as a way and a means to *its own* goal, to a single goal ... Where is the *counterpart* to this closed system of will, goal, and interpretation? Why is this counterpart *missing*? ... Where is the *other* "single goal"? But people tell me that counterpart is *not* missing, claiming it has not only fought a long and successful war with that ideal, but has already mastered that ideal on all major points: all our modern *science* is a testament to that—the whole of our modern science,[1] which, as a true philosophy of reality, evidently believes only in itself, evidently possesses courage and will in itself, and has got along up to this point well enough without God, a world beyond, and virtues which deny. However, I'm not impressed at all with such a fuss and chattering from agitators: these trumpeters of reality are bad musicians. One can hear well enough that their notes do *not* sound out of the depths. The abyss of scientific conscience does *not* speak through them—for today the scientific conscience is an abyss—the phrase "science" in such trumpeting mouths is mere fornication, an abuse, an indecency. The truth is precisely the opposite of what is claimed here: science nowadays has simply *no* faith in itself, to say nothing of an ideal *above* it—and where it consists at all of passion, love, ardour, *suffering*, that doesn't make it the opposite of that ascetic ideal but rather *its newest and most pre-eminent form*. Does that sound strange to you? ... There are indeed a sufficient number

---

1　The discussion of "science" (*Wissenschaft*) that follows encompasses both natural science and scholarship in the humanities.

of upright and modest working people among scholars nowadays, happy in their little corners, and because their work satisfies them, they make noises from time to time, demanding, with some presumption, that people today *should* in general be happy, particularly with science—there are so many useful things to do precisely there. I don't deny that. The last thing I want to do is to ruin the pleasure these honest laborers take in the tasks they perform. For I'm happy about their work. But the fact that people are working rigorously in science these days and that there are satisfied workers is simply *no* proof that science today, as a totality, has a goal, a will, an ideal, a passion in a great faith. As I've said, the opposite is the case: where science is not the most recently appearing form of the ascetic ideal—and then it's a matter of cases too rare, noble, and exceptional to be capable of countering the general judgment—science today is a *hiding place* for all kinds of unhappiness, disbelief, gnawing worms, *despectio sui* [Latin: self-contempt], bad conscience—it is the *anxiety* of the very absence of ideals, suffering from the *lack* of a great love, the dissatisfaction with a condition of *involuntary* modest content. O, what nowadays does science not conceal! How much, at least, it *is meant* to conceal! The efficiency of our best scholars, their mindless diligence, their heads smoking day and night, the very mastery of their handiwork—how often has all that really derived its meaning from the fact that they don't permit some things to become visible to them anymore! Science as a means of putting themselves to sleep. *Are you acquainted with that?* ... People wound scholars to the bone—everyone who associates with them experiences this—sometimes with a harmless word. We make our scholarly friends angry with us when we intend to honor them. We drive them wild, merely because we were too coarse to figure out the people we are truly dealing with, *suffering people*, who don't wish to admit to themselves what they are, narcotized and mindless people, who fear only one thing—coming to consciousness.

24

Now, let's consider, on the other hand, those even rarer cases I mentioned, the last idealists remaining today among the philosophers and scholars. Perhaps in them we have the *opponents* of the ascetic ideal we're looking for, the *counter-idealists?* In fact, that's what they *think* they are, these "unbelievers" (for that's what they are collectively). That, in particular, seems to be their last item of belief, that they are opponents of this ideal, for they are so serious about this stance, their words and gestures are so passionate on this very point:—but is it therefore necessarily the case that what they believe is *true?* We "knowledgeable people" are positively suspicious of all forms of believers. Our suspicion has gradually cultivated the habit in us of concluding the reverse of what people previously concluded: that is, wherever the strength of a faith steps decisively into the foreground, we infer a certain weakness in its ability to demonstrate its truth, even the *improbability* of what it believes. We, too, do not deny that the belief "makes blessed," but *for that very reason* we deny that the belief *proves* something—a strong belief which confers blessedness creates doubts about what it has faith in. It does not ground "truth." It grounds a certain probability—*delusion.* Well, how do things stand in this case?—These people who say no today, these outsiders, these people who are determined on one point, their demand for intellectual probity, these hard, strong, abstemious, heroic spirits, who constitute the honor of our age, all these pale atheists, anti-Christians, immoralists, nihilists, these skeptics, ephectics, *hectics* of the spirit (collectively they are all hectic in some sense or other), the last idealists of knowledge, the only ones in whom intellectual conscience lives and takes on human form nowadays—they really do believe that they are as free as possible from the ascetic ideal, these "free, *very* free spirits," and yet I am revealing to them what they cannot see for themselves—for they are standing too close to themselves— this ascetic ideal is also *their* very own ideal. They themselves represent it today. Perhaps they are the only ones who do. They themselves are its most spiritual offspring, the furthest advanced of its troops and its crowd of scouts, its most awkward, most delicate, most incomprehensibly seductive form. If I am any kind of solver of puzzles, then I want to be that with *this* statement! ... They are not free spirits—not by any stretch—for *they still believe in the truth.* When the Christian crusaders in the Orient came across that unconquerable Order of Assassins,[1] that free-spirited order *par excellence,* whose lowest ranks lived a life of obedience of the sort no order of monks attained, then they also received

---

1 Order of Assassins: a murderous and fanatical religious sect
   founded by Hassan-i-Sabbah (c. 1050–1124) which terrorized
   both Muslim leaders and European Crusaders. The modern term
   assassination is based on their killing methods.

by some means or other a hint about that symbol and slogan which was reserved for only the highest ranks as their *secretus* [Latin: secret], "Nothing is true. Everything is permitted."[1] ... Well now, *that was freedom* of the spirit. *With that* the very belief in truth was canceled.... Has a European, a Christian free spirit ever wandered by mistake into this proposition and its labyrinthine *consequences*? Has he come to know the Minotaur[2] of this cavern *from experience*? ... I doubt it. More than that: I know differently:— nothing is more immediately foreign to people set on one thing, these *so-called* "free spirits," than freedom and emancipation in this sense: in no respect are they more firmly bound; in their very belief in the truth they are, as no one else is, firm and unconditional. Perhaps I understand all this from far too close a distance: that admirable philosophical abstinence which such a belief requires, that intellectual stoicism, which ultimately forbids one to deny just as strongly as it forbids one to affirm, that *desire* to come to a standstill before the facts, the *factum brutum* [Latin: brute fact], that fatalism of the *"petits faits"* [French: small facts] (what I call *ce petit fatalism* [French: this small fatalism]), that quality with which French science nowadays seeks a sort of moral precedence over German science, the attainment of a state where one, in general, abandons interpretation (violating, emending, abbreviating, letting go, filling in the cracks, composing, forging, and the other actions which belong to the *nature* of all interpretation)—generally speaking, this attitude expresses just as much virtuous asceticism as any denial of sensuality (basically it is only one mode of this denial).[3] However, what *compels* a person to this unconditional will for truth is the *faith in the*

---

1 Nietzsche alludes to the famous passage in "The Grand Inquisitor" chapter of Fyodor Dostoevsky's novel *The Brothers Karamazov* (1880) in which Ivan Karamazov claims that if God did not exist, then everything would be permitted.

2 Nietzsche refers to a monster in Greek mythology with the head and tail of a bull and the body of a man. It was imprisoned at the center of a maze-like labyrinth which was built by Daedalus on the orders of the Cretan King Minos.

3 In this passage Nietzsche derides scientific positivism developed in the writings of French philosopher Auguste Comte (1798–1857), which emphasizes the objective value of scientific knowledge and the possibility of attaining certainty through empirical evidence. By contrast, the Kantian and Hegelian idealism of German philosophers, like Nietzsche's approach in *The Joyful Wisdom*, allows for the

ascetic ideal itself, even though it may be its unconscious imperative. We should not deceive ourselves on this point—it is a belief
in a *metaphysical* value, a value of *truth in itself*, something guar-
anteed and affirmed only in that ideal (it stands or falls with that
ideal). Strictly speaking, there is no science "without presuppositions." The idea of such a science is unimaginable, paralogical:
a philosophy, a "belief," must always be there first, so that with
it science can have a direction, a sense, a border, a method, a
right to exist. (Whoever thinks the reverse, whoever, for example,
is preparing to place philosophy "on a strictly scientific foundation," first must place, not just philosophy, but also truth itself *on
its head*—the worst injury to decency one could possibly give to
two such venerable women!). In fact, there is no doubt about this
matter—and here I'm letting my book *The Joyful Wisdom* have a
word (see its fifth book, Section 344)—"The truthful person, in
that daring and ultimate sense which the belief in science presupposes in him, *thus affirms a world different* from the world of life,
of nature, and of history, and to the extent that he affirms this
'other world,' well? Must he not in the process deny its opposite,
this world, *our* world? ... Our faith in science rests on something
which is still a metaphysical belief—even we knowledgeable people of today, we godless and anti-metaphysical people—we, too,
still take *our* fire from that blaze kindled by a thousand years of
old belief, that faith in Christianity, which was also Plato's belief,
that God is the truth, that the truth is *divine*.... But how can we
do that, if this very claim is constantly getting more and more
difficult to believe, if nothing reveals itself as divine any more,
unless it's error, blindness, lies—if even God manifests himself
as our *longest lasting lie*?" At this point it's necessary to pause
and reflect for a long while. Science itself from now on *requires*
some justification (by that I don't yet mean to claim that there
is such a justification for it). People should examine the oldest
and the most recent philosophers on this question. They all lack
an awareness of the problem of the extent to which the will to
truth itself first needs some justification—here is a hole in every
philosophy. How does that come about? It's because the ascetic
ideal up to this point has been *master* of all philosophies, because
truth has been established as being, as god, as the highest authority itself, because truth was not *allowed* to be problematic.

---

interpretation of phenomena and psychological penetration into the
nature of scientific knowledge, which might not be purely selfless,
factual, and disinterested.

Do you understand this "allowed"?—From the moment when the belief in the god of the ascetic ideal is denied, *there is also a new problem*: the problem of the *value* of truth.—The will to truth requires a critique—let us identify our own work with that requirement—for once *to place in question*, as an experiment, the value of truth.... (Anyone who thinks this has been stated too briefly is urged to read over that section of *The Joyful Wisdom*, pp. 160 ff, which carries the title "The Extent to Which We Also Are Still Devout," Section 344—or better, the entire fifth book of that work, as well as the preface to *The Dawn*.)

25

No! People should not come at me with science when I am looking for the natural antagonist of the ascetic ideal, when I ask, "*Where* is the opposing will, in which an *opposing ideal* expresses itself?" For that purpose, science does not stand sufficiently on its own, not nearly; for that it first requires a value ideal, a power to make value, in whose *service* it *could have faith* in itself—science is never in itself something which creates values. Its relationship to the ascetic ideal is still not inherently antagonistic at all. It's even more that case that, for the most part, it represents the forward-driving force in the inner development of this ideal. Its resistance and struggle, when we inspect more closely, are not concerned in any way with the ideal itself, but only with its external trappings, clothing, masquerade, its temporary hardening, petrifaction, dogma. Science makes the life in this ideal free again, since it denies what is exoteric in it. These two things, science and the ascetic ideal—they really stand on a single foundation—I've just clarified the point—namely, on the same overvaluing of the truth (or more correctly, on the same faith in the *in*estimable value of the truth, which is *beyond* criticism). In that very claim they are *necessarily* allies—so that, if someone is going to fight against them, he can only fight them together and place them both in question. An appraisal of the value of the ascetic ideal unavoidably also involves an appraisal of the value of science; while there's still time people should keep their eyes open for that, their ears alert! (As for *art*—let me offer a preliminary remark, for I'll be coming back to it at some point or other at greater length—the very art in which the *lie* sanctifies itself and the *will to deceive* has good conscience on its side is much more fundamentally opposed to the ascetic ideal than is science: that's what Plato's instinct experienced—the greatest enemy of art which Europe has produced up to this point. Plato *versus* Homer: that's the entire, the true antagonism—on one side, the "beyond" of the best will, the great slanderer of life; on the other side, life's unintentional worshipper, the *golden* nature. An artistic bondage in the service of the ascetic ideal is thus the truest *corruption* of the artist there can be. Unfortunately, it's one of the most common, for nothing is more corruptible than an artist.) Physiologically considered, science also rests on the same foundation as the ascetic ideal: a certain *impoverishment of life* is the precondition for both—emotions become cool, the tempo slows down, dialectic replaces instinct, *seriousness* stamped on faces and gestures (seriousness, this most unmistakable sign of a more laborious metabolism, of a life of struggle and hard work). Just look at those periods in a population when the scholars step up into the foreground: they are times of exhaustion, often of evening, of decline. The overflowing force, the certainty about life, the certainty about the *future* have gone. The preponderance of mandarins never indicates anything good—no more than does the arrival of democracy, the peace tribunal instead of war, equal rights for women, the religion of pity, and all the other things symptomatic of a degenerating life. (Science grasped as a problem: what does science mean?—on this point see the Preface to *The Birth of Tragedy*).—No! This "modern science"—keep your eyes open for this—is for the time being the *best* ally of the ascetic ideal, and precisely for this reason: because it is the most unconscious, the most involuntary, the most secret and most subterranean ally! They have up to now been playing a single game, the "poor in spirit"[1] and the scientific opponents of that ideal (we should be careful, incidentally, not to think that these opponents are the opposite of that ideal, something like the *rich* in spirit—that they are *not*; I call them heretics of the spirit). The famous victories of the latter—and they have undoubtedly been victories—but over what? They in no way overcame the ascetic ideal. With those victories, the ideal instead became stronger, that is, harder to understand, more spiritual, more dangerous, as science ruthlessly and continually kept breaking off and demolishing a wall, an external structure which had built itself onto the ideal and coarsened its appearance. Do people really think that, for example, the downfall of theological astronomy indicates a downfall of that ideal? ... Because of that, have human beings

---

1 Matthew 5:3: "Blessed are the poor in spirit: for theirs is the kingdom of heaven."

perhaps become *less dependent* on redemption in a world beyond as a solution for the puzzle of their existence, given that existence since then looks, in the *visible* order of things, even more arbitrary, indolent, and dispensable? Isn't it the case that since Copernicus the very self-diminution of human beings, their *will* to self-diminution, has made inexorable progress?[1] Alas, the faith in their dignity, uniqueness, irreplaceable position in the chain of being has gone—the human being has become an *animal*, not a metaphorical animal, but absolutely and unconditionally—the one who in his earlier faith was almost God ("child of God," "God-man" [*Gottmensch*]) ... Since Copernicus human beings seem to have reached an inclined plane—they're now rolling at an accelerating rate past the mid-point—where to? Into nothingness? Into the "*penetrating* sense of their own nothingness"? ...Well, then, wouldn't this be precisely the way—into the *old* ideal? . . . *All* science (and not just astronomy, about whose humbling and destructive effects Kant made a noteworthy confession, "it destroys my importance"[2] ...)—all science, natural as well as *unnatural*—the name I give to the self-criticism of knowledge—is nowadays keen to talk human beings out of the respect they used to have for themselves, as if the latter were nothing more than a bizarre arrogance about themselves. In this matter we could even say science has its own pride, its characteristically acrid form of stoical *ataraxia* [Greek: imperturbability], in maintaining this laboriously attained *self-contempt* for human beings as their ultimate, most serious demand for self-respect (and, in fact, that's justified, for the one who despises is still one person who "has not forgotten respect" ...). Does doing this

---

1 Nicolaus Copernicus (1473–1543), Polish astronomer who produced a scientifically based theory of a sun-centered solar system which displaced the geocentric or "theological" view of the universe and had the effect of removing humankind as the *raison d'être* of the universe.

2 Nietzsche refers to the opening lines of the Conclusion to *The Critique of Practical Reason* (1788): "Two things fill the mind with ever new and increasing admiration and awe, the oftener and more steadily we reflect on them: *the starry heavens above and the moral law within.*" The suggestion is that the importance of individuals is relativized and diminished by comparison with the immensity of space. However, Kant seeks to compensate for this diminishment by expanding upon the importance of ethics and the role that each individual plays within a moral system.

really *work against* the ascetic ideal? Do people really think in all seriousness (as theologians imagined for quite a while) that, say, Kant's *victory* over dogmatic theological concepts ("God," "Soul," "Freedom," "Immortality")[1] succeeded in breaking up that ideal?—in asking that question, it should not concern us at the moment whether Kant himself had anything at all like that in mind. What is certain is that all sorts of transcendentalists since Kant have once more won the game—they've been emancipated from the theologians. What a stroke of luck!—Kant showed them that secret path by which from now on they could, on their own initiative and with the finest scientific decency, follow their "hearts' desires." Similarly, who could now hold anything against the agnostics, if they, as admirers of what is inherently unknown and secret, worship *the question mark itself* as their God? (Xaver Doudan once spoke of the ravages brought on by *"l'habitude d'admirer l'inintelligible au lieu de rester tout simplement dans l'inconnu"* [French: the habit of admiring the unintelligible instead of simply staying in the unknown]; he claimed that the ancients had not done this).[2] If everything human beings "know" does not satisfy their wishes and, instead, contradicts them and makes them shudder, what a divine excuse to be allowed to seek the blame for this not in "wishes" but in "knowledge"! ... "There is no knowledge. *Consequently*—there is a God"—what a new *elegantia syllogism* [Latin: elegant syllogism]! What a *triumph* of the ascetic ideal!

26

Or does modern historical writing collectively perhaps display an attitude more confident about life, more confident about ideals? Its noblest claim nowadays asserts that it is a *mirror*. It eschews all teleology. It doesn't want to "prove" anything anymore. It spurns playing the role of judge and derives its good taste from that—it affirms as little as it denies. It establishes the facts. It "describes" ... All this is ascetic to a high degree. However, it is also, to an even higher degree, *nihilistic*. We must not deceive ourselves on this point. We see a sad, hard, but determined gaze—an eye which *looks into the distance*, the way a solitary traveler

---

1 In *The Critique of Pure Reason*, Kant attacks these concepts as mere ideas without any factual content.
2 Ximénès Doudan (1800–72), prolific French journalist and politician.

at the North Pole gazes out (perhaps so as not to look inside? not to look behind? ...). Here is snow; here life is quite silent. The final crows that make noise here are called "what for?" "in vain!" "*Nada!*" [Spanish: nothing]—here nothing thrives and grows any more, at most Petersburg metapolitics[1] and Tolstoyan "compassion."[2] But so far as that other style of historian is concerned, maybe an even "more modern" style, which is comfortable and sensual and makes eyes at life as much as at the ascetic ideal—this style uses the word "artist" as a glove and has taken an exclusive lease on the praise of contemplation. O what a thirst these sweet and witty types arouse in people even for ascetics and winter landscapes! No! Let the devil take these "meditative" people! I would much prefer to keep wandering with those historical nihilists through the gloomiest cold gray fog!—In fact, if I had to choose, I might find it better to lend a ear to a completely and essentially unhistorical or anti-historical man (like that Dühring, whose tones intoxicate a species of "beautiful souls" in Germany today,[3] people who up to now have been a still timid, still unassuming species, the *species anarchistica* [Latin: the anarchist kind] within the educated proletariat). The "contemplative ones" are a hundred times worse—: I know nothing that creates so much disgust as such an objective armchair, such a sweet-smelling man luxuriating in history, half cleric, half satyr, with perfume by Renan,[4] who reveals at once in the high falsetto

---

1 The emergence of Russian nationalism as an aggressive pan-Slavist movement.

2 Leo Tolstoy (1828–1910), Russian realistic novelist who, in response to the pathologies of modernity, championed an agrarian Christian utopianism.

3 "Beautiful souls": for a second time, Nietzsche refers to the protagonist of "Confessions of a Beautiful Soul," Book VI of Goethe's novel, *Wilhelm Meister's Apprenticeship* (1795–96), a gifted woman in retreat from conventional life who refuses to compromise her own individuality to get married. Goethe sees such social isolation and self-inflicted suffering as an ascetic form of illness that is consistent with Nietzsche's description of the modern tendency above.

4 Ernest Renan (1823–92), French historian, expert in Semitic languages, and political theorist whose *Life of Jesus* (1863) was notorious, on the one hand, for suggesting that Jesus had physically transformed himself from a Jew into an Aryan. On the other hand, Renan's book was extremely influential in its insistence that both Jesus and the Bible should be subject to the same standards of

of his approval what he lacks, *where* is he deficient, *where* in his case the Fates have wielded their dreadful shears[1] with, alas, so much surgical precision! That affronts my taste as well as my patience: confronted with such sights, let those be patient who have nothing to lose by them—such a picture infuriates me, such "lookers on" make me angry with the "spectacle," even more than the spectacle itself (history itself, you understand). Seeing that, I fall unexpectedly into an Anacreontic mood. This nature, which gave the bull his horns, the lion his *chasm odonton* [Greek: abyss of teeth], why did nature give me a foot? ... To kick with— by holy Anacreon![2]—and not merely to run off, but to kick apart these decrepit armchairs, this cowardly contemplation, this las-civious acting like eunuchs in front of history, the flirting with ascetic ideals, the *Tartufferie* [French: hypocrisy] in the justice of impotence! I grant all honor to the ascetic ideal, *insofar as it is honest*! So long as it believes in itself and does not play games with us! But I can't stand all these coquettish insects, with their insa-tiable ambition to sniff out the infinite, until finally the infinite stinks of bugs. I can't stand these white sepulchers who treat life as play acting. I can't stand the tired and useless people, who wrap themselves up in wisdom and gaze out "objectively." I can't stand the agitators who dress themselves up as heroes, who wear

---

scrutiny as ordinary historical personages. Such a positivistic approach was anticipated by David Friedrich Strauss (1808–74)— the subject of Nietzsche's first *Untimely Meditation*, "David Strauss: The Confessor and the Writer" (1873)—in his *Life of Jesus, Critically Examined* (1835–36), translated into English by the novelist George Eliot (1819–80) in 1846. Strauss controversially treated the miracles described in the Gospels as later additions to the texts that sought to strengthen the case for Jesus as the Messiah prophesied in the Old Testament. Strauss departed from contemporary rationalist interpretations of the New Testament, such as the fragmentary *Life of Jesus* by Hegel, in which the miracles performed by Jesus are naturalized into metaphors consistent with the Hegelian teleological worldview.

1 Fates: Greek mythical figures, one of whom traditionally cut one's threads of life, although here Nietzsche refers to castration.

2 Anacreon (b. c. 570 BCE), Greek lyric poet famous for his drinking songs and the subject of one of Nietzsche's earliest scholarly works completed in 1863. Ode 24 in the *Anacreonta* (a collection of poems attributed to Anacreon) begins, "Nature gave horns to bulls, hooves to horses, fleetness of foot to hares, to lions an abyss of teeth."

a magic hat of ideals on heads stuffed with straw. I can't stand the ambitious artists, who like to present themselves as ascetics and priests, but who are basically tragic clowns. And I can't stand these most recent speculators in idealism, the anti-Semites, who nowadays roll their eyes around in a Christian-Aryan-Philistine[1] way and seek to inflame all the horned-animal elements among the people by abusing the cheapest form of agitation, moral posturing, in a way that exhausts all my patience (—the fact that *every* kind of spiritual fraud succeeds in present-day Germany is the result of the absolutely undeniable and already tangible *desolation* of the German spirit, whose cause I look for in an excessively strict diet limited to newspapers, politics, beer, and Wagnerian music, together with the pre-condition for such a diet: first, a restricting nationalism and vanity, that strong but narrow principle "Germany, Germany, over everything,"[2] as well as the *paralysis agitans* [Latin: trembling palsy] of "modern ideas"). Today Europe is rich and resourceful, above all, in ways of arousing people. Nothing seems to be more important to possess than stimulants and firewater: hence, the monstrous falsification of ideals, the most powerful firewater of the spirit. Hence also the unfavorable, stinking, lying, pseudo-alcoholic air everywhere. I'd like to know how many shiploads of counterfeit idealism, of heroic costumes and rattles full of nonsensical big words, how many tons of sugary spiritual sympathy (its business name: *la religion de la souffrance* [French: the religion of suffering]), how many stilts of "noble indignation" to assist the spiritually flat-footed, and how many *play actors* of the Christian moral ideal would have to be exported from Europe today so that its

---

1 Philistines were originally a crude, warlike people who were enemies of the ancient Israelites, but in modern times the term refers to people who are chiefly motivated by materialism and are indifferent to culture.

2 The opening lines of the German national anthem "Deutschland, Deutschland über alles." The lyrics were written in 1841 by the German nationalist poet August Heinrich Hoffmann von Fallersleben (1798–1874) and set to music originally composed by Joseph Haydn (1732–1809) in 1796 as a hymn to the Austrian emperor. The song was officially adopted as the German national anthem in 1922 during the Weimar Republic, retained with modifications by the Nazi regime, reestablished in 1951 by West Germany, and in 1991, after the fall of the Berlin Wall, reinstated as the national hymn of the reunified country.

air might smell cleaner once again..... Obviously, as far as this overproduction is concerned, a new *commercial* possibility has opened up: obviously there is new "business" to be made with small gods of ideals and their accompanying "idealists"—people should not fail to hear this hint! Who has the courage for it? We have it in our *hands* to "idealize" the entire earth! ... But why am I talking about courage? Only one thing is necessary here, just the hand, an uninhibited, a very uninhibited hand.—

27

Enough! Enough! Let's leave these curiosities and complexities of the most modern spirit, which inspire as much laughter as irritation. Our problem can do without them, the problem of the meaning of the ascetic ideal. What has that to do with yesterday and today! I am going to approach these issues more fundamentally and more forcefully in another connection (under the title *On the History of European Nihilism.* I refer to a work which I am preparing: *The Will to Power: An Attempt at a Revaluation of All Values*).[1] What I have been dealing with here is only the following—to establish that the ascetic ideal has, for the time being, even in the most spiritual sphere, only one kind of true enemy who can inflict harm, and that enemy is those who play-act this ideal—for they awaken distrust. Everywhere else, where the spirit nowadays is strong, powerful, and working without counterfeiting, it generally dispenses with the ideal—the popular expression for this abstinence is "atheism," except for its will to truth. But this will, this remnant of the ideal is, if people wish to believe me, that very ideal in its strongest, most spiritual formulation, thoroughly esoteric, stripped of all its outer structures, and thus not so much a remnant, as its kernel. Consequently, absolutely unconditional atheism (—and that's the only air we breathe, we more spiritual men of this age!) does not stand opposed to this ideal, as it appears to do. It is much rather only one of its last stages of development, one of its concluding forms and internally logical outcomes. It demands reverence, this catastrophe of two thousand years of breeding for the truth which concludes by forbidding itself the lie of a faith in God. (The same

---

1 The work published under this title in 1901, consisting of aphorisms and fragments hastily stitched together, was edited under Elisabeth Förster-Nietzsche's supervision by Peter Gast (Köselitz). It does not reflect Nietzsche's final intentions.

process of development in India, which was fully independent of Europe and therefore proof of something—this same ideal forced things to a similar conclusion. The decisive point was reached five centuries before the European calendar, with Buddha, or more precisely, with the Sankhya philosophy.[1] For this was popularized by Buddha and made into a religion.) Putting the question as forcefully as possible, what really triumphed over the Christian God? The answer stands in my *Gay Science*, p. 290: "Christian morality itself, the increasingly strict understanding of the idea of truthfulness, the subtlety of the father confessor of the Christian conscience, transposed and sublimated into scientific conscience, into intellectual cleanliness at any price. To look at nature as if it were a proof of the goodness and care of a god, to interpret history in such a way as to honor divine reason, as a constant testament to a moral world order and moral intentions, to interpret one's own experiences, as devout men have interpreted them for long enough, as if everything was divine providence, everything was a sign, everything was thought out and sent for the salvation of the soul out of love—now that's over and done with. That has conscience against it. Among more sensitive consciences that counts as something indecent, dishonest, as lying, feminism, weakness, cowardice. With this rigor, if with anything, we are good Europeans and heirs to Europe's longest and bravest overcoming of the self." All great things destroy themselves by an act of self-cancellation [*Selbstaufhebung*]. That's what the law of life wills, that law of the necessary "self-overcoming". [*Selbstüberwindung*] in the essence of life—eventually the call always goes out to the lawmaker himself, "*patere legem, quam ipse tulisti*" [Latin: submit to the law which you yourselves have established]. That's the way Christianity was destroyed as dogma by its own morality; that's the way Christendom as morality must now also be destroyed. We stand on the threshold of this event. After Christian truthfulness has come to a series of conclusions, it will draw its strongest conclusion, its conclusion against itself. However, this will occur when it poses the question: "What is the meaning of all will to truth?" Here I move back again to my problem, to our problem, my unknown friends (—for I still don't know anything about friends): what sense would our whole being have if not for the fact that in us that will

---

1 Sankhya is an ancient school of Hindu philosophy that shares with Buddhism an emphasis on the importance of asceticism and suffering.

to truth became aware of itself as a problem? ... Because this will to truth from now on is growing conscious of itself, morality from now on is dying—there's no doubt about that. That great spectacle in one hundred acts, which remains reserved for the next two centuries in Europe, that most fearful, most questionable, and perhaps also most hopeful of all spectacles ...

28

If we leave aside the ascetic ideal, then man, the *animal* man, has had no meaning up to this point. His existence on earth has had no purpose. "Why man at all?" was a question without an answer. The *will* for man and earth was missing. Behind every great human destiny echoes as refrain an even greater "in vain!" *That*'s just what the ascetic ideal means: that something *is missing*, that a huge *hole* surrounds man—he did not know how to justify himself to himself, to explain, to affirm; he *suffered* from the problem of his meaning. He also suffered in other ways as well: he was for the most part a *pathological* animal, but the suffering itself was *not* his problem, rather the fact that he lacked an answer to the question he screamed out, *"Why* this suffering?" Man, the bravest animal, the one most accustomed to suffering, does *not* deny suffering in itself; he *desires* it; he seeks it out in person, provided that people show him a *meaning* for it, a *purpose* of suffering. The curse that earlier spread itself over men was *not* suffering, but the senselessness of suffering—*and the ascetic ideal offered him a meaning*! The ascetic ideal has been the only meaning offered up to this point. Any meaning is better than no meaning at all; however one looks at it, the ascetic ideal has so far been the *"faute de mieux"* [French: for lack of something better] *par excellence*. In it suffering was *interpreted*, the huge hole appeared filled in, the door shut against all suicidal nihilism. The interpretation undoubtedly brought new suffering with it—more profound, more inner, more poisonous, and more life-gnawing suffering; it brought all suffering under the perspective of *guilt*.... But nevertheless—with it man was *saved*. He had a *meaning*; from that point on he was no longer like a leaf in the wind, a toy ball of nonsense, of "without sense"; he could now *will* something—at first it didn't matter where, why, or how he willed: *the will itself was saved*. We simply cannot conceal from ourselves *what* is really expressed by that total will which received its direction from the ascetic ideal: this hate against what is human, even more against animality, even more against material things—this abhorrence of the senses, of reason itself, this fear of happiness and beauty, this longing for the beyond away from all appearance, change, becoming, death, desire, even longing itself—all this means, let's have the courage to understand this, a *will to nothingness*, an aversion to life, a revolt against the most fundamental preconditions of life—but it is and remains a *will*! ... And to finish up by repeating what I said at the beginning: man will sooner will *nothingness* than *not* will ...

Appendix A: Schopenhauer, Rée, and Nietzsche

1. From Arthur Schopenhauer, *The World as Will and Representation* (1818), translated by Haldane and Kemp, Vol. I, 7th ed. (Kegan, Paul, Trench and Trübner & Co., 1909), pp. 260–61, 262–63

[Schopenhauer (1788–1860), like J.G. Fichte (1762–1814) and F.W.J. Schelling (1775–1854), was an acolyte of Immanuel Kant (1724–1804), whose impact on the modern world is comparable to Aristotle's on the ancient. But while Fichte and Schelling are important figures within the more compact sphere of idealistic philosophy, Schopenhauer, on the strength of his vivid and compulsively readable prose, has reached a far wider audience, extending across international boundaries. His writings exercised an especially powerful influence among writers and artists. Nietzsche was immediately drawn to Schopenhauer's teaching of the will, which begins and ends with the understanding that life consists of a constant state of suffering, strife, and conflict that can be overcome only by an ascetic denial of the will's implacable demands. Salvation from the torments of the will, attempted throughout history by various religions, chief among them Christianity, Buddhism, and Hinduism, is, ultimately, achieved through the contemplation of works of art.]

§ All *willing* arises from want, therefore from deficiency, and therefore from suffering. The satisfaction of a wish ends it; yet for one wish that is satisfied there remain at least ten which are denied. Further, the desire lasts long, the demands are infinite; the satisfaction is short and scantily measured out. But even the final satisfaction is itself only apparent; every satisfied wish at once makes room for a new one; both are illusions; the one is known to be so, the other not yet. No attained object of desire can give lasting satisfaction, but merely a fleeting gratification; it is like the alms thrown to the beggar, that keeps him alive today that his misery may be prolonged till the morrow. Therefore, so long as our consciousness is filled by our will, so long as we are given up to the throng of desires with their constant hopes and fears, so long as we are the subject of willing, we can never have lasting happiness nor peace. It is essentially all the same whether we pursue or flee, fear injury or seek enjoyment; the care for the constant demands of the will, in whatever form it may be, continually occupies and sways the consciousness; but without peace no true well-being is possible. The subject of willing is thus constantly stretched on the revolving wheel of Ixion, pours water into the sieve of the Danaids, is the ever-longing Tantalus.[1]

But when some external cause or inward disposition lifts us suddenly out of the endless stream of willing, delivers knowledge from the slavery of the will, the attention is no longer directed to the motives of willing but comprehends things free from their relation to the will, and thus observes them without personal interest, without subjectivity, purely objectively, gives itself entirely up to them so far as they are ideas, but not in so far as they are motives. Then all at once the peace which we were always seeking, but which always fled from us on the former path of the desires, comes to us of its own accord, and it is well with us. It is the painless state which Epicurus[2] prized as the highest good and as the state of the gods; for we are for the moment set free from the miserable striving of the will; we keep the Sabbath of the penal servitude of willing; the wheel of Ixion stands still....

All this is accomplished by the inner power of an artistic nature alone; but that purely objective disposition is facilitated and assisted from without by suitable objects, by the abundance of natural beauty which invites contemplation, and even presses itself upon us. Whenever it discloses itself suddenly to our view, it almost always succeeds in delivering us, though it may be only for a moment, from subjectivity, from the slavery of the will, and in raising us to the state of pure knowing. This is why the man who is tormented by passion, or want, or care, is so suddenly

---

1 Figures in Greek mythology who exemplify the inescapable, eternal torments of human existence caused by servitude to the will: Ixion is bound to a fiery spinning wheel for eternity; Tantalus is condemned to stand in a pool of water that recedes every time he seeks to drink from it, while above him are branches full of fruit that he cannot reach; the Danaids are fifty sisters who killed their husbands, their punishment consisting of spending eternity carrying water in sieves.

2 The founder of an influential school of ancient Greek philosophy whose professed goal is the attainment of *ataraxia* (freedom from fear) and *aponia* (the absence of pain).

revived, cheered, and restored by a single free glance into nature: the storm of passion, the pressure of desire and fear, and all
the miseries of willing are at once, and in a marvelous manner,
calmed and appeased. For, at the moment at which, freed from
the will, we give ourselves up to pure will-less knowing, we pass
into a world from which everything is absent that influenced our
will and moved us so violently through it. This freeing of knowledge lifts us as wholly and entirely away from all that, as do sleep
and dreams; happiness and unhappiness have disappeared; we
are no longer individual; the individual is forgotten; we are only
pure subject of knowledge; we are only that *one* eye of the world
which looks out from all knowing creatures, but which can become perfectly free from the service of will in man alone. Thus,
all difference of individuality so entirely disappears, that it is all
the same whether the perceiving eye belongs to a mighty king or
to a wretched beggar; for neither joy nor complaining can pass
that boundary with us.

2. From Paul Rée, *The Origin of the Moral Sensations*
   (1877), *Basic Writings*, translated by Robin Small (U of
   Illinois P, 2010 [2003]), pp. 96–97, 98, 114, 117, 118, 121,
   122–23

[The physician and philosopher Paul Rée (1849–1901) was one
of Nietzsche's true intimates and with whom he frequently traveled and occasionally cohabited from 1875 to 1882. What is less
well known or accepted by academic philosophers is how influential Rée was in Nietzsche's intellectual development, from
Human, All-Too Human (1878) onwards. In particular, Nietzsche
assimilates Rée's insight that morality grew out of utilitarian
concepts, such as "good" and "evil," which were originally
deemed beneficial or unbeneficial for *someone* or *something*. In his
interrogation of these concepts, Rée introduces the technique of
etymological reasoning that Nietzsche extends and elaborates
upon in *The Genealogy*. Also, like Rée, Nietzsche rejects the idea
of moral progress because human history demonstrates that
justice and positive moral results can be achieved by selfish motives. Indeed, Rée is responsible for identifying the origins and
interpretation of altruistic behavior as a central ethical problem
detached from any grounding in metaphysics. Stylistically, Rée
(perhaps following the example of Schopenhauer) was influential on Nietzsche in the clarity of his prose, which differentiated
The Origin of the Moral Sensations from the general tendency of

German philosophical writing from the time of Hegel. The footnotes have been added, unless otherwise stated.]

Chapter 1: The Origin of the Concepts "Good" and "Evil"

When, in consequence of the evolution of their reason and their vanity, human beings had become as covetous of others' property, as ambitious and envious as we still find ourselves today, a war of all against all must have broken out among them. But that state of affairs would soon have been felt as unbearable and, to put an end to it, people reached for the only means both effective and ready to hand: punishment. Murder or other injuries to members of the same community were subject to punishment, and executive power was conferred upon the person who, owing to his physical strength or his greater cleverness, was recognized as the head of the community. The fear of this punishment kept individuals in restraint, as it still does today. At the same time, property was instituted, in such a way that members of a community divided its territory among themselves....

In this early period, those people were called good who were useful to other members of the community and refrained from harming them, whatever the motives of their actions may have been. Hence Lubbock expressly emphasizes that savages, when they make any moral judgments at all, never consider the motives of actions, but only their usefulness or harmfulness.[1]

Yet at a higher stage in the evolution of knowledge, one must instinctively have felt that, if someone refrains from harming others only out of fear, peace is only imposed from outside and hence exists only on the surface. In fact, anyone who contains his desire to possess the property of others, his hatred, or his desire for vengeance, only out of fear, will seek to satisfy these drives, partly by actions that are not subject to punishment and partly by actions he believes will not be discovered. On the other hand, when people refrain from harming others not out of fear but for their own sake, peace is not imposed artificially from outside but comes from inside. Not only hostile acts but also hostile feelings such as envy and hate disappear: the mind itself is peaceable and peace extends throughout.

---

1   Sir John Lubbock, *The Origin of Civilisation and the Primitive Condition of Man: Mental and Social Conditions of Savages* (London: Longmans, Green, 1870), 322.

Similarly, if someone pursues the well-being of others only as a means to an end, only for his own advantage, this pursuit seems accidental and uncertain. By itself, others' well-being is indifferent to the egoist: he takes account of it only because he cannot achieve his own advantage otherwise. In contrast, for the person who pursues the well-being of others for their own sake, their well-being is not a means but an end: it is prized by itself, and so it is not uncertain but certain, not accidental but necessary. Indeed, if everyone had truly non-egoistic feelings, if everyone loved his neighbor as himself, then communism would not only be possible, it would already be present at hand.[1]

Thus, non-egoistic behavior would never have been held up as the good if what is at hand coincided with what is desirable, and had always done so, that is, if the non-egoistic drive in human beings were as strong as the egoistic; if it belonged to human nature to care for others as much as for oneself. Some speculative mind may perhaps have arrived at this idea: it would be a good thing if human nature were such that everyone is not concerned only for himself, but just as much for others as well; that he never harbors hostile feelings but only friendly (non-egoistic) feelings toward them. In that case, however, this non-egoism would never have been described as good. For that to occur requires the existence of the bad (egoism): it is just in opposition to this undesirable behavior that non-egoistic behavior is what is desirable, praiseworthy, and good.

Insofar as the degree of non-egoistic feeling and behavior thus became the criterion of moral value, one became used always to looking into motives and to regarding the person who refrains from harming others not out of non-egoistic motives but out of fear of punishment as just as blameworthy as the person who actually does harm others. The action not carried out is morally considered as carried out; for both persons, for example, the murderer and the one who has not committed a murder out of fear of punishment, have an equally low degree of non-egoistic feeling. In the same way, the person who is useful to others out of egoism is not described as morally praiseworthy. The action is morally considered as not carried out.

---

1 [Rée's note:] The communist's error is taking human beings to be good, when they are bad.

Chapter 4: The Origin of Punishment and the Feeling of Justice: On Deterrence and Retribution

Every state or society is a great menagerie in which fear and punishment and the fear of shame are the bars that prevent the beasts from tearing one another to pieces. And sometimes these bars break apart.

After punishment had been introduced to establish peace within a state, the feeling of justice was formed, that is, the feeling on account of which we demand that punishment follow upon bad actions as retribution [*Vergeltung*].

It must be noted that this feeling, which obviously exists in us, does not demand punishment from the same standpoint from which punishment was demanded when it was first established. For the original aim of punishment is, as we have seen, to deter people from bad actions. The feeling of justice, in contrast, does not regard punishment as a means of deterrence for the future, but as retribution for the past. According to this principle, punishment is *quia peccatum est*, not *ne peccutur*.[1]

Nevertheless, the feeling of justice developed out of the original function of punishment and continues to develop even now within each of us during our lives.

The reasoning of the originators of punishment was something like the following. First of all, punishments must be established for bad actions (harming the welfare of one or many members of the community). If this threat is not effective, and someone nevertheless commits an action liable to punishment, that punishment must be inflicted on him, in part because, although the threat of punishment was not enough to deter him, the punishment he now feels will now deter him from similar actions in the future, and in part so that his punishment will also be a warning example for others.

... This future-directed meaning of punishment does not, however, emerge clearly from the punitive process. The judges merely assert that, under these circumstances, this punishment must be inflicted for theft, and they then carry it out. It seems therefore that they are punishing not to prevent other thefts, but

---

1 Rée is quoting from Seneca's "On Anger," Book 19, 10–11: "Num, ut Plato ait, nemo prudens punit, quia peccatum est, sed ne peccetur" ("For, according to Plato, 'A reasonable person does not punish someone because they have sinned, but in order to keep them from sin'").

because of the theft already committed: they seem to be taking retribution for the theft already committed.

Because nothing reminds the judges, the accused, and the spectators of the original meaning of the punishment, they become accustomed to seeing it as what it seems to be, a retribution.

But since retribution has always, as one supposes, been seen to follow lawless actions, then whenever one sees a lawless action, one involuntarily has the feeling that some retribution must follow upon it—that is, the feeling of justice....

Let us suppose now that someone can attain his good end only by inflicting suffering, but that is suffering is less than that which would occur without his intervention. Such a case is that of a man who seeks the well-being of his fellow citizens for their own sake, but who can attain this end only by the assassination of a particular citizen. Here two evils are given, of which one is necessary. Either the whole people perish, or a single person perishes. When someone chooses the lesser of two evils and kills the single person, the motive for this action is reasonable, good, and praiseworthy.

It may perhaps be objected that the agent cannot know in advance with any certainty whether committing his act will actually have such good consequences, or whether refraining from it will have such bad consequences. This is correct but irrelevant. For morality does not look at the outcome, but at the agent's intention or motivation. It is sufficient when the agent has the conviction that the dilemma indicated—either a whole people must perish, or a single individual—does in fact exist....

Certainly justification in terms of morality is quite different from justification in terms of the law. Even when someone uses blameworthy means not only with a good intention but also in fact prevents or eliminates a greater evil through them, the state cannot allow him to go unpunished if he breaks a law. If it did, the authority of the law would suffer. The crowd would not see the good intention there but only the lack of punishment and so would be encouraged, and even think itself justified, in also acting against the law. In this way, the peace of all, maintained solely by fear of punishment, would be endangered. Hence, the state can certainly recognize extenuating circumstances but cannot grant immunity from punishment....

Owing to an imprecise mode of expression, ordinary language attaches the relations that things have to us to the things themselves, as predicates.

What has been said about the predicates "good" and "bad" applies to the predicates "beautiful" and "ugly," "hard" and "soft," "hot" and "cold," "white" and "black," and all the others that Locke called secondary qualities.[1] Nobody believes, for example, that vermilion has a red color in itself, independently of beings provided with appropriate optical nerves…. Nevertheless, we say, "Vermilion is red" and not "Vermilion is red for us," just as we say, "Moderate heat is a good temperature" instead of "Moderate heat is a good temperature for us."

Thus, it is completely senseless to call an object taken by itself good as it is to call vermilion taken by itself red: it is just for beings provided with certain sensory nerves that the vermilion is red and something like moderate heat is good. For beings provide with somewhat different sensory nerves, the vermilion would be yellow, and moderate heat or anything else that we call good would be bad….

In the beginning, people called good that which was useful to others (members of the same community) and bad that which harmed them. Later, they took account not just of whether someone was in fact useful, but of the motives of his actions, and they called good only those actions, useful to others, that were carried out from non-egoistic motives (that is to say, for the sake of others). Motives begin to be examined because, when people help or refrain from harming others out of egoistic motives (such as self-interest and fear of punishment) their accord is accidental, insecure, and externally enforced, whereas if they help or refrain from harming one another out of non-egoistic reasons, their accord is secure, solid, and comes from within.

Non-egoistic behavior is thus called good because it is useful (for achieving social accord), and egoistic behavior is called bad because it is harmful.

Just as a moderate temperature, although it is called good by human beings because it is pleasant to their sensory nerves, is, considered by itself, neither good or bad but just a temperature of a certain nature, so too the non-egoistic person, although he is called good by others because he is useful to them, is nevertheless, considered by himself, not a good person but just a person of a certain nature. To call the non-egoistic person considered by himself good would make no sense, just as it is senseless to call

---

1 John Locke, *Essay Concerning Human Understanding*, ed. John W. Yolton. Rev. ed., 2 vols. (London: Dent, 1965), I:105.

a moderate temperature considered by itself good, or vermilion considered by itself red.

Similarly, the egoistic person, for example, the cruel person, although he is called bad by his neighbors because he harms them, is nevertheless considered by himself, not a bad person but just a person of a certain nature. It would be senseless to call a cruel person considered by himself bad....

This difference is based on the following. Although cruelty and similar kinds of behavior were originally called bad because they are bad for others, in later generations this reason for the designation was not kept in mind, but only the designation itself was maintained out of habit. Suppose someone is asked why cruelty is bad. He will answer: because he feels it is bad. If one inquires into the origin of this feeling, one finds the habit according to which cruelty has been presented to him as bad in itself by everything he has heard, seen, and read from childhood onward. If one inquires further into the first origin of this designation of the behavior in question, one encounters a distant level of culture in which cruelty and similar kinds of behavior were first described as bad, not because they were regarded as bad in themselves, but because they were bad for others. As we have said, this reason was forgotten by later generations since, like us, they were simply taught (i.e., without being given as reason) that cruelty and other similar behaviors are bad. In this way, it came to seem, as pointed out, that cruelty is bad in itself and not just bad insofar as it is harmful to others ...

3. From Friedrich Nietzsche, "On Truth and Falsity in Their Ultramoral Sense" (1873), *The Complete Works of Friedrich Nietzsche*, edited by Oscar Levy, Vol. II, Early Greek Philosophy and Other Essays, translated by Maximilian A. Mügge (T.N. Foulis, 1911), pp. 175–76, 180–81; translation revised by Gregory Maertz

[The following excerpts from Nietzsche's works examine, in a preliminary way, the main themes of *The Genealogy*. As we can see, the origin of morality—human ideas of good and evil—as a cultural construct without any universal values or firm, unchanging ground, is a central concern in the years leading up to the publication of *The Genealogy*.

"On Truth and Falsity in Their Ultramoral Sense" is a seminal essay in Nietzsche's oeuvre in which the role of lies and dissimulation in the formation of morality is explored. Even what we consider to be "truths" are themselves illusions, representations, and metaphors because lying and anthropomorphizing are inextricable from human nature. Of crucial importance to influential thinkers in the twentieth century, such as Michel Foucault (1926–84) and Jacques Derrida (1930–2004), is Nietzsche's understanding that human beings can never step outside of the culture that they create.]

The intellect, as a means for the preservation of the individual, develops its chief power in dissimulation; for it is by dissimulation that the feebler, and less robust individuals preserve themselves, since it has been denied them to fight the battle of existence with horns or the sharp teeth of beasts of prey. In man this art of dissimulation reaches its acme of perfection: in him deception, flattery, falsehood and fraud, slander, display, pretentiousness, disguise, cloaking convention, and acting to others and to himself in short, the continual fluttering to and fro around the one *flame*—Vanity: all these things are so much the rule, and the law, that few things are more incomprehensible than the way in which an honest and pure impulse to truth could have arisen among men. They are deeply immersed in illusions and dream-fancies; their eyes glance only over the surface of things and see "forms"; their sensation nowhere leads to truth, but contents itself with receiving stimuli and, so to say, with playing hide-and-seek on the back of things. In addition to that, at night man allows his dreams to lie to him a whole lifetime long, without his moral sense ever trying to prevent them; whereas men are said to exist who by the exercise of a strong will have overcome the habit of snoring. What indeed *does* man know about himself? Oh! that he could but once see himself complete, placed as it were in an illuminated glass case! Does not nature keep secret from him most things, even about his body, e.g., the convolutions of the intestines, the quick flow of the blood-currents, the intricate vibrations of the fibers, so as to banish and lock him up in proud, delusive knowledge? Nature threw away the key; and woe to the fateful curiosity which might be able for a moment to look out and down through a crevice in the chamber of consciousness, and discover that man, indifferent to his own ignorance, is resting on the pitiless, the greedy, the insatiable, the murderous, and, as it were, hanging in dreams on the back of a tiger. Whence, in the wide world, with this state of affairs, arises the impulse to truth? ...

What therefore is truth? A mobile army of metaphors, metonymies, anthropomorphisms: in short a sum of human relations which became poetically and rhetorically intensified, metamorphosed, adorned, and after long usage seem to a nation fixed, canonic and binding; truth are illusions of which one has forgotten that they *are* illusions; worn-out metaphors which have become powerless to affect the senses; coins which have their obverse effaced and now are no longer of account as coins but merely as metal.

Still, we do not yet know whence the impulse to truth comes, for up to now we have heard only about the obligation which society imposes in order to exist: to be truthful, that is, to use the usual metaphors, therefore expressed morally: we have heard only about the obligation to lie according to a fixed convention, to lie gregariously in a style binding for all. Now man of course forgets that matters are going thus with him; he therefore lies in that fashion pointed out unconsciously and according to habits of centuries' standing—and by *this very unconsciousness*, by this very forgetting, he arrives at a sense for truth.

4. From Friedrich Nietzsche, *Human, All-Too Human: A Book for Free Spirits* (1878), Part One, *The Complete Works of Friedrich Nietzsche: The First Complete and Authorized Translation*, edited by Oscar Levy, Vol. VI, translated by Helen Zimmern (T.N. Foulis, 1911), pp. 38–39; translation revised by Gregory Maertz

[In this book Nietzsche reveals the insight—essential to the development of his later thinking—that human nature is not stable but constantly evolving. History is the medium in which this change occurs.]

§ 2 INHERITED FAULTS OF PHILOSOPHERS.—All philosophers have the common fault that they start from man in his present state and hope to attain their end by an analysis of him. Unconsciously they look upon "man" as an æterna veritas, as a thing unchangeable in all commotion, as a sure standard of things. Yet everything that the philosopher says about man is really nothing more than testimony about the man of a *very limited* period of time. A lack of an historical sense is the hereditary fault of all philosophers; many, indeed, unconsciously mistake the very latest variety of man, such as has arisen under the influence of certain religions, certain political events, for the permanent form from which one must set out. They will not learn that man has developed, that his faculty of knowledge has developed also; while for some of them the entire world is spun out of this faculty of knowledge. Now everything *essential* in human development happened in pre-historic times, long before those four thousand years which we know something of; man may not have changed much during this time. But the philosopher sees "instincts" in the present man and takes it for granted that this is one of the unalterable facts of mankind, and, consequently, can furnish a key to the understanding of the world; the entire teleology is so constructed that man of the last four thousand years is spoken of as an *eternal* being, towards which all things in the world have from the beginning a natural direction. But everything has evolved; there are *no eternal facts*, as there are likewise no absolute truths. Therefore, *historical philosophizing* is henceforth necessary, and with it the virtue of diffidence.

5. From Friedrich Nietzsche, *The Dawn* (1881), *The Complete Works of Friedrich Nietzsche*, edited by Oscar Levy, Vol. IX, translated by John McFarland Kennedy (T.N. Foulis, 1911), pp. 14–17, 97, 98; translation revised by Gregory Maertz

[In this work, Nietzsche describes morality and moral judgments as perpetually mutating as they normalize new forms of behavior, including crimes. Nietzsche provocatively insists that there is nothing moral about submitting to morality: it reflects submission, conformity, and weakness.]

§ 9 CONCEPTION OF THE MORALITY OF CUSTOM.— In comparison with the mode of life which prevailed among men for thousands of years, we men of the present day are living in a very immoral age: the power of custom has been weakened to a remarkable degree, and the sense of morality is so refined and elevated that we might almost describe it as volatilized. That is why we late comers experience such difficulty in obtaining a fundamental conception of the origin of morality: and even if we do obtain it, our words of explanation stick in our throats, so coarse would they sound if we uttered them! Or to so great an extent would they seem to be a slander upon morality! Thus, for example, the fundamental clause: morality is nothing else (and, above all, nothing more) than obedience to customs, of whatsoever nature they may be. But customs are simply the traditional way of acting and valuing. Where there is no tradition there is no morality; and the less life is governed by tradition, the narrower the circle of morality. The free man is immoral, because it is his *will* to depend upon himself and not upon tradition: in all the primitive states of humanity "evil" is equivalent to "individual," "free," "arbitrary," "unaccustomed," "unforeseen," "incalculable." In such primitive conditions, always measured by this standard, any action performed—*not* because tradition commands it, but for other reasons (e.g., on account of its individual utility), even for the same reasons as had been formerly established by custom—is termed immoral and is felt to be so even by the very man who performs it, for it has not been done out of obedience to the tradition.

What is tradition? A higher authority, which is obeyed, not because it commands what is useful to us, but merely because it commands. And in what way can this feeling for tradition be distinguished from a general feeling of fear? It is the fear of a higher intelligence which commands, the fear of an incomprehensible power, of something that is more than personal—there is *superstition* in this fear. In primitive times the domain of morality included education and hygienics, marriage, medicine, agriculture, war, speech and silence, the relationship between man and woman, and between man and the gods—morality required that a man should observe her prescriptions without thinking of *himself* as individual. Everything, therefore, was originally custom, and whoever wished to raise himself above it, had, first of all, to make himself a kind of lawgiver and shaman, a sort of demigod—in other words, he had to create customs, a dangerous and fearful thing to do! ... The most moral man is he who makes the greatest sacrifices to morality; but what are the greatest sacrifices? ... Let us not be deceived as to the motives of that moral law which requires, as an indication of morality, obedience to custom in the most difficult cases! Self-conquest is required, not by reason of its most useful consequences for the individual; but that custom and tradition may appear to be dominant, despite all individual counter desires and advantages. The individual shall sacrifice himself—so demands the morality of custom.

In contrast to this, those moralists who, like the followers of Socrates, recommend self-control and sobriety to the *individual* as his greatest possible advantage and the key to his greatest personal happiness, are *exceptions*—and if we ourselves do not think so, this is simply due to our having been brought up under their influence. They all take a new path, and thereby bring down upon themselves the utmost disapproval of all the representatives of the morality of custom. They sever their connection with the community, as immoralists, and are, in the fullest sense of the word, evil ones. In the same way, every Christian who "sought, above all things, his *own* salvation," must have seemed evil to a virtuous Roman of the old school. Wherever a community exists, and consequently also a morality of custom, the feeling prevails that any punishment for the violation of a custom is inflicted, above all, on the community: this punishment is a supernatural punishment, the manifestations and limits of which are so difficult to understand and are investigated with such superstitious fear. The community can compel any one member of it to make good, either to an individual or to the community itself, any ill consequences which may have followed upon such a member's action. It can also call down a sort of vengeance upon the head of the individual by endeavoring to show that, as the result of his action, a storm of divine anger has burst over the community,—but, above all, it regards the guilt of the individual more particularly as *its own* guilt, and bears the punishment of the isolated individual as its own punishment—"Morals," they bewail in their innermost heart, "morals have grown lax, if such deeds as these are possible." And every individual action, every individual mode of thinking, causes dread. It is impossible to determine how much the more select, rare, and original minds must have suffered in the course of time by being considered as evil and dangerous, *yea, because they even looked upon themselves as such.* Under the dominating influence of the morality of custom, originality of every kind came to acquire a bad conscience; and even now the sky of the best minds seems to be more overcast by this thought than it need be.

§ 97 ONE BECOMES MORAL.—but not because one is moral! Submission to morals may be due to slavishness or vanity, egoism or resignation, dismal fanaticism or thoughtlessness. It may, again, be an act of despair, such as submission to the authority of a ruler; but there is nothing moral about it *per se* [Latin: as such].

§ 98 ALTERATION OF MORALS.—Morals are constantly undergoing changes and transformations, occasioned by successful crimes. (To these, for example, belong all innovations in moral judgments.)

§ 101 OPEN TO DOUBT.—To accept a belief simply because it
is customary implies that one is dishonest, cowardly, and lazy.—
Must dishonesty, cowardice, and laziness, therefore, be the pri-
mary conditions of morality?

6. From Friedrich Nietzsche, *Beyond Good and Evil:
Prelude to a Philosophy of the Future* (1886), *The
Complete Works of Friedrich Nietzsche*, edited by Oscar
Levy, Vol. V, translated by Helen Zimmern (T.N. Foulis,
1909), pp. 10–12, 20, 21–22, 33–34; translation revised by
Gregory Maertz

[Key among the insights expressed in *Beyond Good and Evil*, a
work that immediately preceded *The Genealogy*, are the notions
that 1) the origin of ideas can be traced to the biographies of
philosophers; 2) the will to power is at the core of human needs,
superseding even the survival instinct; and 3) science represents
not "explanations" but subjective interpretations that reflect the
preoccupations, the prejudices, and, above all, the psychology of
scientists.]

§ 6 It has gradually become clear to me what every great philosophy up till now has consisted of—namely, the confession of its
originator, and a species of involuntary and unconscious autobiography; and, moreover, that the moral (or immoral) purpose
in every philosophy has constituted the true vital germ out of
which the entire plant has always grown. Indeed, to understand
how the most abstruse metaphysical claims of a philosopher have
been arrived at, it is always well (and wise) to ask oneself first:
"What morality do they (or does he) aim at?" Accordingly, I do
not believe that an "impulse to knowledge" is the father of philosophy; but that another impulse, here as elsewhere, has only
made use of knowledge (and mistaken knowledge!) as an instrument.... For every drive wants to be master—and it attempts to
philosophize in that spirit.... In the philosopher ... there is absolutely nothing impersonal; and above all, his morality furnishes
a decided and decisive testimony as to who he is,—that is to say,
in what order the deepest impulses of his nature stand to each
other.

§ 13 Psychologists should think before putting down the instinct
of self-preservation as the cardinal instinct of an organic being.

A living thing seeks above all to *discharge* its strength—life itself is *Will to Power*; self-preservation is only one of the indirect and most frequent results thereof. In short, here, as everywhere else, let us beware of superfluous teleological principles![1]

§ 14 It is perhaps just dawning on five or six minds that physics is also only a world-interpretation and world-presentation (to flatter us, if I may say so!) and *not* a world-explanation; but in so far as it is based on belief in the senses, it is regarded as more, and for a long time to come must be regarded as more, namely, as an explanation. It has eyes and fingers of its own, it has ocular evidence and palpableness of its own: this operates fascinatingly, persuasively, and convincingly upon an age with fundamentally plebian tastes—in fact, it follows instinctively the canon of truth of eternal popular sensualism. What is clear, what is "explained"? Only that which can be seen and felt—one must pursue every problem thus far. Conversely, however, the charm of the Platonic mode of thought, which was an *aristocratic* mode, consisted precisely in *resistance to* obvious sense-evidence—perhaps among men who enjoyed even stronger and more fastidious senses than our contemporaries, but who knew how to find a higher triumph in remaining masters of them: and this by means of pale, cold, grey conceptional networks which they hold over the motley whirl of the senses—the mob of the senses, as Plato said. In this overcoming of the world and interpreting of the world in the manner of Plato, there was an enjoyment different from that which the physicists of today offer us—and likewise the Darwinists and anti-teleologists among the workers in physiology, with their principle of the "smallest possible force" and the greatest possible stupidity. "Where man cannot find anything to see or to grasp, he has no further business"—that is certainly an imperative different from the Platonic one, but it may notwithstanding be the right imperative for a hardy, laborious race of machinists and bridge-builders of the future, who have nothing but *rough* work to perform.

§ 23 All psychology so far has run aground on moral prejudices and timidities, it has not dared to push out into the deep water. It seems as if nobody till now has seen in psychology the

---

1 Here Nietzsche is attacking religious and philosophical systems that assert an end purpose as an explanation of human history, such as Christianity, Hegelianism, and Marxism.

morphology and development of the doctrine of *the Will to Power*. The power of moral prejudices has penetrated deeply into the most intellectual world, the world apparently most indifferent and unprejudiced, and has obviously operated in an injurious, obstructive, blinding, and distorting manner. A proper physio-psychology has to contend with unconscious antagonism in the heart of the investigator, it has "the heart" against it: even a doctrine of the reciprocal dependency of the "good" and the "bad" impulses, causes (as refined immorality) distress and aversion in a still strong and manly conscience—still more so, a doctrine of the derivation of all good impulses from bad ones. If, however, a person should regard even the affects of hatred, envy, covetousness, and the drive to rule as conditions of life, as factors which, fundamentally and essentially, in the general economy of life (which must, therefore, be further developed if life is to be further developed), he will suffer from such a view of things as from seasickness. And yet this hypothesis is far from being the strangest and most painful in this immense and almost new domain of dangerous knowledge; and there are in fact a hundred good reasons why everyone should keep away from it who *can* do so! On the other hand, if one has once drifted there in one's bark, well! Very good! Now let us set our teeth firmly! Let us open our eyes and keep our hand fast on the helm! We sail away right *over* morality, we crush, we destroy perhaps the remains of our own morality by daring to make our voyage in that direction—but what do we matter! Never yet did a more profound world of insight reveal itself to daring travelers and adventurers, and the psychologist who thus "makes a sacrifice"—it is not the *sacrifizio dell' intelletto* [Italian: sacrifice of the intellect],[1] on the contrary! We will at least be entitled to demand in return that psychology shall once more be recognized as the queen of the sciences, for whose service and preparation the other sciences exist. For psychology is once more the path to the fundamental problems.

---

1 A concept first articulated in Paul's Second Letter to the
   Corinthians 10:5, which becomes central to Christian thought,
   from St. Ignatius Loyola to Søren Kierkegaard's "leap of faith."

7. From Friedrich Nietzsche, *The Joyful Wisdom: La Gaya Scienza* (1882/1887), *The Complete Works of Friedrich Nietzsche*, edited by Oscar Levy, Vol. X, translated by Thomas Common (T.N. Foulis, 1910), pp. 167–69; translation revised by Gregory Maertz

[In *The Joyful Wisdom* Nietzsche famously declares that "God is dead" and that we humans have killed Him.]

§ 125 THE MADMAN.—Have you ever heard of the madman who on a bright morning lighted a lantern and ran to the marketplace calling out unceasingly: "I seek God! I seek God!"—As there were many people standing about who did not believe in God, he caused a great deal of amusement. Why, is he lost? said one. Has he strayed away like a child? said another. Or does he keep himself hidden? Is he afraid of us? Has he taken a sea voyage? Has he emigrated?—the people cried out laughingly, all in in a hubbub. The insane man jumped into their midst and transfixed them with his glances. "Where is God gone?" he called out. "I mean to tell you! *We have killed him,*—you and I! We are all his murderers! But how have we done it? How were we able to drink up the sea? Who gave us the sponge to wipe away the whole horizon? What did we do when we loosened this earth from its sun? Whither does it now move? Whither do we move? Away from all suns? Do we not dash on unceasingly? Backwards, sideways, forwards, in all directions? Is there still an above and below? Do we not stray, as through infinite nothingness? Does not empty space breathe upon us? Has it not become colder? Does not night come on continually, darker and darker? Shall we not have to light lanterns in the morning? Do we not hear the noise of the gravediggers who are burying God? Do we not smell the divine putrefaction?—for even Gods putrefy! God is dead! God remains dead! And we have killed him! How shall we console ourselves, the most murderous of all murderers? The holiest and the mightiest that the world has hitherto possessed, has bled to death under our knife,—who will wipe the blood from us? With what water could we cleanse ourselves? What lustrums, what sacred games shall we have to devise? Is not the magnitude of this deed too great for us? Shall we not ourselves have to become Gods, merely to seem worthy of it? There never was a greater event,—and on account of it, all who are born after us belong to a higher history than any history hitherto!"—Here the madman was silent and looked again at this hearers; they also were silent and looked at him in surprise. At last, he threw his lantern on the ground, so that it broke in pieces and was extinguished. "I come too early," he then said, "I am not yet at the right time. This prodigious event is still on its way, and is travelling, it has not yet reached men's ears. Lightning and thunder need time, the light of the stars needs time, deeds need time, even after they are done, to be seen and heard. This deed is, as yet, further from them than the furthest star, and yet they have done it!" It is further stated that the madman made his way into different churches on the same day, and there intoned the *Requiem æternam deo* [Latin: eternal rest, grant unto him o Lord].[1] When led out and called to account, he always gave the reply: "What are these churches now, if they are not the tombs and monuments of God?"

8. From Friedrich Nietzsche, *The Will to Power* (1901), Vols. I and II, *The Complete Works of Friedrich Nietzsche*, edited by Oscar Levy, translated by Anthony M. Ludovici (T.N. Foulis, 1914), Books I, II, Vol. XIV, pp. 119–20, 124, 130, 134–35, 149–50, 163–64, 214–15, 226, 228–29, 251, 252–53; Book III, Vol. XV, p. 264; translation revised by Gregory Maertz

[Stitched together by Elisabeth Förster-Nietzsche and Peter Gast from fragments left behind at Nietzsche's death, the aphorisms in *The Will to Power* reiterate themes more fully articulated in *The Genealogy*. Key among them is the idea that morality equals immorality; that is, virtue is achieved by unvirtuous means. There are "no moral phenomena; only moral interpretations—necessarily limited perspectives—of phenomena," and these interpretations bear the imprint of the will to power, subjective self-interest, and the replacement of aristocratic values by the "degenerate" value system that followed in the wake of the Christian slave revolt in morality. Ultimately, Nietzsche rejects Schopenhauer's quietist denial of the will's unbridled desires as a failure to understand that even this solution, fueled by *ressentiment*, expresses the will to power of "the herd," which has replaced the nobler virtues of the pagan-aristocratic world.]

§ 84 ... *Schopenhauer's* cardinal misunderstanding of the *will* (as if passion, instinct, and desire were essential components of the

---

1 The opening line in the Roman Catholic prayer for the dead.

will) is typical: the depreciation of the will to the extent of mistaking it altogether. Likewise, the hatred of willing: the attempt at seeing something superior—indeed, in seeing superiority itself, and that which really matters, in non-willing, in the "subject being *without* aim or intention." Great symptom of *fatigue or of the weakness of will*: for this, in reality, is what treats desire as master, and directs the passions as to the way and to the measure ...

§ 140 The philosopher considered as a further development of the priestly type:—He has the heritage of the priest in his blood; even as rival he is compelled to fight with the same weapons as the priest of his time;—he aspires to the *highest authority*.

What is it that bestows *authority* upon those who have no physical power to wield (no army, no weapons at all)? How do they gain authority over those who are in possession of material power and actual authority? (Philosophers enter the lists against princes, victorious conquerors, and wise statesmen.)

They can do it only by establishing the belief that they are in possession of a power which is higher and stronger—*God*. Nothing is strong enough: everyone is in *need* of the mediation and the service of priests. They establish themselves as indispensable *intercessors* ...

§ 141 Critique of the holy lie.—That a lie is permitted in pursuit of holy objectives is a principle that belongs to the theory of all priestcraft ...

But philosophers, too, whenever they intend taking over the leadership of mankind, with the ulterior motives of priests in their minds, have never failed to arrogate to themselves the right to lie: Plato above all ...[1]

§ 142 ... We find a class of people, the sacerdotal class, who consider themselves the norm, the highest example and the most perfect expression of the human type. The notion of "improving" mankind, to this class of people, means to make mankind like themselves. They believe in their own superiority; they will be superior in practice: the origin of the holy lie is the *Will to Power*.

---

1 Nietzsche refers to the altruistic rationale for factitious religious or patriotic myths. From his perspective, the "good lie" reflects the will to power—to exert control, to dominate, to enslave others.

§ 154 ... *Christianity* is a degenerative movement, consisting of all kinds of decaying and excremental elements: it is *not* the expression of the downfall of a race, it is, from the root, a concretion of all the morbid elements which are mutually attractive and which gravitate to one another.... It is therefore *not* a national religion, not determined by race: it appeals to the disinherited everywhere; it consists of a foundation of resentment against all that is successful and dominant: it is in need of a symbol which represents the damnation of everything successful and dominant. It is opposed to every form of *intellectual* movement, to all philosophy: it takes up the cudgels for idiots and utters a curse upon all intellect. Resentment against those who are gifted, learned, intellectually independent: in all these it suspects the element of success and domination.

§ 163 Jesus bids us:—not to resist, either by deeds or in our heart, him who ill-treats us; He bids us admit of no grounds for separating ourselves from our wives; He bids us make no distinction between foreigners and fellow-countrymen, strangers and familiars; He bids us show anger to no one, and treat no one with contempt;—give alms secretly; not to desire to become rich;—not to swear;—not to stand in judgment;—become reconciled with our enemies and forgive offenses;—not to worship in public.

"Blessedness" is nothing promised: it is here, with us, if we only wish to live and act in a particular way.

§ 166 Jesus opposed a real life, a life in truth, to ordinary life: nothing could have been more foreign to His mind than the somewhat heavy nonsense of an "eternal Peter,"—of the eternal duration of a single person. Precisely what He combats is the exaggerated importance of the "person": how can He wish to immortalize it?

He likewise combats the hierarchy within the community; He never promises a certain proportion of reward for a certain proportion of deserts: how can He have meant to teach the doctrine of punishment and reward in a Beyond?[1]

§ 179 On the psychological problem of Christianity.—The driving forces are: ressentiment, popular insurrection, the revolt of the needy ...

---

1 In §163 and §166, Nietzsche critiques organized Christianity's exploitation and perversion of the original teachings in the Gospel of Jesus.

This party, which stands for freedom, understands that *the renunciation of enmity in thought and deed* is a condition of distinction and preservation. Here lies the psychological difficulty which has stood in the way of understanding Christianity: the drive that created it forces one to struggle against it out of principle.

Only as a party standing for *peace* and *innocence* can this insurrectionary movement hope to be successful: it must conquer through excessive mildness, sweetness, softness, and its instincts are aware of this. The masterstroke was to deny and condemn the drive, of which man is the expression, and to press the opposite of that drive continually to the fore, by word and deed.

§ 200 I regard Christianity as the most fatal and seductive lie that has ever yet existed—as the greatest and most *impious lie*: I can discern the last sprouts and branches of its ideal beneath every form of disguise, I refuse to enter into any compromise or false position in reference to it—I urge people to declare open war with it.

The *morality of paltry people* [*ressentiment*] as the measure of all things: this is the most repugnant kind of degeneracy that civilization has ever yet brought into existence. And this *kind of ideal* is hanging still, under the name of "God," over mankind.

§ 258 I have tried to understand all moral judgments as symptoms and a language of signs in which the processes of physiological prosperity or failure, as also the consciousness of the conditions of preservation and growth, are betrayed—a mode of interpretation equal in worth to astrology, prejudices, created by instincts (peculiar to races, communities, and different stages of existence, as, for example, youth or decay, etc.).

Applying this principle to the morality of Christian Europe more particularly, we find that our moral values are signs of decline, of a disbelief in *Life*, and of a preparation for pessimism.

My leading doctrine is this: *there are no moral phenomena, but only a moral interpretation of phenomena. The origin of this interpretation itself lies outside of morality.*

What is the meaning of the fact that we have imagined a *contradiction* in existence? This is of decisive importance: behind all other valuations those moral valuations stand in command. Supposing they disappear, according to what standard shall we then measure? And then of what value would knowledge be, etc. etc. ? ? ?

§ 259 Insight: all valuations are made from a definite perspective: the preservation of the individual, a community, a race, a state, a church, a faith, or a culture.—Thanks to the fact that people forget that all valuing occurs from a particular perspective, each individual is subject to a host of contradictory valuations, and *therefore also to a host of contradictory impulses or drives.* This is the *expression of disease* in man as opposed to the health of animals, in which all the instincts answer to certain definite purposes....

§ 274 *Whose will to power is morality?*—The *common factor* in the history of Europe since *Socrates* is the attempt to make *moral values* dominate over all other values, so that they should not only be the leader and judge of life, but also: (1) knowledge, (2) art, (3) political and social aspirations. "Amelioration" regarded as the sole duty, everything else used as a *means* to it (or a disturbance, hindrance, danger to it: therefore to be opposed and annihilated—)....

What is the meaning of this *will to power on the part of moral values* which has played a major role in the world's development?

Answer:—*Three powers lie concealed behind it:* (1) the instinct of the herd opposed to the strong and independent; (2) the instinct of all *sufferers* and the underclass opposed to the happy and fortunate; (3) the instinct of the mediocre opposed to the exceptional.—*Enormous advantage of this movement,* despite the cruelty, falseness, and narrow-mindedness which have assisted it (for the history of *the struggle of morality with the fundamental instincts of life* is in itself the greatest piece of immorality that has ever yet been witnessed on earth ...).

§ 276 The whole of European morality is based upon the values *useful to the herd:* the sorrow of all higher and exceptional men is explained by the fact that everything which distinguished them from others reaches their consciousness in the form of a feeling of their own smallness and egregiousness. It is the *virtues* of modern men which are the causes of pessimistic gloominess; the mediocre, like the herd, are not troubled much with questions or with conscience—they are cheerful. (Among the gloomy strong men, Pascal and Schopenhauer are noted examples.) *The more dangerous a quality seems to the herd, the more completely it is condemned.*

§ 306 The victory of a moral idea is achieved by the same "immoral" means as any other victory: violence, lies, slander, injustice.

§ 308 Morality is just as "immoral" as any other thing on earth; morality is itself a form of immorality. The great liberation which this insight brings. The contradiction between things disappears, the homogeneity of all phenomena is *saved*—

§ 311 *By what means does a virtue come to power?*—By exactly the same means as a political party: slander, suspicion, the undermining of virtues that oppose it and are already in power, by renaming them, systematic persecution and mockery; in short, *by means of acts of general "immorality."*

What must a *desire* do with itself in order to become a *virtue?*—A process of rechristening; systematic denial of its intentions; practice in misunderstanding itself; alliance with established and recognized virtues; ostentatious hostility toward its adversaries. If possible, it purchases the protection of sanctifying powers; people must also be intoxicated and fired with enthusiasm; idealistic tartuffery must be employed, and it forms a party which *either* triumphs or perishes—it becomes *unconscious and naïve.*

§ 822 If I have sufficiently initiated my readers into the doctrine that even "goodness," in the whole comedy of existence, represents a form of *exhaustion*, they will credit Christianity with consistency for having conceived the good to be the ugly. Christianity was right.

It is absolutely unworthy of a philosopher to say that "the good and the beautiful are one"; if he should add "and also the true," he deserves to be thrashed. Truth is ugly.

We have *art* so as not to *perish of the truth.*[1]

---

1 Unlike Schopenhauer, who elevates art as the most powerful medium of escape from the will's hold over us, Nietzsche insists that art provides pleasing illusions that mask the truths of our existence which would otherwise be too painful or repugnant to bear.

Appendix B: Plato

1. From Plato, *The Republic*, Book I, *The Dialogues of Plato*, translated by Benjamin Jowett, Vol. III (London: Oxford UP, 1892), pp. 331–39

[In this excerpt from *The Republic*, Socrates leads a discussion of the true basis of justice, beginning with a suggestion that justice lies in the distribution of credits and debits (an idea that re-emerges in *The Genealogy*) and concluding with the judgment that "justice is nothing else than the interest of the stronger."]

The first Definition of Justice

Well said, Cephalus, I [Socrates] replied; but as concerning justice, more than this? And even to this are there not exceptions? Suppose that a friend when in his right mind has deposited arms with me and he asks for them when he is not in his right mind, ought I to give them back to him? No one would say that I ought or that I should be right in doing so, any more than they would say that I ought always to speak the truth to one who is in his condition.

You are quite right, he replied.

But then, I said, speaking the truth and paying your debts is not a correct definition of justice.

Quite correct, Socrates, if Simonides is to be believed, said Polemarchus interposing.

I fear, said Cephalus, that I must go now, for I have to look after the sacrifices, and I hand over the argument to Polemarchus and the company.

Is not Polemarchus your heir? I said.

To be sure, he answered, and went away laughing to the sacrifices.

Tell me, then, O thou heir of the argument, what did Simonides say, and according to you truly say, about justice?

He said that the re-payment of a debt is just, and in saying so he appears to me to be right.

I should be sorry to doubt the word of such a wise and inspired man, but his meaning, though probably clear to you, is the reverse of clear to me. For he certainly does not mean, as we were just now saying, that I ought to return a deposit of arms or of anything else to one who asks for it when he is not in his right senses; and yet a deposit cannot be denied to be a debt.

True.

Then when the person who asks me is not in his right mind I am by no means to make the return?

Certainly not.

When Simonides said that the repayment of a debt was justice, he did not mean to include that case?

Certainly not; for he thinks that a friend ought always to do good to a friend and never evil.

You mean that the return of a deposit of gold which is to the injury of the receiver, if the two parties are friends, is not the repayment of a debt,—that is what you would imagine him to say?

Yes.

And are enemies also to receive what we owe to them?

To be sure, he said, they are to receive what we owe them, and an enemy, as I take it, owes to an enemy that which is due or proper to him—that is to say, evil.

Simonides, then, after the manner of poets, would seem to have spoken darkly of the nature of justice; for he really meant to say that justice is the giving to each man what is proper to him, and this he termed a debt.

That must have been his meaning, he said.

By heaven! I replied; and if we asked him what due or proper thing is given by medicine, and to whom, what answer do you think that he would make to us?

He would surely reply that medicine gives drugs and meat and drink to human bodies.

And what due or proper thing is given by cookery, and to what?

Seasoning to food.

And what is that which justice gives, and to whom?

If, Socrates [said Simonides], we are to be guided at all by the analogy of the preceding instances, then justice is the art which gives good to friends and evil to enemies....

And so [said Socrates], you and Homer and Simonides are agreed that justice is an art of theft; to be practiced however "for the good of friends and for the harm of enemies,"—that was what you were saying?

No, certainly not that, though I do not know what I did say; but I still stand by the latter words.

Well, there is another question: By friends and enemies do we mean those who are so really, or only in seeming?

Surely, he said, a man may be expected to love those whom he thinks good, and to hate those whom he thinks evil.

Yes [said Socrates], but do not persons often err about good and evil: many who are not good seem to be so, and conversely?

That is true.

Then to them the good will be enemies and the evil will be their friends?

True.

And in that case they will be right in doing good to the evil and evil to the good?

Clearly.

But the good are just and would not do an injustice?

True.

Then according to your argument it is just to injure those who do no wrong?

Nay, Socrates; the doctrine is immoral.

Then I suppose that we ought to do good to the just and harm to the unjust?

I like that better.

But see the consequences:—Many a man who is ignorant of human nature has friends who are bad friends, and in that case he ought to do harm to them; and he has good enemies whom he ought to benefit; but, if so, we shall be saying the very opposite of that which we affirmed to be the meaning of Simonides.

Very true, he said; and I think that we had better correct an error into which we seem to have fallen in the use of the words "friend" and "enemy."

What was the error, Polemarchus? I [Socrates] asked.

We assumed that he is a friend who seems to be or who is thought good.

And how is the error to be corrected?

We should rather say that he is a friend who is, as well as seems, good; and that he who seems only and is not good, only seems to be and is not a friend; and of an enemy the same may be said.

You would argue that the good are our friends and the bad our enemies?

Yes.

And instead of saying simply as we did at first, that it is just to do good to our friends and harm to our enemies, we should further say: It is just to do good to our friends when they are good and harm to our enemies when they are evil?

Yes, that appears to me to be the truth.

But ought the just to injure any one at all?

Undoubtedly he ought to injure those who are both wicked and his enemies.

When horses are injured, are they improved or deteriorated?

The latter.

Deteriorated, that is to say, in the good qualities of horses, not of dogs?

Yes, of horses.

And dogs are deteriorated in the good qualities of dogs, and not of horses?

Of course.

And will not men who are injured be deteriorated in that which is the proper virtue of men?

Certainly.

And that human virtue is justice?

To be sure.

Then men who are injured are of necessity made unjust?

That is the result.

But can the musician by his art make men unmusical?

Certainly not.

Or the horseman by his art make them bad horsemen?

Impossible.

And can the just by justice make men unjust, or speaking generally, can the good by virtue make them bad?

Assuredly not.

Any more than heat can produce cold?

It cannot.

Or drought moisture?

Clearly not.

Nor can the good harm anyone?

Impossible.

And the just is the good?

Certainly.

Then to injure a friend or anyone else is not the act of a just man, but of the opposite, who is the unjust?

I think that what you say is quite true, Socrates.

Then if a man says that justice consists in the repayment of debts, and that good is the debt which a just man owes to his friends, and evil the debt which he owes to his enemies,—to say this is not wise; for it is not true, if, as has been clearly shown, the injuring of another can be in no case just.

I agree with you, Polemarchus....

Glaucon and the rest of the company joined in my request [to describe what they know], and Thrasymachus, as any one might see, was in reality eager to speak; for he thought that he had an excellent answer, and would distinguish himself. But at first he affected to insist on my answering; at length he consented to begin. Behold, he said, the wisdom of Socrates; he refuses to teach himself, and goes about learning of others, to whom he never even says Thank you.

That I learn of others, I [Socrates] replied, is quite true; but that I am ungrateful I wholly deny. Money I have none, and therefore I pay in praise, which is all I have; and how ready I am to praise anyone who appears to me to speak well you will very soon find out when you answer; for I expect that you will answer well.

Listen, then, he [Thrasymachus] said; I proclaim that justice is nothing else than the interest of the stronger. And now why do you not praise me? But of course you won't.

Let me first understand you, I replied. Justice, as you say, is the interest of the stronger. What, Thrasymachus, is the meaning of this? You cannot mean to say that because Polydamas, the pancratiast,[1] is stronger than we are, and finds the eating of beef conducive to his bodily strength, that to eat beef is therefore equally for our good who are weaker than he is, and right and just for us?

That's abominable of you, Socrates; you take the words in the sense which is most damaging to the argument.

Not at all, my good sir, I said; I am trying to understand them; and I wish that you would be a little clearer.

Well, he said, have you never heard that forms of government differ; there are tyrannies, and there are democracies, and there are aristocracies?

Yes, I know.

And the government is the ruling power in each state?

Certainly.

And the different forms of government make laws democratic, aristocratic, tyrannical, with a view to their several interests; and these laws, which are made by them for their own interests,

---

1 A participant in the pancratium, an athletic event combining box-
ing and wrestling.

are the justice which they deliver to their subjects, and him who transgresses them they punish as a breaker of the law, and unjust. And that is what I mean when I say that in all states there is the same principle of justice, which is the interest of the government; and as the government must be supposed to have power, the only reasonable conclusion is, that everywhere there is one principle of justice, which is the interest of the stronger.

Now I understand you, I said; and whether you are right or not I will try to discover. But let me remark, that in defining justice you have yourself used the word "interest" which you forbade me to use. It is true, however, that in your definition the words "of the stronger" are added.

A small addition, you must allow, he said.

Great or small, never mind about that: we must first enquire whether what you are saying is the truth. Now we are both agreed that justice is interest of some sort, but you go on to say "of the stronger"; about this addition I am not so sure, and must therefore consider further.

Proceed.

I will; and first tell me, Do you admit that it is just for subjects to obey their rulers?

I do.

But are rulers of states absolutely infallible, or are they sometimes liable to err?

To be sure, he replied, they are liable to err.

Then in making their laws they may sometimes make them rightly, and sometimes not?

True.

When they make them rightly, they make them agreeably to their interest; when they are mistaken, contrary to their interest; you admit that?

Yes.

And the laws which they make must be obeyed by their subjects,—and that is what you call justice?

Doubtless.

Then justice, according to your argument, is not only obedience to the interest of the stronger but the reverse?

What is that you are saying? he asked.

I am only repeating what you are saying, I believe. But let us consider: Have we not admitted that the rulers may be mistaken about their own interest in what they command, and also that to obey them is justice? Has not that been admitted?

Yes.

Then you must also have acknowledged justice not to be for the interest of the stronger, when the rulers unintentionally command things to be done which are to their own injury. For if, as you say, justice is the obedience which the subject renders to their commands, in that case, O wisest of men, is there any escape from the conclusion that the weaker are commanded to do, not what is for the interest, but what is for the injury of the stronger?

Nothing can be clearer, Socrates, said Polemarchus.

Appendix C: Old and New Testaments

[In these excerpts from the Christian Old and New Testaments (from the authorized 1611 King James version), we can see the original expression of the values that Nietzsche derides as issuing from the slave revolt in morality initiated by Judaism and, via assimilation, culminating in Christianity.]

1. Exodus 20:1–26

1 And God spake all these words, saying

2 I am the LORD thy God, which have brought thee out of the land of Egypt, out of the house of bondage.

3 Thou shalt have no other gods before me.

4 Thou shalt not make unto thee any graven image, or any likeness of *any thing* that *is* in heaven above, or that *is* in the earth beneath, or that *is* in the water under the earth:

5 Thou shalt not bow down thyself to them, nor serve them: for I the LORD thy God *am* a jealous God, visiting the iniquity of the fathers upon the children unto the third and fourth *generation* of them that hate me;

6 And shewing mercy unto thousands of them that love me, and keep my commandments.

7 Thou shalt not take the name of the LORD thy God in vain; for the LORD will not hold him guiltless that taketh his name in vain.

8 Remember the sabbath day, to keep it holy.

9 Six days shalt thou labor, and do all thy work:

10 But the seventh day is the sabbath of the LORD thy God: *in it* thou shalt not do any work, thou, nor thy son, nor thy daughter, thy manservant, nor thy maidservant, nor thy cattle, nor thy stranger that is within thy gates:

11 For in six days the LORD made heaven and earth, the sea, and all that in them *is*, and rested the seventh day: wherefore the LORD blessed the sabbath day, and hallowed it.

12 Honour thy father and thy mother: that thy days may be long upon the land which the LORD thy God giveth thee.

13 Thou shalt not kill.

14 Thou shalt not commit adultery.

15 Thou shalt not steal.

16 Thou shalt not bear false witness against thy neighbour.

17 Thou shalt not covet thy neighbour's house, thou shalt not covet thy neighbour's wife, nor his manservant, nor his maidservant, nor his ox, nor his ass, nor any thing that *is* thy neighbour's.

18 And all the people saw the thunderings, and the lightnings, and the noise of the trumpet, and the mountain smoking: and when the people saw *it*, they removed and stood afar off.

19 And they said unto Moses, Speak thou with us, and we will hear: but let not God speak with us, lest we die.

20 And Moses said unto the people, Fear not: for God is come to love you, and that his fear may be before your faces, that ye sin not.

21 And the people stood afar off, and Moses drew near unto the thick darkness where God *was*.

22 And the LORD said unto Moses, Thus thou shalt say unto the children of Israel, Ye have seen that I have talked with you from heaven.

23 Ye shall not make with me gods of silver, neither shall ye make unto you gods of gold.

24 An altar of earth thou shalt make unto me, and shalt sacrifice thereon thy burnt offerings, and thy peace offerings, thy sheep, and thine oxen: in all places where I record my name I will come unto thee, and I will bless thee.

25 And if thou wilt make me an altar of stone, thou shalt not build it of hewn stone: for if thou lift thy tool upon it, thou hast polluted it.

26 Neither shalt thou go up by steps unto mine altar, that thy nakedness be not discovered thereon.

2. Matthew 5:1–21; 27–48

1 And seeing the multitudes, he went up into a mountain: and when he was set his disciples came unto him:

2 And he opened his mouth, and taught them, saying,

3 Blessed *are* the poor in spirit: for theirs is the kingdom of heaven.

4 Blessed *are* they that mourn: for they shall be comforted.

5 Blessed *are* the meek: for they shall inherit the earth.

6 Blessed *are* they which do hunger and thirst after righteousness: for they shall be filled.

7 Blessed *are* the merciful: for they shall obtain mercy.

8 Blessed *are* the pure in heart: for they shall see God.

9 Blessed *are* peacemakers: for they shall be called children of God.

10 Blessed *are* they which are persecuted for righteousness's sake: for theirs is the kingdom of heaven.

11 Blessed are ye, when *men* shall revile you, and persecute you, and shall say all manner of evil against you falsely, for my sake.

12 Rejoice, and be exceeding glad: for great *is* your reward in heaven: for so persecuted they the prophets which were before you.

13 Ye are the salt of the earth: but if the salt have lost his savour, wherewith shall it be salted? It is thenceforth good for nothing, but to be cast out, and to be trodden under foot of men.

14 Ye are the light of the world. A city that is set on an hill cannot be hid.

15 Neither do men light a candle, and put it under a bushel, but on a candlestick; and it giveth light unto all that are in the house.

16 Let your light so shine before men that they may see your good works, and glorify your Father which is in heaven.

17 Think not that I am come to destroy the law, or the prophets: I am not come to destroy, but to fulfil.

18 For verily I say unto you, Till heaven and earth pass, one jot or one tittle shall in no wise pass from the law, till all be fulfilled.

19 Whosoever therefore shall break one of these least commandments, and shall teach men so, he shall be called the least in the kingdom of heaven: but whosoever shall do and teach *them*, the same shall be called great in the kingdom of heaven.

20 For I say unto you, That except your righteousness shall exceed *the righteousness* of the scribes and Pharisees, ye shall in no case enter into the kingdom of heaven.

21 Ye have heard that it was said by them of old time, Thou shalt not kill; and whosoever shall kill shall be in danger of the judgment:

27 Ye have heard that it was said by them of old time, Thou shalt not commit adultery:

28 But I say unto you, That whosoever looketh on a woman to lust after her hath committed adultery already in his heart.

29 And if thy right eye offend thee, pluck it out, and cast *it* from thee: for it is profitable for thee that one of thy members

should perish, and not that thy whole body should be cast into hell.

30 And if thy right hand offend thee, cut it off, and cast *it* from thee: for it is profitable for thee that one of thy members should perish, and not *that* thy whole body should be cast into hell.

31 It hath been said, Whosoever shall put away his wife, let him give her a writing of divorcement:

32 But I say unto you, That whosoever shall put away his wife, saving for the cause of fornication, causeth her to commit adultery: and whosoever shall marry her that is divorced committeth adultery.

33 Again, ye have heard that it hath been said by them of old time, Thou shalt not forswear thyself, but shalt perform unto the Lord thine oaths:

34 But I say unto you, Swear not at all; neither by heaven; for it is God's throne:

38 Ye have heard that it hath been said, An eye for an eye, and a tooth for a tooth:

39 But I say unto you, That ye resist not evil: but whosoever shall smite thee on thy right cheek, turn to him the other also.

40 And if any man will sue thee at the law, and take away thy coat, let him have thy cloak also.

41 And whosoever shall compel thee to go a mile, go with him twain.

42 Give to him that asketh thee, and from him that would borrow of thee turn not thou away.

43 Ye have heard that it hath been said, Thou shalt love thy neighbour, and hate thine enemy.

44 But I say unto you, Love your enemies, bless them that curse you, do good to them that hate you, and pray for them which despitefully use you, and persecute you;

45 That ye may be the children of your Father which is in heaven: for he maketh his sun to rise on the evil and on the good, and sendeth rain on the just and on the unjust.

46 For if ye love them which love you, what reward have ye? Do not even the publicans do the same?

47 And if ye salute your brethren only, what do ye more *than others?* Do not even the publicans so?

48 Be ye therefore perfect, even as your Father which is in heaven is perfect.

3. Matthew 19:13–30

13 Then there were brought unto him little children, that he should put *his* hands on them, and pray: and the disciples rebuked them.

14 But Jesus said, Suffer little children, and forbid them not, to come unto me: for of such is the kingdom of heaven.

15 And he laid *his* hands on them, and departed thence.

16 And, behold, one came and said unto him, Good Master, what good thing shall I do, that I may have eternal life?

17 And he said unto him, Why callest thou me good? There is none good but one, that is, God: but if thou wilt enter into life, keep the commandments.

18 He saith unto him, Which? Jesus said, Thou shalt do no murder, Thou shalt not commit adultery, Thou shalt not steal, Thou shalt not bear false witness,

19 Honour thy father and *thy* mother: and Thou shalt love thy neighbour as thyself.

20 The young man saith unto him, All these things have I kept from my youth up: what lack I yet?

21 Jesus said unto him, If thou wilt be perfect, go *and* sell that thou hast, and give it to the poor, and thou shalt have treasure in heaven: and come *and* follow me.

22 But when the young man heard him saying, he went away sorrowful: for he had great possessions.

23 Then said Jesus unto his disciples, Verily I say unto you, That a rich man shall hardly enter into the kingdom of heaven.

24 And again I say unto you, It is easier for a camel to go through the eye of a needle, than for a rich man to enter into the kingdom of God.

25 When his disciples heard *it*, they were exceedingly amazed, saying, Who then can be saved?

26 But Jesus beheld *them*, and said unto them, With men this is impossible; but with God all things are possible.

27 Then answered Peter and said unto him, Behold, we have forsaken all, and followed thee; what shall we have therefore?

28 And Jesus said unto them, Verily I say unto you, That ye which have followed me, in the regeneration when the Son of man shall sit in the throne of his glory, ye also shall sit upon twelve thrones, judging the twelve tribes of Israel.

29 And every one that hath forsaken houses, or brethren, or

sisters, or father, or mother, or wife, or children, or lands, for my name's sake, shall receive an hundredfold, and shall inherit everlasting life.

30 But many *that are* first shall be last; and the last *shall be* first.

4. Luke 6:20–38

20 And he lifted up his eyes on his disciples, and said, Blessed *be ye* poor: for yours is the kingdom of God.

21 Blessed *are ye* that hunger now: for ye shall be filled. Blessed *are ye* that weep now: for ye shall laugh.

22 Blessed are ye, when men shall hate you, and when they shall separate you from their company, and shall reproach you, and cast out your name as evil, for the Son of man's sake.

24 But woe unto you that are rich! For ye have received your consolation.

25 Woe unto you that are full! For ye shall hunger. Woe unto you that laugh now! For ye shall mourn and weep.

27 But I say unto you which hear, Love your enemies, do good to them which hate you.

28 Bless them that curse you, and pray for them which despitefully use you.

29 And unto him that smiteth thee on the *one* cheek offer also the other; and him that taketh away thy cloak forbid not *to take thy* coat also.

30 Give to every man that asketh of thee; and of him that taketh away thy goods ask *them* not again.

31 And as ye would that men should do to you, do ye also to them likewise.

32 For if ye love them which love you, what thank have ye? For sinners also love those that love them.

33 And if ye do good to them which do good to you, what thank have ye? For sinners also do even the same.

34 And if ye lend to them of whom ye hope to receive, what thank have ye? For sinners also lend to sinners, to receive as much again.

35 But love ye your enemies, and do good, and lend, hoping for nothing again; and your reward shall be great, and ye shall be the children of the Highest: for he is kind unto the unthankful and *to* the evil.

36 Be ye therefore merciful, as your Father also is merciful.

37 Judge not, and ye shall not be judged: condemn not, and yet shall not be condemned: forgive and ye shall be forgiven:

38 Give, and it shall be given unto you; good measure, pressed down, and shaken together, and running over, shall men give into your bosom. For with the same measure that ye mete withal it shall be measured to you again.

Appendix D: British Philosophy, History, and Science

1. From Thomas Hobbes, *Leviathan* (London: Printed for Andrew Crooke, 1651), Chapter XIII, "Of the Natural Condition of Mankind as Concerning their Felicity and Misery," pp. 62, 63

[Hobbes's (1588–1679) well-known conception of the state of nature as violent and war-like—based on reports concerning the manners of Indigenous peoples in the New World as well as contemporary European evidence of barbarism—serves as a counterweight to idealized notions of pre-literate societies made popular by the works of John Locke (1632–1704) and, later, by Jean-Jacques Rousseau (1712–78). Nietzsche's contempt for utopianism, particularly where he provides readers with an historically inflected conception of the state-forming capacities of the violent and rapacious "blond beast," can thus be seen as an instance of a post-Hobbesian critique of Romantic idealism in political and social theory.]

From Diffidence Warre

Hereby it is manifest, that during the time men live without a common Power to keep them all in awe, they are in that condition which is called Warre; and such a warre, as is of every man, against every man. For WARRE, consisteth not in Battell onely, or the act of fighting; but in a tract of time, wherein the Will to contend by Battell is sufficiently known: and therefore the notion of *Time*, is to be considered in the nature of Warre; as it is in the nature of Weather. For as the nature of Foule weather, lyeth not in a showre or two of rain; but in an inclination thereto of many dayes together; So the nature of War, consisteth not in actuall fighting; but in the known disposition thereto, during all the time there is no assurance to the contrary. All other time is PEACE....

It may peradventure be thought, there was never such a time, nor condition of warre as this; and I believe it was never generally so, over all the world: but there are many places, where they live so now. For the savage people in many places of *America*, except the government of small Families, the concord whereof dependeth on naturall lust, have no government at all; and live at this day in that brutish manner, as I said before. Howsoever, it may be perceived what manner of life there would be, where there were no common Power to feare; by the manner of life, which men that have formerly lived under a peacefull government, use to degenerate into, in a civill Warre....

To this warre of every man against every man, this also is consequent; that nothing can be Unjust. The notions of Right and Wrong, Justice and Injustice have there no place. Where there is no common Power, there is no Law: where no Law, no Injustice. Force, and Fraud, are in warre the two Cardinall vertues. Justice, and Injustice are none of the Faculties neither of the Body, nor Mind. If they were, they might be in a man that were alone in the world, as well as his Senses, and Passions. They are Qualities, that relate to men in Society, not in Solitude. It is consequent also to the same condition, that there be no Propriety, no Dominion, no *Mine* and *Thine* distinct; but onely that to be every mans, that he can get; and for so long, as he can keep it. And thus much for the ill condition, which man by meer Nature is actually placed in; though with a possibility to come out of it, consisting partly in the Passions, partly in his Reason.

2. From Jeremy Bentham, *Introduction to the Principles of Morals and Legislation* (London: Printed for T. Payne, and Son, 1789), Chapter XIV, "Of the Proportion Between Punishments and Offences," pp. 216–18

[The following passages illustrate Bentham's (1748–1832) concept of the "efficacy" of punishment in relation to crimes committed. From this perspective, the "first Object" of punishment is "to prevent, in as far as it is possible, and worthwhile, all sorts of offenses whatsoever," and that a "proportion of punishments to offenses" has been and continues to be maintained throughout human history. Of course, Bentham's utilitarian conception of punishment is totally antithetical to Nietzsche's view of the problem, which holds that punishment arose within a specific relationship between equals, specifically, the creditor-debtor relationship. In addition, Bentham's cost-benefit analysis of crime and punishment conflicts with Nietzsche's psychological insight into the symbolic and performative value of punishment.]

I. We have seen that the general object of all laws is to prevent mischief; that is to say, when it is worthwhile; but that, where there are no other means of doing this than punishment, there are four cases in which it is *not* worthwhile.

II. When it *is* worthwhile, there are four subordinate designs or objects, which, in the course of his endeavors to compass, as far as may be, that one general object, a legislator, whose views are governed by the principle of utility, comes naturally to propose to himself.

III. 1. His first, most extensive, and most eligible object, is to prevent, in as far as it is possible, and worthwhile, all sorts of offenses whatsoever: in other words, so to manage, that no offense whatsoever may be committed.

IV. 2. But if a man must needs commit an offense of some kind or other, the next object is to induce him to commit an offense *less* mischievous, *rather* than one *more* mischievous: in other words, to choose always the *least* mischievous, of two offenses that will either of them suit his purpose.

V. 3. When a man has resolved upon a particular offense, the next object is to dispose him to do *no more* mischief than is *necessary* to his purpose: in other words, to do as little mischief as is consistent with the benefit he has in view.

VI. 4. The last object is, whatever the mischief be, which it is proposed to prevent, to prevent it at as *cheap* a rate as possible.

VII. Subservient to these four objects, or purposes, must be the rules or canons by which the proportion of punishments to offenses is to be governed.

VIII. Rule 1. The first object, it has been seen, is to prevent, in as far as it is worthwhile, all sorts of offenses; therefore,

The value of the punishment must not less in any case than what is sufficient to outweigh that of the profit of the offense.

If it be, the offense (unless some other considerations, independent of the punishment, should intervene and operate efficaciously in the character of tutelary motives) will be sure to be committed notwithstanding: the whole lot of punishment will be thrown away: it will be altogether *inefficacious.*

IX. The above rule has been often objected to, on account of its seeming harshness: but this can only have happened for want of its being properly understood. The strength of the temptation, *cæteris paribus* [Latin: all other things being equal], is as the profit of the offense: the quantum of the punishment must rise with the profit of the offense: *cæteris paribus,* it must therefore rise with the strength of the temptation. This there is no disputing. True it is, that the stronger the temptation, the less conclusive is the indication which the act of delinquency affords of the depravity of the offender's disposition. So far then as the absence of any aggravation, arising from extraordinary depravity of disposition, may operate, or at the utmost, so far as the presence of a ground of extenuation, resulting from the innocence or beneficence of the offender's disposition, can operate, the strength of the temptation may operate in abatement of the demand for punishment. But it can never operate so far as to indicate the propriety of making the punishment ineffectual, which it is sure to be when brought below the level of the apparent profit of the offense.

The partial benevolence which should prevail for the reduction of it below this level, would counteract as well those purposes which such a motive would actually have in view, as those more extensive purposes which benevolence ought to have in view: it would be cruelty not only to the public, but to the very persons in whose behalf it pleads: in its effects, I mean, however opposite in its intention. Cruelty to the public, that is cruelty to the innocent, by suffering them, for want of an adequate protection, to lie exposed to the mischief of the offense: cruelty even to the offender himself, by punishing him to no purpose, and without the chance of compassing that beneficial end, by which alone the introduction of the evil of punishment is to be justified.

3. From John Stuart Mill, *Utilitarianism* (London: Parker, Son, and Bourn, 1863), Chapter II: "What Utilitarianism Is," pp. 9–10, 16–17

[In this definitive post-Benthamite exposition of the main tenets of "utilitarianism," Mill (1806–73) argues that the value of any social and political policy, including the functions of the criminal justice system, resides principally in whether such policies do or do not promote happiness for the greatest number of individuals. Mill identifies the "principal of utility" or the "greatest-happiness principle" as the foundation of all ethics. Implicit in Mill's theory is the idea of the continuous, inevitable progress of enlightenment and the progressive defeat of irrationalism. Although Mill admittedly enlarges the concepts of pleasure and happiness to include non-hedonistic pursuits and sources of gratification, his simplistic and mechanistic psychology of human behavior is in stark contrast to the position of Nietzsche, who argues in *The Genealogy* that the prime mover of human action is overcoming resistances, which often includes some element of humiliation and subordination. Pain and pleasure are merely minor consequences of such overcoming. For Nietzsche, utilitarian calculations of pain and pleasure are not key elements in human motivation.]

The creed which accepts as the foundation of morals, Utility, or the Greatest Happiness Principle, holds that actions are right in proportion as they tend to promote happiness, wrong as they tend to produce the reverse of happiness. By happiness is intended pleasure, and the absence of pain; by unhappiness, pain, and the privation of pleasure. To give a clear view of the moral standard set up by the theory, much more requires to be said; in particular, what things it includes in the ideas of pain and pleasure; and to what extent this is left an open question. But these supplementary explanations do not affect the theory of life on which this theory of morality is grounded—namely, that pleasure, and freedom from pain, are the only things desirable as ends; and that all desirable things (which are as numerous in the utilitarian as in any other scheme) are desirable either for the pleasure inherent in themselves, or as means to the promotion of pleasure and the prevention of pain ...

I have dwelt on this point, as being a necessary part of a perfectly just conception of Utility or Happiness, considered as the directive rule of human conduct. But it is by no means an indispensable condition to the acceptance of the utilitarian standard; for that standard is not the agent's own greatest happiness, but the greatest amount of happiness altogether; and if it may possibly be doubted whether a noble character is always the happier for its nobleness, there can be no doubt that it makes other people happier, and that the world in general is immensely a gainer by it. Utilitarianism, therefore, could only attain its end by the general cultivation of nobleness of character, even if each individual were only benefited by the nobleness of others, and his own, so far as happiness is concerned, were a sheer deduction from the benefit. But the bare enunciation of such an absurdity as this last, renders refutation superfluous.

According to the Greatest Happiness Principle, as above explained, the ultimate end, with reference to and for the sake of which all other things are desirable (whether we are considering our own good or that of other people), is an existence exempt as far as possible from pain, and as rich as possible in enjoyments, both in point of quantity and quality; the test of quality, and the rule for measuring it against quantity, being the preference felt by those who, in their opportunities of experience, to which must be added their habits of self-consciousness and self-observation, are best furnished with the means of comparison. This, being, according to the utilitarian opinion, the end of human action, is necessarily also the standard of morality; which may accordingly be defined, the rules and precepts for human conduct, by the observance of which an existence such as has been described might be, to the greatest extent possible, secured to all mankind; and not to them only, but, so far as the nature of things admits, to the whole sentient creation.

4. From Charles Darwin, *On the Origin of Species by Means of Natural Selection, or the Preservation of Favoured Races in the Struggle for Life* (London: John Murray, 1859), pp. 83–84

[Based on evidence gathered on the *Beagle* expedition in the 1830s to the Galapagos Islands, this incredibly influential work by Darwin (1809–82) supplied the foundation for evolutionary biology, first, with the suggestion that species diversity can be traced from common descent through a branching pattern of evolution and, second, that all creatures are subject to change through natural selection. From this insight grew the application of the analogous idea that the history of nations evolves with alterations in climate and other external factors. Nietzsche's critique of Darwin is based on both an aesthetic objection— namely, that Darwin's approach demystifies and thus diminishes the status of humans to just another organism competing for survival and thus subject to the same external influences—and an intellectual objection: that Darwin seeks to know too much.]

CHAPTER IV

NATURAL SELECTION; OR THE SURVIVAL OF THE FITTEST

... [Nature] cares nothing for appearances, except in so far as they are useful to any being. She can act on every internal organ, on every shade of constitutional difference, on the whole machinery of life. Man selects only for his own good; Nature only for that of the being which she tends. Every selected character is fully exercised by her; and the being is placed under well-suited conditions of life. Man keeps the natives of many climates in the same country; he seldom exercises each selected character in some peculiar and fitting manner; he feeds a long and a short beaked pigeon on the same food; he does not exercise a long-backed or long-legged quadruped in any peculiar manner; he exposes sheep with long and short wool to the same climate. He does not allow the most vigorous males to struggle for the females. He does not rigidly destroy all inferior animals, but protects during each varying season, as far as lies in his power, all his productions. He often begins his selection by some half-monstrous form; or at least by some modification prominent enough to catch the eye, or to be plainly useful to him. Under nature, the slightest differences of structure or constitution may well turn the nicely-balanced scale in the struggle for life, and so be preserved. How fleeting are the wishes and efforts of man! how short his time! and consequently how poor will his products be, compared with those accumulated by Nature during whole geological periods. Can we wonder, then, that Nature's productions should be far "truer" in character than man's productions; that they should be infinitely better adapted to the most complex conditions of life, and should plainly bear the stamp of far higher workmanship?

It may be said that natural selection is daily and hourly scrutinizing, throughout the world, every variation, even the slightest; rejecting that which is bad, preserving and adding up all that is good; silently and insensibly working, whenever and wherever opportunity offers, at the improvement of each organic being in relation to its organic and inorganic conditions of life. We see nothing of these slow changes in progress, until the hand of time has marked the long lapse of ages, and then so imperfect is our view into long past geological ages that we see only that the forms of life are now different from what they formerly were ...

5. From Charles Darwin, *The Descent of Man, and Selection in Relation to Sex* (London: John Murray, 1871), Vol. II, Chapter XXI, pp. 392–94

[In this follow up to *On the Origin of Species*, Darwin applies the theory of evolution described in the previous work specifically to human evolution. Nietzsche views Darwin's assertion of the adaptation of a species to its external environment as vulgar English positivism. For Nietzsche, one of the signs of the strength and dignity of a species is its ability to overcome, shape, and exploit its natural and social environments.]

CHAPTER XXI

A moral being is one who is capable of reflecting on his past actions and their motives—of approving of some and disapproving of others; and the fact that man is the one being who certainly deserves this designation, is the greatest of all distinctions between him and the lower animals.... I have endeavored to shew that the moral sense follows, firstly, from the enduring and ever-present nature of the social instincts; secondly, from man's appreciation of the approbation and disapprobation of his fellows; and thirdly, from the high activity of his mental faculties, with past impressions extremely vivid; and in these latter respects he differs from the lower animals. Owing to this condition of mind, man cannot avoid looking both backwards and forwards, and comparing past impressions. Hence after some temporary desire or passion has mastered his social instincts, he reflects and compares the now weakened impression of such past impulses with the ever-present social instincts; and he then feels that sense of dissatisfaction which all unsatisfied instincts leave behind them, he therefore resolves to act differently for the future,—and this is conscience. Any instinct, permanently stronger or more enduring than another, gives rise to a feeling which we express by saying that it ought to be obeyed. A pointer dog, if able to reflect on his past conduct, would say to himself, I ought (as indeed we say of him) to have pointed at that hare and not have yielded to the passing temptation of hunting it.

Social animals are impelled partly by a wish to aid the members of their community in a general manner, but more commonly to perform certain definite actions. Man is impelled by the same general wish to aid his fellows; but has few or no special instincts. He differs also from the lower animals in the power of expressing his desires by words, which thus become a guide to the aid required and bestowed. The motive to give aid is likewise much modified in man: it no longer consists solely of a blind instinctive impulse but is much influenced by the praise or blame of his fellows. The appreciation and the bestowal of praise and blame both rest on sympathy; and this emotion, as we have seen, is one of the most important elements of the social instincts. Sympathy, though gained as an instinct, is also much strengthened by exercise or habit. As all men desire their own happiness, praise or blame is bestowed on actions and motives, according as they lead to this end; and as happiness is an essential part of the general good, the greatest-happiness principle indirectly serves as a nearly safe standard of right and wrong. As the reasoning powers advance and experience is gained, the remoter effects of certain lines of conduct on the character of the individual, and on the general good, are perceived; and then the self-regarding virtues come within the scope of public opinion, and receive praise, and their opposites blame. But with the less civilized nations reason often errs, and many bad customs and base superstitions come within the same scope, and are then esteemed as high virtues, and their breach as heavy crimes.

The moral faculties are generally and justly esteemed as of higher value than the intellectual powers. But we should bear in mind that the activity of the mind in vividly recalling past impressions is one of the fundamental though secondary bases of conscience. This affords the strongest argument for educating and stimulating in all possible ways the intellectual faculties of every human being. No doubt a man with a torpid mind, if his social affections and sympathies are well developed, will be led to good actions, and may have a fairly sensitive conscience. But whatever renders the imagination more vivid and strengthens the habit of recalling and comparing past impressions, will make the conscience more sensitive, and may even somewhat compensate for weak social affections and sympathies.

The moral nature of man has reached its present standard, partly through the advancement of his reasoning powers and consequently of a just public opinion, but especially from his sympathies having been rendered more tender and widely diffused through the effects of habit, example, instruction, and reflection. It is not improbable that after long practice virtuous tendencies may be inherited. With the more civilized races, the conviction of the existence of an all-seeing Deity has had a potent influence on the advance of morality. Ultimately man does not accept the praise or blame of his fellows as his sole guide, though few escape this influence, but his habitual convictions, controlled by reason, afford him the safest rule. His conscience then becomes the supreme judge and monitor. Nevertheless, the first foundation or origin of the moral sense lies in the social instincts, including sympathy; and these instincts no doubt were primarily gained, as in the case of the lower animals, through natural selection.

6. From Sir John Lubbock, 1st Baron Avebury, *Pre-historic Times, As Illustrated by Ancient Remains, and the Customs of Modern Savages* (London: Williams and Norgate, 1865), pp. 489–90

[Polymath, entrepreneur, philanthropist, and ethnologist, Lubbock (1834–1913) was one of the remarkable characters of the Victorian era. As a boy he worked as an assistant to his neighbor, Charles Darwin, and he was thus inspired to establish archaeology on scientific principles. In this pioneering application of Darwin's idea of "natural selection" to a broad overview of pre-historical human cultural development (which reached seven editions before 1913), in which he popularized the terms "Paleolithic" and "Neolithic," Lubbock offers an anthropological narrative and conception of the origins and development of so-called "savages" or "primitive peoples." Consistent with the utilitarian assumptions of the era, Lubbock drew an equivalence between physical and moral evolution—progressive improvement as a direct consequence of natural selection—and treated archaeological discoveries in a rationalist, positivist, scientific evidence-based manner. Lubbock's account is useful in putting into perspective Nietzsche's ideas in *The Genealogy* regarding "Aryans" and non-Europeans—representatives of prehistoric peoples—and their respective social instincts. Lubbock contributed to the racist assumptions of modern anthropology by assuming that the different paths of cultural development taken by various human groups reflected biological differences among them. In his evocative treatment of prehistoric man, Lubbock seems to strike a Hobbesian note with something like wistful nostalgia for nature "red in tooth and claw," as the Victorian poet Tennyson once called it.]

Chapter XIV Concluding Remarks

... Men do not sin for the sake of sinning; they yield to temptation. Most of our unhappiness arises from a mistaken pursuit of pleasure; from a misapprehension of that which constitutes true happiness. Men do wrong, either from ignorance, or in the unexpressed hope that they may enjoy the pleasure, and yet avoid the penalty of sin. In this respect there can be no doubt that religious teaching is widely mistaken. Repentance is too often regarded as a substitute for punishment. Sin it is thought is followed either by the one or the other. So far, however, as our world is concerned, this is not the case; repentance may enable a man to avoid punishment in future but has no effect on the consequences of the past. The laws of nature are just, and they are salutary, but they are also inexorable. All men admit that "the wages of sin is death," but they seem to think that this is a general rule to which there may be many exceptions, that *some* sins may possibly tend to happiness; as if there could be any thorns that would grow grapes, any thistles which could produce figs. That suffering is the inevitable consequence of sin, as surely as night follows day, is, however, the stern yet salutary teaching of Science. And surely if this lesson were thoroughly impressed upon our minds, if we really believed in the certainty of punishment; that sin could not conduce to happiness, temptation, which is at the very root of crime, would be cut away, and mankind must necessarily become more innocent....

In reality we are but on the threshold of civilization. Far from showing any indications of having come to an end, the tendency to improvement seems latterly to have proceeded with augmented impetus and accelerated rapidity. Why, then, should we suppose that it must now cease? Man has surely not reached the limits of his intellectual development, and it is certain that he has not exhausted the infinite capabilities of nature. There are many things which are not as yet dreamt of in our philosophy; many discoveries which will immortalise those who make them, and confer upon the human race advantages which as yet, perhaps, we are not in a condition to appreciate. We may still say with our great countryman, Sir Isaac Newton, that we have been but like children, playing on the seashore, and picking up here and there a smoother pebble or a prettier shell than ordinary, while the great ocean of truth lies all undiscovered before us.

Thus, then, the most sanguine hopes for the future are justified by the whole experience of the past. It is surely unreasonable to suppose that a process which has been going on for so many thousand years, should have now suddenly ceased; and he must be blind indeed who imagines that our civilization is unsusceptible of improvement, or that we ourselves are in the highest state attainable by man ...

7. From Herbert Spencer, *The Principles of Psychology*, 1st ed. (London: Longman, Brown, Green, and Longmans, 1855), Section 105, pp. 334–35; 2nd ed. (London: Williams and Norgate, 1870), Section 129, pp. 291–93; Section 220, p. 503; and Section 273, pp. 627–28

[Coiner of the phrase "survival of the fittest" and thus the thinker most closely associated with "Social Darwinism," the concept that pervaded intellectual discourse in the later nineteenth century and into the twentieth, Spencer (1820–1903) popularizes the idea of a biological paradigm for human communities with the phrase "social organism." What is pertinent to Nietzsche's critique of the "English psychologists" in *The Genealogy* is Spencer's insistence that the development of human consciousness—and culture, including ethics and morality—must be viewed through the lens of organic and cognitive evolution. In his earliest works, Spencer provides a mechanistic and historicist theory of human development that is predicated upon utilitarian principles. For example, what is "good" in human experience is that which is "useful," regardless of the potentially dark origins of what is deemed socially expedient. Ethics are therefore based on immutable natural laws. In a highly prescient observation, Spencer urges the usurpation of man's unchallenged status as a moral being. Animals, too, he asserts, exhibit the capacity for cooperation and altruistic self-sacrifice for the benefit of other members of their communities. Indeed, Spencer sees evolution not merely as a physical or biocentric process but rather as primarily a moral one, according to which human development moves toward a more refined embodiment of altruistic fellow-feeling. Nietzsche, of course, objected to the "leveling" of human beings to the status of "mere" animals, for the creation of moral systems was man's prerogative. Moreover, Nietzsche identified altruism with the slave revolt in morality.]

§105. ... When it is remembered that the laws of structure and function must necessarily harmonize; and that the structure and functions of the nervous system must conform to the laws of structure and function in general; it will be seen that the parallelism here roughly indicated, is such as might be expected to hold. It will be seen that the ultimate generalizations of Psychology and Physiology, must be, as they here appear, different sides of the same primordial truth. It will be seen that they are both expressions of the same fundamental principle of Life.

§ 129. If the doctrine of Evolution is true, the inevitable implication is that Mind can be understood only by observing how Mind is evolved. If creatures of the most elevated kinds have reached those highly integrated, very definite, and extremely heterogeneous organizations they possess, through modifications upon modifications accumulated during an immeasurable past—if the developed nervous systems of such creatures have gained their complex structures and functions little by little; then, necessarily, the involved forms of consciousness which are the correlatives of these complex structures and functions must have arisen by degrees. And as it is impossible truly to comprehend the organization of the body in general, or of the nervous system in particular, without tracing its successive stages of complication; so it must be impossible to comprehend mental organization without similarly tracing its stages.

§ 220. To reduce the general question to its simplest form: — Psychical changes either conform to law or they do not. If they do not conform to law, this work, in common with all works on the subject, is sheer nonsense: no science of Psychology is possible. If they do conform to law, there cannot be any such thing as free will. I will only further say that freedom of the will, did it exist, would be at variance with the beneficent necessity displayed in the evolution of the correspondence between the organism and its environment. That gradual molding of inner relations to outer relations which has been delineated in the foregoing pages—that ever-extending adaptation of the cohesions of psychical states to the connections between the answering phenomena, which we have seen results from the accumulation of experiences, would be hindered did there exist anything which otherwise caused their cohesions. As it is, we see that the continuous adjustment of the vital activities to activities in the environment must become more accurate and exhaustive. The life must become higher and the happiness greater—must do so because the inner relations are determined by the outer relations. But were the inner relations partly determined by some other agency, the harmony at any moment existing would be disturbed, and the advance to a higher harmony impeded. There would be a retardation of that grand progress which is bearing Humanity onwards to a higher intelligence and a nobler character.

§ 273. And this brings us to the true conclusion implied throughout the foregoing pages—the conclusion that it is one and the same Ultimate Reality which is manifested to us subjectively and objectively. For while the nature of that which is manifested under either form proves to be inscrutable, the order of its manifestations throughout all mental phenomena proves to be the same as the order of its manifestations throughout all material phenomena.

The Law of Evolution holds of the inner world as it does of the outer world. On tracing up from its low and vague beginnings the intelligence which becomes so marvelous in the highest beings, we find that under whatever aspect contemplated, it presents a progressive transformation of like nature with the progressive transformation we trace in the Universe as a whole, no less than in each of its parts. If we study the development of the nervous system, we see it advancing in integration, in complexity, in definiteness. If we turn to its functions, we find these similarly show an ever-increasing inter-dependence, an augmentation in number and heterogeneity, and a greater precision. If we examine the relations of these functions to the actions going on in the world around, we see that the correspondence between them progresses in range and amount, becomes continually more complex and more special, and advances through differentiations and integrations like those everywhere going on. And when we observe the correlative states of consciousness, we discover that these, too, beginning as simple, vague, and incoherent, become increasingly numerous in their kinds, are united into aggregates which are larger, more multitudinous, and more multiform, and eventually assume those finished shapes we see in scientific generalizations, where definitely quantitative elements are coordinated in definitely quantitative relations.

Appendix E: The Reception of Nietzsche in Germany

1. From Max Nordau, *Degeneration* (1892), Book III: "Egomania," Chapter V: "Friedrich Nietzsche," 2nd ed. (London: William Heinemann, 1898), pp. 415–17, 419–20, 420–21, 430–31, 443–44; anonymous translation revised by Gregory Maertz

[The treatise on Western spiritual and cultural decay by Nordau (1849–1923) appeared on the doorstep of the twentieth century and joined Cesare Lombroso's diagnosis of human atavism in *Uomo Deliquente* [*Criminal Man*] (1876) and works of fiction—e.g., Robert Louis Stevenson's *Strange Case of Dr. Jekyll and Mr. Hyde* (1886) and Bram Stoker's *Dracula* (1897)—in sounding the alarm. Nordau privileges the scientific method of the Enlightenment as well as its aesthetic values of lucidity, beauty, and morally improving purpose. Nietzsche's bombastic, contradictory, and fragmentary style violated this tradition. Ironically for a critic of Jewish heritage, Nordau's withering attack on modernist literature as "decadent" and "degenerate" was co-opted by the architects of the cultural program of National Socialism.]

As in Ibsen egomania has found its poet, so in Nietzsche it has found its philosopher. The deification of filth by the Parnassians with ink, paint, and clay; the censing among the Diabolists and Decadents of licentiousness, disease, and corruption; the glorification, by Ibsen, of the person who "wills," is "free" and "wholly himself"—of all this Nietzsche supplies the theory, or something which proclaims itself as such....

From the first to the last page of Nietzsche's writings the careful reader seems to hear a madman, with flashing eyes, wild gestures, and foaming mouth, spouting forth deafening bombast; and through it all, now breaking out into frenzied laughter, now sputtering expressions of filthy abuse and invective, now skipping about in a giddily agile dance, and now bursting upon the auditors with threatening mien and clenched fists. So far as any meaning at all can be extracted from the endless stream of phrases, it shows, as its fundamental elements, a series of constantly reiterated delirious ideas, having their source in illusions of sense and diseased organic processes.... Here and there emerges a distinct idea, which, as is always the case with the insane, assumes the form of an imperious assertion, a sort of despotic command. Nietzsche never tries to argue. If the thought of the possibility of an objection arises in his mind, he treats it lightly, or sneers at it, or curtly and rudely decrees, "That is false!" ("How much more rational is that ... theory, for example, represented by Herbert Spencer! ... According to this theory, good is that which has hitherto always proved itself to be useful, so that it may be estimated as valuable in the highest degree, as valuable in itself. Although this mode of explanation is also false, the explanation itself is at least rational and psychologically tenable."—*Zur Genealogie der Moral*, 2 Auflage, p. 5 [see above, p. 58]. "This mode of explanation is also false." Full-stop! Why is it false? Where is it false? Because Nietzsche so orders it. The reader has no right to inquire further.) For that matter, he himself contradicts almost every one of his violently dictatorial dogmas. He first asserts something and then its opposite, and both with equal vehemence, most frequently in the same book, often on the same page....

... In the dozen volumes, thick or thin, which he has published it is always the same. His books bear various titles, for the most part characteristically crack-brained, but they all amount to one single book. They can be changed by mistake in reading, and the fact will not be noticed. They are a succession of disconnected sallies, prose and doggerel mixed, without beginning or ending. Rarely is a thought developed to any extent; rarely are a few consecutive pages connected by any unity of purpose or logical argument. Nietzsche evidently had the habit of throwing on paper with feverish haste all that passed through his head, and when he had collected a heap of snippings he sent them to the printer, and there was a book. These sweepings of ideas he himself proudly terms "aphorisms," and the very incoherence of his language is regarded by his admirers as a special merit. When Nietzsche's moral system is spoken of, it must not be imagined that he has anywhere developed one. Through all his books, from the first to the last, there are scattered only views on moral problems, and on the relation of man to the species and to the universe, from which, taken together, there may be discerned something like a fundamental conception. This is what has been called Nietzsche's philosophy....

Nietzsche's doctrine, promulgated as orthodox by his disciples, criticizes the foundations of ethics, investigates the genesis of the concept of good and evil, examines the value of that which is called virtue and vice, both for the individual and for society, explains the origin of conscience, and seeks to give an idea of the end of the evolution of the race, and, consequently, of man's ideal—the "over man" (Übermensch). I desire to condense these doctrines as closely as possible, and, for the most part, in Nietzsche's own words, but without the cackle of his mazy digressions or useless phrases....

... Nietzsche is uncommonly proud of his discovery, that the conception of *Schuld* [guilt] is derived from the very narrow and material conception of *Schulden* [debts]. Even if we admit the accuracy of this derivation, what has his theory gained by it? This would only prove that, in the course of time, the crudely material and limited conception had become enlarged, deepened, and spiritualized. To whom has it ever occurred to contest this fact? What dabbler in the history of civilization does not know that conceptions develop themselves? Did love and friendship, as primitively understood, ever convey the idea of the delicate and manifold states of mind now expressed by these words? It is possible that the first guilt of which men were conscious was the duty of restoring a loan. But neither can guilt, in the sense of a material obligation, arise amongst "blond brutes," or "cruel beasts of prey." It already presupposes a relation of contract, the recognition of a right of possession, respect for other individuals. It is not possible if there does not exist, on the part of the lender, the disposition to be agreeable to a fellow creature, and a trust in the readiness of the latter to requite the benefit; and, on the part of the borrower, a voluntary submission to the disagreeable necessity of repayment. And all these feelings are really already morality—a simple, but true, morality—the real "slave morality" of duty, consideration, sympathy, self-constraint; not the "master morality" of selfishness, cruel violence, unbounded desires! Even if single words like the German *schlecht (schlicht)* [bad, plain, or straight] have today a meaning the opposite of their original one, this is not to be explained by a fabulous "transvaluation of values," but, naturally and obviously, by Abel's theory of the "contrary double meaning of primitive words." The same sound originally served to designate the two opposites of the same concept, appearing, in agreement with the law of association, simultaneously in consciousness, and it was only in the later life of language that the word became the exclusive vehicle of one or other of the contrary concepts. This phenomenon has not the remotest connection with a change in the moral valuation of feelings and acts....

In other places, again, we find the current of thought and almost the very words of Oscar Wilde, Huysmans, and other Diabolists and Decadents.[1] The passage in *Zur Genealogie der Moral* (p. 171 [see above, p. 180]) in which he glorifies art, because "in it the lie sanctifies itself, and the will to deceive has a quiet conscience on its side," might be in the chapter in Wilde's *Intentions* on "The Decay of Lying," as, conversely, Wilde's aphorisms: "There is no sin except stupidity." "An idea that is not dangerous is unworthy of being called an idea at all." And his praises of Wainewright,[2] the poisoner, are in exact agreement with Nietzsche's "morality of assassins," and the latter's remarks that crime is calumniated, and that the defender of the criminal is "oftenest not artist enough to turn the beautiful terribleness of the crime to the advantage of the doer." Again, by way of joke, compare these passages: "It is necessary to get rid of the bad taste of wishing to agree with many. Good is no longer good when a neighbor says it's good" (Nietzsche, *Jenseits von Gute und Böse*, p. 54), and "Ah! don't say that you agree with me. When people agree with me, I always feel that I must be wrong" (Oscar Wilde, *Intentions*, p. 202). This is more than a resemblance, is it not? To avoid being too diffuse, I abstain from citing passages exactly resembling these from Huysmans' *À Rebours*, and from Ibsen.[3] At the same time, it is unquestionable that Nietzsche could not have known the French Decadents and English Aesthetes whom he so frequently approaches, because his books are in part antecedent to those of the latter: and neither could they have drawn from him, because, perhaps with the exception of Ibsen, it is only about two years since they could have heard as much as Nietzsche's name. The similarity, or rather identity, is not

---

1 Oscar Wilde (1854–1900), Irish poet, playwright, and renowned aesthete. Joris-Karl Huysmans (1848–1907), French novelist and author of *À rebours* (*Against Nature*) (1884), a definitive work of the "Decadent" movement.
2 Thomas Griffiths Wainewright (1794–1847), English artist, journalist, and suspected serial killer who became a *cause célèbre* among prominent English writers such as Charles Dickens (1812–70) and Oscar Wilde.
3 Henrik Ibsen (1828–1906), realist Norwegian playwright and founding figure of modernism.

explained by plagiarism; it is explained by the identity of mental qualities in Nietzsche and the other egomaniacal degenerates.

2. From Stefan George, "Nietzsche," *Der Siebente Ring* (*The Seventh Ring*) (Blätter für die Kunst, 1907), pp. 12–13; translated by Gregory Maertz

[The lyric poet George (1868–1933) was the focus of a Heidelberg-based cult of aesthetic experience that included the prominent literary scholar Friedrich Gundolf (1880–1931) and Claus von Stauffenberg (1907–44), leader of the 20 July 1944 assassination plot against the Nazi dictator Adolf Hitler. Cult members believed that George would usher in an era of cultural and spiritual renewal. George's poetry is characterized by an extreme preference for beauty over reason and ethics as well as an esoteric vocabulary and symbolism accessible only to initiates. With this poem George contributed to the cultic status of Nietzsche, who had died only seven years earlier.]

> Heavy yellow clouds are pulled over the hill,
> Bringing cooling storms—half of the autumn offering
> And half of the early spring … So this mighty fortress
> Encastled the Thunderer—who stood apart
> From the thousands who emerged out of the dust and
>   smoke surrounding him.
> Here he sent out over the flat midlands
> And the dead city the last dull lightning bolts
> And the world went from a longer to the longest night.
>
> Stupidity drags the crowd under—but do not be afraid!
> What matters the poisonous sting of sea creatures?
> Let's cut down the weeds choking our path!
> For a while longer, there will be pious silence
> And then the beast will stain you with praise
> As you continue to fatten yourself in the darkness.
> He who helped strangle you has just died,[1]
> Allowing you to stand radiant before the times
> While wearing the bloody crown of supreme leadership.

---

1 A reference to Richard Wagner, Nietzsche's early mentor, who died on 13 February 1883.

You are the redeemer! Even the most unfortunate
Are burdened with the weight of the lost ones.
Have you never seen the land of the yearning smile?
Did you create gods just to overthrow them?
Are you never to take a rest or to take pleasure in some-
    thing you created?
You have killed the next god inside yourself
Allowing you to tremble after him with a new desire
And to cry out in the pain of loneliness.

Then the late arriving supplicant pleaded with you:
There is no longer any path over the icy cliffs
And the nests of cruel birds—now it is necessary:
Confine yourself within the circle that is formed by love ...
And if the austere and tormented voices
Then intone a song of praise in the lilac-tinted night
That forms a bright flood like a lamentation:
The new soul should not speak but sing!

3. From Ernst Bertram, *Nietzsche: An Attempt at a
   Mythology* (Bondi, 1918), pp. 1, 6, 8–10; translated by
   Gregory Maertz

[This study of Nietzsche by Bertram (1884–1957), originally an
adherent of the mystical poet Stefan George and a close friend of
the Nobel Prize-winning novelist Thomas Mann (their friendship ended with the rise of Adolf Hitler), is a prime example
of *Gestaltsbiographie*—further developed by Wilhelm Dilthey
(1833–1911) and Hans-Georg Gadamer (1900–2002)—an approach to biography which insists that historical objectivity is
an illusion. Bertram was prized as a German stylist, and there
is an untranslatable quality to his writing, which is inherently
poetic and features an abundance of German wordplay. In contrast to the rationalist Nordau, Bertram embraces the circularity
and contradictory nature of Nietzsche's insights and appreciates
the deeper tensions, the unsettledness, the self-negation, and
the musical structure of Nietzsche's works. Bertram emphasizes Nietzsche's aristocratic radicalism as the inheritance of
Socrates—they both sought to undermine myths and religious
mysteries—and identifies Nietzsche as a rebel against the leveling impact of mass democracy and the legacy of the French
Revolution.]

Do we serve those who came before?
We serve those who are coming.

EVERYTHING has been just a parable. No historical method, as a naive historical realism of the nineteenth century so often seems to believe, helps us to see the physical reality "as it actually was." History, after all soul science and soul provocation, is never synonymous with the reconstruction of any past, with the closest possible approach even to a past reality. Rather, it is precisely the realization of this former reality, its conversion into a completely different category of being: it is a value-setting, not a reality-making.... This becomes clear above all where history is in the most intense sense, the story of individuals who have remained visible or have become visible again. We do not visualize a past life, we counter it by looking at it historically. We do not save it in our time, we make it timeless. By clarifying it, we already interpret it. Whatever remains of him, as we always seek to brighten, to explore, to relive, is never life, but always his legend. What remains as a history of all events, is always the last—the word taken without any ecclesiastical or even romantic overtones—the legend.

... History is active image creation, not reporting, illustration, or a preservation of the past. Legend is really what that is: the Word in the most naked sense says. Not something written as a stable entity, but something that is always to be read anew, that only comes through via a new, a different reading. In the sense that Burckhardt says (in the introduction to Greek cultural history as well as in the world-historical considerations) of the nature of the historical source, a fact of the first order may be reported in Thucydides but which will only be noticed in a hundred years. And next to that historian Burckhardt, the philologist Nietzsche: "The same text allows innumerable interpretations: there is no 'correct' interpretation." ... Everything that has happened wants to become image, all living beings seek to become legend, all reality seeks to become myth....

In spite of its eternal transformation, every legend strives for a unique, extreme and purest embodiment, which represents a supreme possibility of the human, a dense formation of the soul eschewing the last remnant of the earth, effective through its mere existence as a parable until the end of our human world. Most legends, according to their given intensity ... remain mythical possibilities only and are like painful shadows in relationship to a great archetype, destined to drink the blood of the soul and of perfection....

The memory of humankind is generally ungrateful, but where it thanks, it gratefully plunders all the small altars of the past to decorate their greatest images of thought. Plato and Alexander, Francis and Dante, Leonardo, Rembrandt and Goethe[1] have become worlds out of powerful individuals. And only for the glory of the greatest kings have all the smaller ones achieved their victories; only for the glory of the greatest have poets celebrated the less mighty ones....

Nietzsche, too, on the forehead of his much-blessed and much-maligned name, seems to magnetically draw down the destinies and memory of countless forebears. He appears, today, as the last and greatest heir of all those who are of the tribe of Luciferic defiance, but of a defiance that is puzzlingly mixed with and almost identical to divine nostalgia; the heir of all Promethean heights, all Promethean willing for the new godless divine man.[2] He is the heir and brother of the destiny of all, who not only strive Goethically out of the dark into the light, but who drive a deep distress out of the bright, all too illuminated dawn into the dark, into the unknown; their nature, "one and double" like the songs of the *West-Eastern Divan*,[3] like Proserpina,[4] must belong to two realms of the soul. And if Nietzsche, the murderer

---

1 Plato, Athenian philosopher (see Appendix B). Alexander the Great (356–323 BCE), king of Macedon renowned for his extensive conquests. St. Francis of Assisi (1181 or 1182–1226 CE), Italian Catholic friar and founder of various orders, associated with the blessing of animals. Dante Alighieri (c. 1265–1321), Italian poet whose *Divine Comedy* (1320) is considered a masterwork of world literature. Leonardo da Vinci (1452–1519), Renaissance Italian polymath, artist, and architect. Rembrandt van Rijn (1606–69), Dutch painter of wide-ranging influence. Johann Wolfgang von Goethe (1749–1832), polymath, poet, playwright, and novelist who is considered Germany's answer to Dante and Shakespeare.

2 In comparing Nietzsche to Prometheus, the Titan god who defied Zeus by stealing fire from heaven and gifting it to humankind, Bertram highlights Nietzsche as a benefactor and liberator as well as a martyr who suffered on behalf of humanity.

3 Goethe's *West-östlicher Divan* (1819 and 1827), a collection of lyric poems, was inspired by the Persian poet Hafiz (1315–90).

4 Proserpina is a goddess of Roman mythology (Persephone in Greek) who was abducted by Pluto, the god of the underworld (Hades); she returns to the earth in the spring but must spend the winter in Hades.

of God, is also the proclaimer of a god in his own singular way, this new god is certainly a god who, in addition to the light name of a god, also bears a very dark name—like the Eros of Plato and the "twice-born" Dionysus.

4. **From Oswald Spengler, *Nietzsche and His Century* (1924), an address delivered on the occasion of Friedrich Nietzsche's eightieth birthday at the Nietzsche Archive, Weimar, 15 October 1924; first published in *Reden und Aufsätze* (C.H. Beck, 1937), pp. 109–23; translated by Gregory Maertz**

[Aligned with Nordau politically, to the tradition of cultural pessimism, and methodologically, to scientific positivism, Spengler (1880–1936) authored an influential bestseller, *The Decline of the West* (1918), which describes the inevitable collapse of Western or "Faustian" civilization and characterizes the present epoch as the "winter" of European culture. Delivered in 1924 at the Nietzsche Archive in Weimar on the occasion of Nietzsche's eightieth birthday, at a time of lingering shock following the catastrophic German defeat in World War I and of deep, widespread resentment at the draconian provisions of the Treaty of Versailles (1919) imposed on Germany by the victorious Allies, Spengler's address presents Nietzsche as the direct descendent and rightful heir of the great Goethe. Together they will provide the foundation for Germany's cultural rebirth. The address concludes with a rousing call to action that builds upon the existing cult status of Nietzsche as a reactionary icon and that will contribute to his exploitation by the National Socialists as a Party mascot.]

Anyone looking back to the nineteenth century today and allowing its great people to pass by will find something astonishing in Nietzsche's appearance, as his own time hardly could have felt. All others, including Wagner, including Strindberg, and Tolstoy,[1] too, have somehow carried the color and shape of those years, but have somehow been imprisoned along with the flat

---

1 Richard Wagner (1813–83), German composer who revolutionized music in the nineteenth century with his idea of the "total work of art." August Strindberg (1849–1912), Swedish *avant-garde* playwright, novelist, and poet. Leo Tolstoy (1828–1910), famed Russian realist novelist.

optimism of their progressive philosophers, their utilitarian and socially responsible ethics. Their worldview of strength and substance, of adaptation and expediency, has made sacrifice obsolete in our most unspiritual age. A ruthless exception is made only by one, and if the word "untimely," which he himself coined, is still valid today for anyone, then it is valid for Nietzsche himself. For in his whole life and the whole attitude of his thinking one will search in vain for something in which he would inwardly succumb to anything fashionable. He stands in opposition to this and in doing so, he forms a profound relationship with the second German of importance to modern times, whose life has also been a great symbol: Goethe. They are the only two Germans of rank whose existence abounds both outside and beside their works, and because they have both felt themselves from the beginning and kept themselves accounted for, they have become the common property of their nation and an integral part of their intellectual history is similarly bound to their nation.

It was, of course, Goethe's good fortune that he was born at the apex of occidental culture, when a mature and saturated spirituality prevailed, which he represented, and that he needed nothing but to be the man of his time, to attain that formal serenity, which was later described as Olympian. Nietzsche lived a century after that, and meanwhile the momentous cultural turn had come, which we understand only today. It was his doom to appear after the Rococo, right amid the total lack of culture in the 1860s and 1870s. In what atrocious streets and houses he lived! Not to mention the dreadful manners, clothes, and furniture around him! In what horrid forms did social interaction take place? How one thought, how one wrote, how one felt! Goethe lived in a time full of form, but Nietzsche passed away longing for forms that were irrevocably broken and past; and as Goethe only needed to affirm what he saw and experienced, there was nothing left for Nietzsche to do but to lodge a passionate protest against everything present, for he was determined to save what he could of the cultural heritage of his ancestors. Goethe and Nietzsche both strove throughout their lives to achieve strict inner form. But the eighteenth century was still culturally rich. It possessed the highest level of civilized society that Western Europe has ever known. The nineteenth century, on the other hand, had neither proper social ranks nor any social structure at all. Apart from the casual manners of a metropolitan upper class, it was only here and there that it knew a laboriously maintained courtly or bourgeois tradition. And while Goethe, as a recognized leader of society, was able to grasp and solve all the great questions of his time, as *Wilhelm Meister* and the *Elective Affinities*[1] teach, Nietzsche had nothing to cling to but his great philosophical mission. His ghastly loneliness contrasts with Goethe's cheerful sociability. While Goethe works with what is given, Nietzsche ponders the nonexistent and seeks to articulate a ruling form that he will assert against a prevailing formlessness.

Today we can grasp the antagonism which prevailed throughout Western Europe around 1800, including literary Petersburg, and was objectified by the words classicism and romanticism. Goethe was a classicist to the same extent that Nietzsche was a romantic. Each of them also possessed the capacity to embody the other sensibility, which sometimes came to the fore; and just as Goethe, whose Faust Monologue and *West-East Divan* represent the climax of a romantic world-feeling, constantly endeavored to master this penchant for the far-off and the limitless and to subordinate it to a clear and strict, traditional form, Nietzsche not only has his philologist's bias in favor of the classically rational, he also inclined toward what he called the Dionysian or the romantic. They both stood at the border between the two worlds of sensibility. Goethe was just as much the last classicist as Nietzsche was, along with Richard Wagner, the last romantic. Each of them exhausted the circle of these possibilities, living and creative. According to them, the meaning of the times could no longer be expressed in words and pictures, as the epigones of classical drama and the followers of Zarathustra and the Ring of the Nibelungen[2] proved. But it is equally impossible to open up to them a new way of seeing and speaking. No matter how powerful a creator may appear in Germany they will always linger in the shadow of Goethe and Nietzsche because the great line of development is over as well.

It is part of the essence of Western classicism that, under the balanced control of opposing impulses, it adheres completely to the here and now, and seeks to dissolve the past and future in a sensuous engagement with the present moment. Goethe's statement about the "demands of the day," and the near unanimous contemporary testimony regarding his "cheery disposition"

---

1 *Wilhelm Meister's Apprenticeship* (1795–96) and *Elective Affinities* (1809) are novels by Goethe.

2 *The Ring of the Nibelungs* (1869–76), a cycle of four operas by Wagner; considered one of the greatest creative achievements of the nineteenth century.

signify that he took upon himself the task of incorporating and personalizing every epoch of the past, resulting in the representation of *his* Greeks, *his* Renaissance as well as *his* Götz and Faust and Egmont.[1] He makes *Tasso* and *Iphigenie*[2] so intimately his own and present that they do not even come across as historical documents. Conversely, what is distant is the real homeland of the romantics. Their yearning is detached from the present, which seems to them faraway and strange, and is projected into the past and the future simultaneously. No romantic has been able to form a deep relationship with what surrounded him. Indeed, the romantic is attracted to what is essentially alien to him. The classicist, by contrast, *belongs* fully at home in his own nature. The romantics are noble dreamers and noble conquerors of dreams. They rave about the despots, rebels, and criminals of the past or fantasize about ideal future states and supermen, while classicists understood or even practiced the craft and method of statesmanship, such as Goethe and Humboldt[3] did. The conversation between Egmont and Orange is one of Goethe's masterpieces.[4] He admired Napoleon not as an apparition but as one whose deeds he observed closely.[5] Goethe never knew what to do with the violent men of the past as soon as he tried to make them present. Consequently, his *Caesar* remained unwritten. But Nietzsche could only admire such beings from a distance. Those nearby, such as Bismarck, were unbearable for him to perceive. He would not have tolerated Napoleon either. He would have seemed to him crude, empty, and flat, like the Napoleonic natures who lived in his time, the great politicians of Europe and the robber barons who ruled the economy, whom

---

1   *Götz von Berlichingen* (1773), *Faust* (1808 and 1832), and *Egmont* (1788), plays by Goethe.

2   *Torquato Tasso* (1790) and *Iphigenie auf Tauris* (1780–86), plays by Goethe.

3   Wilhelm von Humboldt (1767–1835), Prussian philosopher of language, diplomat, and founder of what would become Humboldt University in Berlin.

4   Count Lamoral Egmont and William of Orange are characters in Goethe's play *Egmont*.

5   The Battle of Jena (14 October 1806) was a crushing victory by Napoleon over the Prussian and Saxon armies. Afterwards, French troops sacked Weimar and some soldiers were billeted in Goethe's house. The carnage of the battlefield (34,000 dead) contributed to Goethe's studies of human anatomy.

he had not even seen, let alone understood. Nietzsche required a vast distance between the "here and now" to feel related to a reality, and so he created the *Übermensch*, and no less freely, the figure of Cesare Borgia[1] ...

Goethe, who was fully aware of his superior social rank, had never been an aristocrat in the passionate theoretical sense of Nietzsche, who did not have the habit of real personal experience as a member of the nobility. After all, he never really got to know the democracy of his time in its power and powerlessness. If Nietzsche revolted against the feelings of the herd with the wrath of a deeply soul-sensitive man, then his rebellion could be traced to some moment in the historical past. He saw, inexorably, that in all great cultures and epochs of the past, the multitude is nothing, that it does not survive history, that the herd is the perpetual sacrifice and object of the will of the ruling classes. This was often enough acknowledged, but, except for Nietzsche, it was deemed impossible to dismantle the traditional image of "humanity," whose development seemed to be the progressive solution of a utopian task and whose leaders seemed to be the agents of this objective. Herein lies the immeasurable distance between the historiographical method of Niebuhr and Ranke,[2] which as a concept was, obviously, of romantic origin. This stands in sharp contrast to Nietzsche's perspective. His gaze, which penetrated into the soul of times past and the nations that lived then, was not concerned with the mere pragmatic order of facts.

Having arrived at this height, Nietzsche raises the question of the value of the world, a task which lay ready for him from the time of his childhood. Thus was the period of Western philosophy completely closed, at the center of which was the question of the form that knowledge should take. Here, too, there was both a classical and romantic or, to put it in terms of Nietzsche's era, a socialist and an aristocratic answer. Life is worth so much because it benefits the whole. This was the answer of the educated

---

1 Cesare Borgia (1475–1507), illegitimate son of Pope Alexander VI, cardinal of the Church, infamous mercenary, model for Niccolò Machiavelli's *The Prince* (1532), and Nietzsche's ultimate embodiment of the will to power.

2 Barthold Georg Niebuhr (1776–1831) and Leopold von Ranke (1795–1886), German historians who believed that they could accurately recover history by a more scientific reconstruction of the past.

Englishmen who had learned to distinguish between what was presented as honorable intuition and what one performed at crucial moments as a politician or as a businessman. Life is all the more valuable the stronger its instincts for self-preservation. That was the answer of Nietzsche, whose own life, ironically, was delicate and vulnerable. After all, because he was so alienated from this active life, he understood his secret that the will to power is stronger than all the principles and doctrines that have ever made history or will do so in the future. Whatever may be proved or preached against the will to power, it is the definitive medium for the understanding of actual history. Any conceptual dissection of the "will" is of no interest to him because the image of the active, creative, and destructive will at work in history means everything to him. Nietzsche does not teach, but he observes how the will is and will be in future. Despite what the theoretical and priestly people want, the primitive instincts of life will remain the stronger ones. What a gap between Schopenhauer's worldview and this one! Between Nietzsche's contemporaries with their sentimental plans for improving the world and this finding of a hard fact! Nietzsche's success has placed a romantic thinker at the head of his century. Whether we like it or not, whether we know it or not, we are all his disciples. This perspective has, unnoticed, already conquered the present world. No one writes history today without seeing things this way....

Goethe, the privy councilor and minister, the celebrated center of European spirituality, confessed in the last year of his life, in the last act of his Faust, that he regarded his life as fulfilled. "Tarry a while, you are so beautiful!"[1] speaks the word of blissful saturation in the moment when the work of active intimacy with life, under the command of Faust, completes itself and is presented in a form that will last forever. That was the great and final symbolic act of classicism, to which Goethe's life was dedicated, and which led from the strict education of the eighteenth century to the conquest of the nineteenth.

But the distance cannot be created, only proclaimed. And just as Faust's death and transfiguration marked the end of classicism, so the spirit of the loneliest of wanderers—Nietzsche's—dispenses a final curse on his time and ours. Just as in those enigmatic days of Turin when Nietzsche clearly saw the image of his world before he disappeared into the mist and the farthest

---

1 *Faust*, Part One, line 1700: "Verweile doch! Du bist so schön!"

peaks of madness. That is why Nietzsche's existence exerts the stronger effect on posterity. It also lies in the fulfillment of Goethe's life that it represented the end of something. Countless Germans will, of course, continue to worship Goethe, live with him, and confront him, but he will not, in the end, transform them. The effect of Nietzsche is precisely transforming because the melody of his vision did not end with him. Romantic thinking is infinite, influencing form but never reaching fulfillment. It always seizes new territories, consuming them or melting them. Nietzsche's way of seeing is conveyed to both friends and enemies of his thought and is passed on from them to new successors and to new opponents. Even if one day no one reads his works, his perspective will nonetheless endure and inspire creativity.

Works Cited and Recommended Reading

Works by Nietzsche

The Birth of Tragedy, 1872.
On Truth and Falsity in their Ultramoral Sense, 1873.
Philosophy in the Tragic Age of the Greeks, 1873.
Untimely Meditations, 1876.
Human, All-Too Human, 1878.
The Dawn, 1881.
The Joyful Wisdom, 1882.
Thus Spoke Zarathustra, 1883.
Beyond Good and Evil, 1886.
On the Genealogy of Morality, 1887.
The Case of Wagner, 1888.
Twilight of the Idols, 1888.
The Antichrist, 1888.
Ecco Homo, 1888; first published 1908.
Nietzsche contra Wagner, 1888.
The Will to Power, posthumously edited by Elisabeth Förster-Nietzsche.

The best English edition of Nietzsche's major works is published in the Cambridge Texts in the History of Political Thought series.

The standard German edition of the collected works is *Kritische Gesammtausgabe: Werke*, edited by Giorgio Colli and Mazzino Montinari (Walter de Gruyter, 1967–).

Selected Letters of Friedrich Nietzsche, edited by Christopher Middleton (Hackett Publishing, 1969).

Works on Nietzsche

Acompora, Christa Davis, editor. *Nietzsche's On the Genealogy of Morals: Critical Essays*. Rowman and Littlefield Publishers, 2001.
Ahern, Daniel. *The Smile of Tragedy: Nietzsche and the Art of Virtue*. Penn State UP, 2012.

Ansell-Pearson, Keith, editor. *A Companion to Nietzsche.*
Blackwell, 2006.
——. *How to Read Nietzsche.* Norton, 2005.
Benders, R., and S. Oettermann. *Friedrich Nietzsche Chronik in Bildern und Texten.* Carl Hanser, 2000.
Bertram, Ernst. *Nietzsche: Attempt at a Mythology.* Translated and edited by Robert B. Norton, U of Illinois P, 2009.
Bishop, Paul, editor. *A Companion to Friedrich Nietzsche, Life and Works.* Camden House, 2012.
Blue, Daniel. *The Making of Friedrich Nietzsche: The Quest for Identity 1844–1869.* Cambridge UP, 2016.
Brobjer, Thomas H. *Nietzsche's Philosophical Context: An Intellectual Biography.* U of Illinois P, 2008.
Cate, Curtis. *Friedrich Nietzsche: A Biography.* Pimlico, 2003.
Clark, Maudemarie. *Nietzsche on Ethics and Politics.* Oxford UP, 2015.
——. *Nietzsche on Truth and Philosophy.* Cambridge UP, 1990.
Danto, Arthur C. *Nietzsche as Philosopher.* Columbia UP, 2005.
Deleuze, Gilles. *Nietzsche and Philosophy.* Columbia UP, 1983.
De Man, Paul. *Allegories of Reading: Figural Language in Rousseau, Nietzsche, Rilke, and Proust.* Yale UP, 1979.
Diethe, Carol. *The A to Z of Nietzscheanism.* Scarecrow Press, 2010.
——. *Nietzsche's Sister and the Will to Power.* U of Illinois P, 2003.
——. *Nietzsche's Women: Beyond the Whip.* Walter de Gruyter, 1996.
Fornari, Giuseppe. *A God Torn to Pieces: The Nietzsche Case.* Translated by Keith Buck, Michigan State UP, 2013.
Gooding-Williams, Robert. "Nietzsche's Pursuit of Modernism." *New German Critique,* vol. 41, 1987, pp. 95–108.
Guthke, Karl. "Die Geburt des Nietzsche-Mythos aus dem Ungeist Elisabeths." *Nietzsche-Studien,* vol. 26, 1997, pp. 537–50.
Hanauer, Tom R. "Strangers to Ourselves: Self-Knowledge in Nietzsche's *Genealogy.*" *Journal of Nietzsche Studies,* vol. 50, no. 2, 2019, pp. 250–71.
Harris, Daniel I. "Compassion and Affirmation in Nietzsche." *Journal of Nietzsche Studies,* vol. 48, no. 1, 2017, pp. 17–28.
Hatab, Lawrence. *'On the Genealogy of Morality': An Introduction.* Cambridge UP, 2008.
Hayman, Ronald. *Nietzsche, A Critical Life.* Weidenfeld and Nicolson, 1980.

Heidegger, Martin. *Nietzsche, Volumes One and Two* (Vol. I. *The Will to Power as Art*; Vol. II. *The Eternal Recurrence of the Same*). 1979, 1984. Translated by David Farrell Krell, HarperCollins, 1991.

———. *Nietzsche, Volumes Three and Four* (Vol. III. *The Will to Power as Knowledge and as Metaphysics*; Vol. IV. *Nihilism*). 1987, 1984. Translated by David Farrell Krell, HarperCollins, 1991.

Heller, Erich. *The Importance of Nietzsche*. U of Chicago P, 1988.

Hollingdale, R.J. *Nietzsche, The Man and His Philosophy*. Cambridge UP, 1999.

Huddleston, Andrew. *Nietzsche on the Decadence and Flourishing of Culture*. Oxford UP, 2019.

———. "Why (and How) We Read Nietzsche." *Journal of Nietzsche Studies*, vol. 49, no. 2, 2018, pp. 233–40.

Janaway, Christopher. *Beyond Selflessness: Reading Nietzsche's Genealogy*. Oxford UP, 2009.

Janz, Curt Paul. *Friedrich Nietzsche Biographie*. 1978. Hanser, 1993.

Kaufmann, Walter A. *Nietzsche: Philosopher, Psychologist, Antichrist*. 1968. Princeton UP, 2013.

Köhler, Joachim. *Nietzsche and Wagner: A Lesson in Subjugation*. Translated by Ronald Taylor, Yale UP, 1998.

Kuehne, Tobias. "Nietzsche's Ethics of Danger." *Journal of Nietzsche Studies*, vol. 49, no. 1, 2018, pp. 78–101.

Kuhn, Elizabeth. "Towards an Anti-Humanism of Life: The Modernism of Nietzsche, Hulme, and Yeats." *Journal of Modern Literature*, vol. 34, no. 4, 2011, pp. 1–20.

Laforce, Daisy. "Three Modes of History in *On the Genealogy of Morality*." *Journal of Nietzsche Studies*, vol. 50, no. 2, 2019, pp. 292–309.

Leiter, Brian. *Nietzsche on Morality*. Routledge, 2002.

Love, Frederick R. *Young Nietzsche and the Wagnerian Experience*. U of North Carolina P, 1963.

Luchte, James. *The Peacock and the Buffalo: The Poetry of Nietzsche*. Continuum, 2010.

Metzger, Jeffrey. *The Rise of Politics and Morality in Nietzsche's Genealogy: From Chaos to Conscience*. Lexington Books, 2020.

Moore, Gregory. *Nietzsche, Biology and Metaphor*. Cambridge UP, 2002.

Nehemas, Alexander. *Nietzsche, Life as Literature*. Harvard UP, 2002.

Owen, David. *Nietzsche's Genealogy of Morality.* McGill-Queen's UP, 2007.

Peters, H.F. *Zarathustra's Sister.* Crown, 1977.

Prideaux, Sue. *I Am Dynamite! A Life of Nietzsche.* Tim Duggan Books, 2018.

Ratner-Rosenhagen, Jennifer. *American Nietzsche: A History of an Icon and His Ideas.* U of Chicago P, 2012.

Remhof, Justin. "Naturalism, Causality, and Nietzsche's Conception of Science." *Journal of Nietzsche Studies,* vol. 46, no. 1, 2015, pp. 110–19.

Richardson, John. "Nietzsche Studies as Historical Philosophizing." *Journal of Nietzsche Studies,* vol. 49, no. 2, 2018, pp. 271–77.

Ridley, Aaron. *Nietzsche's Conscience: Six Character Studies from the Genealogy.* Cornell UP, 2018.

Safranski, Rüdiger. *Nietzsche: A Philosophical Biography.* Translated by Shelley Frisch, Norton, 2003.

Schuringa, Christoph. "Nietzsche's Genealogical Histories and His Project of Revaluation." *History of Philosophy Quarterly,* vol. 31, no. 3, 2014, pp. 249–69.

Tanner, Michael. *Nietzsche: A Very Short Introduction.* Oxford UP, 2000.

Van Fossen, Joel A. "Nietzsche, Self-Disgust, and Disgusting Morality." *Journal of Nietzsche Studies,* vol. 50, no. 1, 2019, pp. 79–105.

Van Tongeren, Paul. *Reinterpreting Modern Culture: An Introduction to Friedrich Nietzsche's Philosophy.* Purdue UP, 2000.

Young, Julian. *Nietzsche's Philosophy of Art.* Cambridge UP, 1992.

Zweig, Stefan. *Nietzsche.* Translated by Will Stone, Hesperus Press, 2013.

Background

Andreas-Salomé, Lou. *Looking Back: Memoirs.* Translated by Breon Mitchell, Paragon House, 1990.

Ascheim, Steven E. *The Nietzsche Legacy in Germany 1890–1990.* U of California P, 1992.

Binion, Rudolf. *Frau Lou: Nietzsche's Wayward Disciple.* Princeton UP, 1968.

Galindo, Martha Zapata. *Triumph des Willens, Zur Nietzsche-Rezeption im NS-Staat.* Argument, 1995.

Gossman, Lionel. *Basel in the Age of Burckhardt: A Study in Unseasonable Ideas.* U of Chicago P, 2002.

Hoffmann, David Marc. *Zur Geschichte des Nietzsche-Archivs.* Walter de Gruyter, 1991.

MacIntyre, Ben. *Forgotten Fatherland: The Search for Elisabeth Nietzsche.* Macmillan, 1992.

Meysenburg, Malwida von. *Rebel in a Crinoline: Memoirs of Malwida von Meysenburg.* Translated by Elsa von Meysenburg Lyons, George Allen & Unwin, 1937.

Moritzen, Julius. *Georg Brandes in Life and Letters.* Colyer, 1922.

Pfeiffer, Ernst, editor. *Friedrich Nietzsche, Paul Rée, Lou von Salomé: Die Dokumente ihrer Begegnung.* Insel, 1970.

Schain, Richard. *The Legend of Nietzsche's Syphilis.* Greenwood, 2001.

Small, Robin. *Nietzsche and Rée, A Star Friendship.* Clarendon, 2007.

Stern, Fritz. *The Politics of Cultural Despair.* U of California P, 1961.

Vickers, Julia. *Lou von Salomé. A Biography of the Woman Who Inspired Freud, Nietzsche and Rilke.* McFarland, 2008.

Watson, Peter. *The German Genius, Europe's Third Renaissance, The Second Scientific Revolution and the Twentieth Century.* Simon & Schuster, 2010.

This book is made of paper from well-managed FSC® - certified forests, recycled materials, and other controlled sources.